DESIGN CITY
MELBOURNE
LEON VAN SCHAIK
PHOTOGRAPHY BY JOHN GOLLINGS

Published in Great Britain in 2006 by Wiley-Academy, a division of John Wiley & Sons Ltd

Copyright © 2006

John Wiley & Sons Ltd, The Atrium, Southern Gate, Chichester, West Sussex, PO19 8SQ, England Telephone (+44) 1243 779777

Email (for orders and customer service enquires): cs-books@wiley.co.uk

Visit our Home Page on www.wiley.co.uk or www.wiley.com

Other Wiley Editorial Offices

John Wiley & Sons Inc., 111 River Street, Hoboken, NJ 07030, USA

Jossey-Bass, 989 Market Street, San Francisco, CA 94103-1741, USA

Wiley-VCH Verlag GmbH, Boschstr. 12, D-69469 Weinheim, Germany

John Wiley & Sons Australia Ltd, 42 McDougall Street, Milton, Queensland 4064, Australia

John Wiley & Sons (Asia) Pte Ltd, 2 Clementi Loop #02-01, Jin Xing Distripark, Singapore 129809

John Wiley & Sons Canada Ltd, 22 Worcester Road, Etobicoke, Ontario, Canada M9W 1L1

ISBN 978 470 01041 1

Executive Commissioning Editor: Helen Castle
Development Editor: Mariangela Palazzi-Williams
Content Editor: Louise Porter
Publishing Assistant: Calver Lezama

Book and cover design by Warren Dean Bonett (www.wdbonett.com)

Printed and bound by Markono Print Media Pte Ltd, Singapore

DESIGN CITY
MELBOURNE

Contents

Acknowledgments

This book is about the many layers of curatorship that come together when a city blooms as a design city. While I have tried to convey the characteristics of this process through the stories of those included, I know that constraints of space have meant that just as many have been excluded. They should take comfort from the fact that there are so many other radar screens tuned in on this fortunate city that they are bound to show up somewhere else.

In the course of preparing this book a collaboration has developed with photographer John Gollings that had its seeds in his decision to accept an invitation to examine the nature of his mastery in my programme for masters at RMIT. The text has prompted him to search for the perfect image, and those images in turn have had a defining impact on the text. Collaboration is not easy, but it is certainly very rewarding.

I want, however, to note that many photographers, of whom John is certainly the doyen, have played a very significant role in the beneficial curatorial culture of Melbourne over the past 20 years. Mary Beard observed that Sir John Soane haunts the imaginations of architects around the world thanks to his delineators, Gandy and Basevi. Their renditions of his architectural creations subtly amplify and suppress alternately characteristics of the works that are idiosyncratic, emphasising the inherent ideas.

In Melbourne, John Gollings, Peter Bennets, Tim Griffiths and Trevor Mein are among those who have competed to provide this service to architects, revealing to them as much as to their audience what their architecture 'wants to be'. I take my hat off to them all – no architect should be without such support.

Around the architects cluster a series of practices that this book touches on only lightly, but I hope with respect. For what Robert Buckingham and his friends did for fashion, Kjell Grant for furniture, the gallery owners and directors for the arts, and for what journalists and theorists have done for us all, we can only be grateful, because anything that raises up one of us, raises up us all.

The others who are not mentioned are engineers like Peter Feliccetti, whose deep understanding of and appreciation for architectural ambitions support so many of the works that are illustrated in this book. There are the contractors who fall in love with the ideas of the buildings and pursue these with a passion that matches that of the architects – like the aptly named Probuild at TarraWarra Museum of Art, or the joiners who work so tirelessly with John Wardle. And there is then that band of utterly dedicated architects who devote their careers to working on the most interesting buildings in the city, without whom Lab Architecture could not have realised Federation Square. There are people like Jen Rippon who did so much to work out how to build Storey Hall, like Nigel Fitton, Peter Bickle, Michael Dredge and Hamish Lyon, who contributed to so many of the projects included in this book (see p 124 for a photographic portrait of many of these project architects).

My thanks go very pointedly to my colleagues in the practice of architecture whose work I have reviewed. I sometimes feel that having in a sense forsaken the practice of architecture for the practice of observing that practice, I must at times seem to be a drain on the slender resources that these extraordinarily idealistic people bring to bear on building a city worthy of its inhabitants' best aspirations. I simply hope that the little I have been able to do to affect climates of patronage and criticism is some recompense for the enormous amount of their time and patience which the business of observing entails of them. Conversations take two parties, and you have all been so generous in your parts. For my part, I have learned so much, chiefly not to take work at face value, always to look deeper.

My thanks go to the people who have made this work possible, the difficult but always present potential of RMIT, my colleagues in and around Architecture and Design who have made working here a delight, the team at Wiley-Academy with whom I have had a long-distance electronic relationship – an attenuated medium that must have tried their patience over and again – but particularly for Helen Castle's guidance. It is easy to underestimate the contribution made by Bronwen Jacobs, with whom I have worked for 20 years, so calmly and coolly has she organised, eased paths and done that which has made this book possible. My community of friends around the world has watched over this venture with a kindly eye and convinced me that it was worthwhile – Kate Heron and Julian Feary, Ranulph Glanville and Aartje Hulstein, Colin Fournier and Doris Metzin in the UK; Kevin Alter, Grahame Shane and Graeme Hardy in the USA; Iain Low and Gill Butler in South Africa; Andreas and Ilke Ruby in Germany; and my friends from our years together in undergraduate study at the University of Newcastle-upon-Tyne – Stephen Buckley, Elspeth Clements, Bryan Ferry and Andrew Keen. Among these was the author David Sweetman, now deceased, who treated every book of mine as if it was a major event in his life too. I want also to acknowledge Peter Cook's enduring curiosity about my work and my friends! For me, as for so many, he is a source of continuing encouragement.

And there is that support of my extended family, my mother and my stepmother, my son Jan, my daughter Andrée, their mother Cath. I had often wished that I could work with my father, it was never possible. But now I have had the enormous pleasure of working with Jan, his grandson, for whom he had great ambitions!

To whom should this book be dedicated? In my mind's eye is the character of Diotima created by Robert Musil in his *The Man Without Qualities*.[1] She was entrusted with the search for an idea that would keep the Austro-Hungarian Empire alive in the face of a tide of nationalism. To this end she interviewed people from the cities and redoubts the length and breadth of the empire. She failed, of course, but the account of the journey alone is a testament to our human purpose – a search for awareness and meaning.

1 Robert Musil, *The Man Without Qualities*, Picador (London), 1995.

Preface

What is a 'design city'? All cities teem with creativity because all humans are creative. Creativity is a human capability. It's unavoidable. Sitting on the pavement outside *The Wall* in East St Kilda with Tom Kovac and John Warwicker, two internationally renowned creatives, I notice a bicycle chained to a pole. It is a black mountain bike with wide tyres. Its owner has fashioned mudguards from carefully selected translucent plastic bottles, cut in half and joined to the frame with ties that are threaded through the salvaged handles of the bottles. We are talking about 'design cities'. As I alert the others to the bicycle, we eye every cleverly edited bottle, every piece chosen to catch and deflect water thrown up by the tyres, every handing of throat to base and every found connector elegantly and parsimoniously fit to purpose. We fall silent. John explodes first: 'Design is everywhere! You just have to recognise it!'

And yet from time to time we, the international community of designers, become aware that one or other city is 'hot'. In the 1970s it was Graz. In the 1980s it was Barcelona. In the 1990s it was the Dutch 'Randstat' including Amsterdam and Rotterdam. Now Antwerp and Brussels. And in the first decade of the 21st century Melbourne seems to be a place that excites our curiosity. Of course, matters are not that simple: the great conurbations muster such power that their centres can be seen to be 'design cities' over and again, simply because they regularly import the best from other cities. But it is less often that they surface as generators of design from their own internal processes of nurturing mastery and supporting the innovation that is launched from those platforms of mastery. London could not lay claim to the design city epithet through the three decades after Mary Quant's heyday until the patronage of the Jubilee line put a full range of its architectural talent on display.

Warwicker's intuition is correct. Recognition is the core of this business, but what kind of recognition? Journalistic recognition is easily won and as easily withdrawn. That Graz was more than a nine-days'-wonder lay in the fact that there was more going on than the mere production of pointy architecture. The school of Graz begins as a regional literary phenomenon, becomes a project for the architects, is the focus of an intense self-examination by the city intelligentsia, and in the 1990s there was a popular decision to import into the city the Trojan Horse – in the sense that its impact on the future direction of the culture is unpredictable – of the Kunsthalle by outsiders Peter Cook and Colin Fournier. In a way this decision could also be read as an attempt to regain international attention. But has recognition been withdrawn from Graz? Not really. The school of Graz sits on the edge of everyone's design consciousness as a phenomenon against which one has to register one's own position. Nowhere can stay 'front of mind' all of the time. It would be better for Graz if their school's intention had been to disrupt their own culture with a new but aligned work.

What in Graz was a deliberate project of differentiation undertaken by the intellectuals of Austria's second city is echoed in the origins of Barcelona's emergence as a design city in the 1980s. For two golden decades around the 1986 Olympics we all knew what a design city was – it was Barcelona. And this was indeed a supremely 'designed' city, laid out in an epic of analysis, design and politics as the first designed modern city, led by Cerdà (active as an urbanist 1844–76).[1]

In 1986 a series of urban interventions, workshopped over a decade by the local College of Architects (CoA), was thrown into relief by the spotlight of the international event and it stunned the world of design. People flocked there over the following years to discover for themselves what these works were saying about Barcelona's emergence from the suppression of the Franco era. Design was seen as evidence of the vigour of the local culture, and outside architecture this continues to be a dynamic design city, filled with ateliers and streaming with ideas – and the opportunity to realise them. How did this come about?

Here, during the last years of Franco's regime – a period in which Barcelona was starved of funds as a punishment for its resistance to the dominance of Madrid – the CoA ran workshops on many of the problematic sites in the city, engaging the communities around the sites in the process. When the time came for the normalisation of Barcelona's relationship to the centre the city was ready to act. A flood of pocket urban projects flowed and burst upon the international scene with a freshness that astounded. *Quaderns*, the magazine of the CoA, disseminated the works in a bilingual format (Catalan/English) and pioneered new ways of showing work in its urban and social context. The CoA capitalised on this in the bid for the 1984 Olympics, cementing in place major opportunities for local architects alongside works by internationally

From top: Jubilee line redevelopment in London; Austria, Graz, Island of the Mur at dusk

renowned talent from elsewhere, and millions became aware that Barcelona was once again (following on from the intense Catalan nationalism that threw up opportunities for the school that nurtured Antoni Gaudí) a 'design city'. The College also bid for and hosted the 1996 UIA Congress, but by this time the vision that had fuelled the wave of innovative works was faltering. In a process in which, as Ignasi de Sola Morales lamented, the College of Architects had lost the initiative, the view from the Ramblas across the harbour mole came to be blocked by 80,000 square metres of indifferent commercial accommodation designed by New York architect IM Pei. Other similar decisions have robbed locals of the most important commissions in the city, even though Carlos Ferrater, in the Barcelona Botanical Garden, Mediterranean section (winning fractal competition project 1989, design 1995, completion 1999), and others continue to produce works of outstanding innovative importance.

What has happened? The creativity has not waned, but the city's curatorial vision has collapsed – ironically, the victim of its own success. Politicians noticed the impact of the city's design reputation and reasoned something like this: 'If we have been so successful with local unknown architects, how much more successful will we be if we use great architects from elsewhere?' Perhaps because they are intent on capturing an export market for themselves, the CoA seems unable to mount a counter argument. There is evidence for this in the way that the major project of extending the Diagonal to the sea has been curated. It appears that the CoA was unable to argue for this to be a design process open to many local architects – as were all the Cerdà blocks that give the Eixample its distinctively pluralist character. Instead, they have been content for the entire project aside from the plum job – the Forum (2001–04), an indifferent Herzog & De Meuron – to go to one local firm. As in this last case and unfortunately for architecture, most major new commissions in the past decade have gone to outsiders, and works that simply do not generate the excitement that the endemic architectural culture previously engendered are overshadowing the culture. The politics of procurement has slipped into a paradigm of collecting great works rather than sustaining local creativity.

It is important to dwell on this, the counter creative impulse that imports external work rather than nurturing local creativity, because if we are to understand the 'design city' phenomenon, the mechanisms by which a city harnesses the creativity of its people, nurturing collegiate processes through which creativity becomes mastery and then innovation, need to be understood.

In Graz and Barcelona the conditions for flowering as a design city were created by intellectuals, who are integrated into the local culture in ways that are unusual in Anglophone countries. And what has been achieved is directly related to the power of the arguments that they have been able to mount. In the Netherlands, by contrast, the 'Super Dutch' phenomenon arose through government policy, extending into design from a more general concern with the physical and social environments. There, measures supporting innovative design by architects and landscape architects were the envy of the design world in the 1990s. The well-funded Netherlands Architecture Institute (NAI) was fortunate to coax Kristin Feirreis, co-founder of Aedes Architecture Forum in Berlin and a curator of genius, into its directorship. So while public

Above: Night view of Ben Van Berkel's Erasmus Bridge (1997), Rotterdam

clients were commissioning works that would challenge the uniformity of a largely manufactured country, the NAI captured the curatorial high ground in international design, mounting a series of exhibitions on local and international architecture and supporting a series of publications that established some Dutch architects as world players. Two events have diminished this flowering: Kristin Feirreis had to withdraw from the NAI for health reasons, and a conservative government came into power, unconvinced of the purpose of innovative design.

Knowing this, what do we need to look for in Melbourne as we seek to understand its emergence in Deyan Sudjic's International Architecture Biennale of Venice in 2000 as the only city in the world to be represented in every category of design in the Arsenale? We need to understand the curatorial arguments that have marshalled the creative energies of designers into collectives that mastery consciously pursue. Victoria Newhouse draws a parallel between the role of the auteur in film and that of a curator: 'The curator's hand is visible in varying degrees. Like a film director, who works with a studio, actors, a cinematographer, technicians, and a producer, a curator heads a team...'.[2] In this book I extend the notion of curation to the shaping of the stories that we tell in order to guide what we do. We need to understand the source of those arguments, individual and institutional. They are the channels through which recognition flows. We can be certain that, as in other cities, these were laid down in the previous decade. And we need to examine the patronage that has opened up opportunities for the architects of this city to innovate on the basis of that mastery.

This is Melbourne's decade as an acknowledged 'design city'. Will that recognition fade, as it has for other design cities? Perhaps understanding the design city phenomenon will enable this city to extend the benefits of being a design city to the next generation. Be that as it may, it is my hope that in understanding these processes you will be better able to read cities and understand how they bloom, and why, while always creative, they are perhaps not always in flower.

1 'Ildefons Cerdà' in Arturo Soria y Puig (ed), *Cerdà: The Five Bases of the General Theory of Urbanization*, Electa (Madrid), 1999. The Eixample plan that was implemented was first proposed in 1859 and amended in 1869.
2 Victoria Newhouse, *Art and the Power of Placement*, Monacelli Press, (New York), 2005.

TRIPOLAR
DESIGN
CULTURE

Previous spread: View of the city across the new riverside Birrarung Marr park upstream from Federation Square showing the most recent work in reclaiming the river front for the citizens, here progressively covering the railway tracks that had previously separated the centre from the river. The path through the middle leads directly to 101 Collins Street (DCM 1988), the only locally designed tower in this view. The major sporting venues of the city, the MCG and the Tennis Centre, lie to the right. The picture gives an accurate archaeology of the city's design culture, emerging from the foreground, with 101 marking the financial spine of Collins Street running parallel to the river after the bend, and with Federation Square marking the crossing of the river by the civic spine along which the new work of Melbourne's architects is arrayed

Opposite: Ideogram C by Leon van Schaik. Bringing a curatorial intelligence to bear on the procurement of architecture by RMIT involved an assessment of current processes that favoured out-of-town architects (see left curtain), the establishment of criterion for the selection of architects (signboard), and a view of the relationships between the positions being pursued by the architects of Melbourne (centre ground). It was also based on the university mission (top drop); precedents (rear flat); and a broad political position (trailing ribbons). The resulting artefacts are shown on the stage

Tripolar Design Culture

THE CURATORIAL ARMATURES OF THE CITY

This introductory essay seeks to outline the emergence of the tripolar design culture that has fuelled Melbourne's take-off as a world design city, and to draw threads to the other cultural and economic phenomena that relate to this emergence. The aim is to uncover the basic forms of curatorial intelligence at work in Melbourne over the period since the city was founded in 1840.

Infrastructure: How generations of surveyors, engineers and urban architects have bequeathed to the city its grids and subdivisions; highways, boulevards, streets, roads, lanes and arcades; its domains, reserves, parks and gardens; and the basic public hygiene services that form the armature around which the creativity of the citizens of the city has crystallised.

Patronage: How clients have taken the opportunity to contribute to the local culture through their commissioning of architecture.

The canon: How architects have argued for a skewing of the international canon to meet local ambitions, and have laid down works that no future generation at work in the city could ignore.

Reflection: How critics and curators have engaged practitioners in a deepened understanding of the process by which creativity becomes mastery, and that in turn becomes a platform for innovation in design.

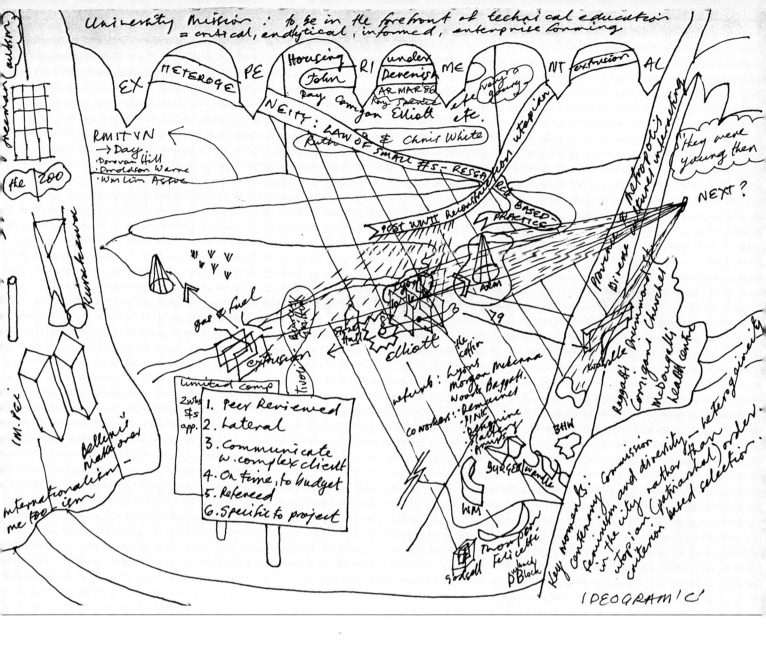

Is Melbourne a design city? Viewed from certain angles, say from the new Birrarung Marr Park looking towards the city along the Yarra River that defined one edge of the original settlement, just as its fresh water gave it a locational rationale, the view of Melbourne is sheer Alpha Ville, and involuntarily I exclaim 'Design city my foot!' From other more distant vantage points, seeing the cluster of towers that defines what planners now refer to as the Central Activities District, I recall the patronising remarks of a Texan matron commenting on the changes made in the city over the past 15 years: 'My! Haven't you come a long way! The skyline is almost like part of Houston!' Melbourne doesn't look like a 'design city'.

Into the new millennium London has enjoyed the benefit of New Labour identifying design culture as a key attribute of a successful Britain. No such easy alignment between government and design exists here: sport takes it all. Every Australian Olympic Gold Medal had over $8 million invested in it. The most any designer could point to is the government contribution to their higher education, an amount including a capital contribution that could not be greater than $25,000 a year for three to five years, depending on their degree. There is not even a Design Council promoting research and excellence. Were it not for writer Peter Rose's account of how Australian Rules Football enabled his farming family to escape poverty, and of how supportive of different creative abilities his

a former St Kilda Football Club rookie, the other a
Hawthorn Football Club player), there is after all a
latent understanding that the intensity and joy in
performance that underlie sport also underlie design.
Both of these sporting heroes have turned seamlessly
to design, and with as much concern for excellence in
their new domain as they displayed in their old, and
with as sure a confidence that what they do matters to
everyone. Even Justin Madden, our Minister for Sport,
is a footballer turned architect turned politician! Maybe
in time this settler society will accord them, designer
and sportsperson alike, their equal due, but this will not
happen until the underlying processes of design are as
well understood and wittily commented upon in
newspapers as is sport in Australia. Even in journalism,
the most coveted awards for investigative work, the
Walkley awards, often as not go to the sports pages – of
the Sydney Morning Herald. And yet, in this post 2000
Olympic decade, sporting eminence is attributed to
Sydney, while architecture has brought Melbourne the
'design city' accolade.

Sydney looks the part of a design city, with
Utzon's iconic Opera House, wonderfully and
unforgettably sited, but (as with Gehry in Bilbao) with as
much consequence for the local design culture as if it
were from Mars. The 2000 Olympics saw no Barcelona-
like rush of recognition by the world of Sydney's local
design culture. Little opportunity was given to avant-
garde designers, but where it was given – as in the
Archery Pavilion by Stutchbury and Pape – it was seized
upon. There seemed little understanding of how to
represent the local architecture other than the 'me too-
ism' of 'as Minimalist as New York/Tokyo/
London/etc'. Settler societies such as Australia move
only slowly towards supporting a local design culture.
At first their energies are tied up in surveying,

sporting family were when it became evident that his
own skills lay in words, it would be difficult to reconcile
the Australian obsession with sport with the equally
intense business of design.[1] Equally striking is his
account of how his non-conforming sexuality was
accepted in this family, and in its wider sporting social
milieu. As we will see in the stories of two sportsmen
turned designer, Sean Godsell[2] and Greg Burgess (one

subdividing and exploiting.[3] For many generations the chief function of design is to replicate some notion of 'home'. This takes extreme forms; the rivers of Australia did not resemble the rivers of Europe to settlers, consisting as they did for much of the year of disconnected billabongs, oxbow lakes and the like. The Murray River was dynamited into conforming to the European notion of a continuously flowing river – the ecological sense of the pre-existing condition cavalierly ignored. Botanical gardens in every town and city were filled with imported plants as settlers studied how to normalise this newly settled continent to their familiar landscapes. At the same time tides of architectural styles washed across the cities, only fitfully developing a local cultural capital.

It is in some invisible ways that Melbourne first merits consideration as a 'design city'. The city has an outfall sewer. The almost completely land-encircled, 60-kilometre diameter bay on which it sits is rarely unfit for swimming in (only after rain storms have flushed out the storm channels that do not meet the embrace of the system that runs the sewers to Werribee and Carrum Downs for treatment). The bay teems with life. The city also has clean air. Design cities lay claim to infrastructural foresight, Barcelona through adopting Cerdà's plan, London by building the original outfall sewer. Such considerations of geographical hygiene seem to underpin a self-consciousness about the environment that – as is indeed endemic in the Netherlands and Belgium, urban regions that consistently profile as design cities – encourages people to think of their city as a site for improvement through design.

How does this self-consciousness play out towards a culture that could be designated 'design city'? Redmond Barry, a prominent early citizen of Melbourne, wrote a weekly architectural column in the first newspaper in the city, and caused a set of photographs of 10 great buildings to be hung in what is now the State Library (the photographs were sourced from the Architectural Association in London, founded almost contemporaneously in 1846 – Melbourne was officially gazetted as a settlement in 1840). Barry was the judge who sentenced Ned Kelly to death, thus creating the local myth of a highway robber who is famous for the design of his own armour, the horizontal viewing slit of which, set in its black cylinder, is as much an icon of Australia as anyone has achieved. Barry did not intend these 10 buildings to be mimicked; in his column he challenged his fellow citizens to achieve their like. Local scholar and landscape architect Paul Fox has shown that in taking up this challenge citizens came to be divided between those who continued the quest for a re-creation of 'home', and those who began to embrace the notion of the 'New World' that was already prevalent in the centuries older settlement society of the USA.[4]

In agriculture this embrace of the new led unfortunately to even more rapacious exploitation of the land, causing trees to be cleared so effectively that Australia faces salinity problems that are a slowly unfolding local equivalent of the Kansas Dust Bowl. In the architecture of the cities these mental affiliations to either the old or the new are played out through the work of prodigies who, in cities awash with wealth from the goldfields, designed and built numerous 19th-century Australian landmarks. There is the neo-Italian Renaissance Treasury (1857–62) in Melbourne, designed by 19-year-old JJ Clark, and in the booming gold town of Bendigo, two hours' drive northwest of Melbourne, a neo-French Renaissance ensemble of

Clockwise from top left: Shamrock Hotel in Bendigo; Bendigo Law Courts; Sacred Heart Cathedral, Bendigo; Bendigo Post Office, now a visitor centre; St Paul's Cathedral, Melbourne; and Bendigo Town Hall

the City Hall (1872–85) by William C Vahland; there are the Law Courts (1890) and Post Office (1883) by George Watson, and the Shamrock Hotel (1896) by Vahland's Bendigo-born and bred protégé Philip Albert Kennedy. The Gold Rush town of Ballarat, situated a similar distance to the west of Melbourne, had a more classical architecture. Cathedrals were either imported like the radical St Paul's on Swanston Street, designed in England in 1878 by William Butterfield, and placed as close to the originating point of the city as was feasible, adjacent to the bridge over the river; or they were designed in a simulation of European exemplars like St Patrick's in Melbourne (1858–97) by the local William Wardell and the Sacred Heart Cathedral in Bendigo, the latter by John Reed and completed in two stages (1895–1901, 1954–77).

Strangely in this instance it is Butterfield who seems to have been thinking of new worlds, while the locals were all in thrall to 'dreaming spires'. Certainly it is St Paul's that has disturbed the local revanchist culture, which in the 20th century (1931) dumbed down the blunt Romanesque profile of his design by surmounting it with pretty Gothic towers, views of which, dreamily across the river, are today regarded as sacrosanct by conservative politicians. But Wardell's St Patrick's, the largest Catholic church in Australia, was also surmounted with romanticising spires, taller than designed and added in 1939.[5] This may have been an attempt to forestall the effects of a proposed dome on the state parliament, proposed by the Protestant ascendancy in order, some believe, to block the view to the church up Bourke Street, where today these spires make a picturesque closure above the neo-classical facade of parliament. The early years of Melbourne are littered with works of almost autistic mastery – so complete is their recall of their origins elsewhere. The buildings are very fine in their way, but they are so tied to their origins in other societies and in the thinking of theorists embedded in the imperial metropolis that they speak little of Melbourne except of its progeny's imitative ambitions. Even radical works like the 'blood and bandages' Independent Church, now St Michael's (1867 by Joseph Reed), on the corner of Russell and Collins, with its extraordinary pancake of internal space offering an unusual interpretation of Ruskin's strictures, began an experiment in spatial organisation that could have created a new approach, but ran into the sand for want of local discourse. This often brilliant replicative mode of operating has persisted generation after generation without building any local cultural capital. Among these 'fall from the skies' masterpieces are a Wrightian town hall in Brighton, a Miesian office block (former BHP HQ by Yuncken Freeman on the corner of Bourke and William, 1967–72), Heide, a superb Modern house by David McGlashan at Bulleen (1964–8), and the catenary Sidney Myer music bowl (Yuncken Freeman, 1956–9). All very 'me too'! So many locals did not find, as did Londoner Butterfield, in the midst of the gold boom, that the Melbourne site offered new challenges in terms of scale or type. For Butterfield this was a rare opportunity to do a cathedral, but nothing out of the ordinary in the office tower stakes flowed a century later. There are both IM Pei (Collins Place, 1970s–81) and Kiso Kurakawa (Melbourne, Central, late 1980s) asleep at the wheel: nothing, despite popular belief, is ever 'kick-started' in the culture through these imports. Only when designers come to live in the city for which they are designing, employing the local talent as did the Burley Griffins and as did Don Bates and Peter Davidson of Lab Architecture on Federation Square (2003; in partnership with Bates Smart McCutcheon, the oldest firm of architects in the state), does that very particular design alchemy that binds a work to the culture occur. Without a local grounding and a determined construction of a local culture, there are so many brave starts, many dim resonances of works elsewhere and so few enduring consequences.

What are the factors that support a city in the development of its own culture? In Europe and Asia, in metropolitan centres with ancient histories, longevity alone can promote such cultures. Here each generation can look at what preceding generations have done, and by subtly changing an emphasis make a big statement about their generation's contribution. Not so in settler cities. There, an independent culture only arises when the city becomes diverse enough to break the stranglehold of the home country on the popular imagination of the city.

Only when such a city's population is cosmopolitan enough to embrace difference can it begin to accept its own culture as something of significance in its own right, not simply a pale reflection of the imperial origin. Australians know this in their marrow, coining the term 'cultural cringe' and yet succumbing to it all the more for having put a name to it. Lacking confidence in their own hold on beauty, they feel in their hearts that the best conversations are indeed taking place in London, that the best Sissinghurst is – believe it or not – in Kent. Not in sport, however. What really has changed in Melbourne since the mid 1980s is the slow erosion of the monocular view of Europe through Bloomsbury, or of Washington through the Camelot of the Kennedy period. As we will see, Melbournians of Greek and

Italian origin have transformed this city, naming their buildings sometimes for homelands other than Anglo – the Rialto Tower (Gerard de Preu and Perrott Lyon Matheson, 1986) for example as an explicit reference in name and design (the building's top is arced like the bridge) for the place of origin of its builders and major investors. But even more significantly, they are naming their work for an alternative and local vision – the Republic Tower (Katsalidis, 2000) and the Eureka Tower (Katsalidis, 2005) both signal, as we shall see, a radical Australian identity forged from what is here, not from nostalgia. What has opened Melbourne up to be a design city is the emergence into public life of its citizens of Greek, Italian, Dutch, Vietnamese, Maltese and other origins, and its opening up to people of Catholic and Jewish faith. Prior to 1985, this was the 'wowser' city of Australia, prim and Protestant, dominated by patriarchies descended from the ascendancy in Northern Ireland, run by the old school tie. Not for nothing do cartoons of the prewar years represent Melbournians as always carrying umbrellas and revolvers. Not for nothing even today do people talk of the old money of Melbourne as a conservative force.

It was my good fortune to arrive in the city in 1986, just as it began to be multipolar – as we shall see, a phenomenon essential to creativity. In the 19th century the lure of gold brought people from all over the world, and a China Town remains in Little Bourke Street in the city centre, but the colonial situation enforced one view of the world. In the 20th century wave on wave of migration washed across the city – Italians and then Greeks to the inner suburbs, the Dutch heading for the hills and growing tulips on the slopes of the Dandenong Range, the Maltese to the flats of Sunshine in the west, the Vietnamese to Richmond. While migration is still dominated by

Melbourne has the most highly educated population of any city in Australia, containing 40 per cent of the people in the country with a higher degree, and it is far and away the most liberal (small 'l') place in the country, so much so that to journey to its outer suburbs is to acquire a sense that you need a passport. As we shall see, this inner city community has created a market for high design in several fields. The outer suburbs are, however, another world, less educated, more static – most people live one suburb away from where they were born. Aside from Perth, but less extremely than Melbourne, all Australian cities are characterised by the same bipolar culture, a feature that means that politics is played to the outer suburbs and seldom overtly to the high culture supported by the inner cities. If any credence can be given to Richard Florida's thesis that tolerance and diversity generate a creative class,[6] then Melbourne's inner city is where you would expect – *pace* Sydney – to find the biggest concentration of such talents in Australia.

But, until design finds its way on to a continuum between DIY decorating and the highest aspirations of designers, a continuum such as that which exists between playing ball in the backyard and marvelling at a great player's skills on the field, you will not find much political support for design or higher education. Almost everything that happens to nurture ambitious design is dependent on individual initiatives. So while the environment was ripe, in a sense, 20 years ago when I took up my appointment at RMIT, there was little idea of what needed to be done to make the local design culture flourish. The largest commitment to design that the city of Melbourne then supported was the so-called 'International Series', a lecture series that imported famous architects from around the world and presented them on stage in the Dallas

Anglo-Saxons, this is now a very cosmopolitan city. In terms of internal migration flows, Melbourne, regarded as an industrial rust bucket in the 1980s, has become a youthful city, attracting young professionals from all of the other cities in Australia, and exporting its retirees to the Gold Coast in Queensland. It is also an educated city, at least at its core. Today inner

Brooks Hall (one of the largest auditoriums in the inner city) to an audience of 1,000 architects. After observing this for a time, I asked how many local architects were being asked back to the countries of origin of these 'stars' and hearing, as I'd suspected I would, that no one had ever been so invited, I pulled the plug on this ritual. Such money as we had, I determined, would go into ventures that would lead to architects from Melbourne going overseas to explain what they were achieving.

The first task, I thought, was to get those architects who were ambitious to think about their achievements in a conversation that could be international, and so I developed the idea of inviting architects and designers who had already established a mastery at least as advanced as anything I had seen overseas to consider the nature of their mastery and speculate on how future practice might evolve.[7] This involved a more systematic capturing of the design knowledge being generated locally in publications; indeed, I supported the struggling journal *Transition* until it had created a market for a series of other journals such as *Monument*, and embarked on a series of monographs on local heroes such as Guilford Bell[8] and Peter Corrigan.[9] These began slowly to circulate in the wider world. And I put our resources into getting the talent exposed at the foremost forums for experimental architecture: the biennales of Venice (Wood Marsh in 1991, Lyons in 2000, Kovac in 2002 and 2004) and Rotterdam (2003 and 2005); Archilab in Orleans (2000, 2001, 2002); Architectures Non Standard at the Pompidou (Kovac 2003/4), and so on. And then, despite fears that I would import stars from overseas, as did most people in a position to influence commissioning in Australia up until the end of the 20th century, I looked instead for ways to commission the adventurous

Australia-based architects to do buildings in the inner city – as has now become routine in Melbourne.

This last is utterly crucial. No one has ever created a design culture by importing design. The story of a design city is the story of when and how it embraces its own ideas and works through them to generate local cultural capital. And then when and how that capital is exported. Such ideas, as say, what a place is this! How noble in form and majesty! The enemies of this process are those who always think that the good comes from somewhere else, those who never pause to live here, saying to themselves all the time: 'Oh! That is so like Tuscany! I wish I were there!' The proponents of my approach are those who have stayed here long enough to engage with the wonders of the place without succumbing to endless analogy. How can anyone who has walked down Brunswick Street in the inner city suburb of Fitzroy as I did in 1987, aiming to post a letter, wearing a sweat shirt, not perspiring at all in the dry 40 degree mid summer heat, and who has crossed through 'the change' into the relative coolness of 20 degrees half way to the Post Office, shivered, and on their return noted that they are stepping back into the heat two shops further up than they left it, not wonder what a local culture might be? And yet the most internationally vociferous Australians are expatriates who aim to make at last a proper garden in England, or grow proper vines in Tuscany, or seek out true wealth in the cultural institutions of the USA (where ironically they succeed as remnant English). Those who have focused their energies on what is here and have worked with what is where they are have laced this culture with obstacles, areas of resistance in the field like the lost remains of a Roman villa under an English meadow that anyone who begins yet again to plough across its increasingly wrinkled surface cannot avoid noticing. These acts of the particular are the nuggets of which the design city culture is formed, as when Paul Carter describes a Christmas in Brunswick, a second ring inner suburb, where everything becomes 'surface' because nothing has an inner story that can be read, and then designs the scoriated surface of the amphitheatre of Federation Square, incising it with letters from the alphabet that look to mean something, but are about us being lost in translation – the settler condition.

What I look for, what we connoisseurs of wherever we are seek, are the ideas that have taken hold, and that – even if avoided for a generation – turn up again as soon as someone serious begins to work across the terrain of the culture. A design city is one in which enough people are interested in finding these resistances, resistances that are always sufficiently densely laid down to be attached to the culture in a chain of linkages that, once noticed, seem to be the inevitable context for working in a place. I see myself as an identifier and an espouser of these positions. But also as an enemy of the mediocre. Most of what I have seen officially embraced as design culture in this city is provincial in the most excruciating sense of the word. And that continues to be the case, because good design is always marginal, edgy and difficult and it cannot be wrapped up in pink bows and festooned with butterflies without real designers gagging in disbelief.

In Melbourne the emergence of a strand of thinking, neither Old World nor New World in focus, but dreaming about here, a strand that has become a cornerstone of local design culture, was invited by Redmond Barry, and then denied. It recommenced

with the arrival and temporary migration of a radical architectural duo, Marian Mahoney and Walter Burley Griffin, designers and theorists, embraced and then denied. It had a conflicted flowering when Robin Boyd was at the height of his curatorial powers in the 1960s, conflicted because he was torn between the romantic Europhile position of his distinguished family and his talent for the modern. His designs speak for the latter, his writing collapses into a retreat from the New World. It recommences with the return from study at Yale of Peter Corrigan in 1976, determined to attack the politesse theorised by Boyd, determined to find the architecture in the ordinary instinctive preferences of suburban Australia excoriated by Boyd as the 'Australian Ugliness'. And then it finds its moment again in the levers I was fortunate to find and provide in the late 1980s.

So, Melbourne has a history of curatorial ambitions that forms an invisible but essential infrastructure. Even though much of this has been innocent of a conscious curatorial agenda, it has edged the city over and again towards design ambition. Wittingly or not, Redmond Barry opened up a curatorial arena when in the 1860s he purchased the 10 photographs of great buildings, posing the question as it were, 'What will our great buildings be?' In the 1960s Melbourne architect and critic Robin Boyd created a curatorial space with his writings on Australian design, but then fell into the trap of proscription, attacking an 'Australian Ugliness'. He denigrated everything suburban or in any sense related to Las Vegas (that Las Vegas which Venturi Scott Brown by contrast later saw as the beginnings of a new beauty), eschewing the popular culture of the New World, revealing as he did so his deep family connection to the Old-World-recreated colonial project. But Boyd's failure of self-awareness opened the door to Peter Corrigan's counter attack, freshly returned from postgraduate study at Yale and promoting the difficult beauty of that New World. *Transition* (1979–2000), the journal that Corrigan inspired Ian McDougall and Richard Munday to establish, became the voice for writings by architects. The writing was lampooned by critics but curatorially vital, because a design culture grows through the expression of the aims of its designers in media other than that in which it has been designed.

When I arrived the main story in design in the city was about Boyd's heritage – who was related most closely, who indeed most closely married into it. Corrigan's push to reconcile high culture with the suburban reality of most of the city was seen as 'larrikin', and lacking in seriousness. It was far from either, and was manifesting itself in a series of small buildings on the fringe of the city and in ways that will always haunt the architects here. Then, to show a visitor work of ambition took three days, driving to three or so projects on the city fringe each day. The establishment was completely oblivious to any local talent, as indeed much of it is to this day, with incredulity being the reaction of wealthy patrons of the arts when told that one is writing about Melbourne as a design city. For them, now as then, such a thing is only possible in Florence. As we will see, Corrigan was not alone in producing profoundly important work on the fringes of the city, and it is from this experience that the proposition of this book is derived, namely that Melbourne itself has become a curatorial armature. Invention takes place – in a satisfying alignment with the theory of creativity – on Melbourne's margins, that productive creativity being recognised eventually with a position on the

civic spine of the city and, as we shall also see, with postscripts being written again on the margins of the city region.

It was indeed my good fortune to arrive in time to embrace the energies of a new generation of architects, with their just-emerging new ways of thinking about design; their diverse intellectual and technical approaches are in the main the subject of this book. I have no doubt that they would have succeeded without my being here, but in the event, the way in which they have succeeded has been affected by what I was able to do through my good luck in having been able to capture the procurement process of RMIT, strategically situated in the heart of the city, on the civic spine, and suddenly – in the year of its centenary – aware of the need to make amends for an unspeakably insensitive and activity-deadening building along two-thirds of a city block frontage to that spine. My appointment also coincided with a time when RMIT was about to invest in a series of new buildings, partly in defiance of a state government that had energetically tried to remove it from the city centre, and partly in the process of reinventing itself as an independent university after 20 years of quiescent decline. In this I was fortunate to gain the confidence of the new university's first Vice Chancellor and its first Deputy Vice Chancellor Resources, who were able to surround my radical suggestions for selecting consultants with a veil of retired senior professionals. From engineering came John Connell, founding partner of Connell Wagner (now an international consultancy), a daring inventor who proposed freezing the ground to enable construction of the Arts Centre. Then there was Don Little, former Director General of Public Works in Victoria. To my delight both embraced the challenge of the new with the enthusiasm for

Below: Two of the award-winning designs now making up the RMIT complex. Left: Ashton Raggatt McDougall's Storey Hall (1995); and right: Allan Powell's B94 building (1996)

which they had been famous in their early careers, and convinced the university council that this was all a good idea. I was able to convince everyone of the urgent need for our building programme to express our desire to be at the forefront of technical education and research, and that every commission should therefore in some sense be an experiment, and that the results would be both heterogeneous, reflecting our city context, and a collection of works by a wide array of our most ambitious emerging architects. Over and again I would go to selection meetings with my heart in my mouth, only to find that these old warhorses and I were of one mind. Never say that becoming old dulls the appetite for adventure. Our most determined opposition was always from the young fogies from planning. An unprecedented string of innovative and award-winning designs resulted, transforming the commissioning culture of universities across Australia, and then within the city itself. These buildings include Edmond and Corrigan's Building 8 (1994), Ashton Raggatt McDougall's Storey Hall (1995), Allan Powell's B94

(1996) and Wood Marsh's B220 (1998), Wardle's Graphic Technologies building in Brunswick (2001) and, in collaboration with DesignInc, the Biosciences building at Bundoora (2001).

Paradoxically, despite Melbourne's claims to an intellectual life, on my arrival I had to assert that design is an intellectual activity. Boyd's heritage was a series of shibboleths, not the encouragement of the thinking process. More Beverly Nichols than Rossi or Smithson. The former purveyed a world of charm and grace that found its expression in thatched cottages, that fatal Anglo-Saxon dream of the country so antithetical to good cities.[10] I do not – cannot – lay claim to the singular visions of the latter, but I do believe that I have been able to bring to the city a curatorial understanding that I saw underlying the unarticulated programme of Alvin Boyarsky, and the political programme espoused by Fred Koetter on behalf of Colin Rowe at Boyarsky's International Institute of Design (1970), on which I believe

Boyarsky's position was built. This anti-totalitarian approach seeks out difference, looking for ways of articulating contrasting visions of the good-life and arguing that it is indeed in the rubbing up against each other of these ideas that the city builds its energy, and its utility as a forger of human creativity. It does indeed seem to me that design without theory is unable to connect, to embed, to become part of the cultural substrate, even though – as Mary Beard[11] has shown with Soane – that expression is often conveyed through design renders rather than through words. But I am even more persuaded as a South African by origin, and therefore with firsthand experience of totalitarian rule, that there must always be more than one theory in contest, preferably – as I have latterly come to understand – three, and that where this is not the case, it is our duty to rebel until it is. And as a practitioner first, I see theory as being built from practice, as much as it then builds towards practice in turn. In fact, as my psychotherapist colleague Grahame Barnes, EB Fellow of the Institute of Transactional Analysis has shown in doctoral research conducted at RMIT, theory applied to practice denies the real at great cost to human individuals. I have long eschewed the academic models of North America in favour of a direct engagement with what ambitious designers actually do.

As my friend Celeste Olalquiaga has so entertainingly shown, all around the world a tension between the local and the imported persists in popular consumer culture, with the metropolitans self-satisfyingly assuming that all flows towards them and from them, while real interest lies in the local anywhere.[12] In Melbourne, the culture manifests through local car design and the fads and fancies of all the designer venues of grungy Fitzroy or chic Prahran. Here streamline and Formica succeed one another in cycles that, without a local curatorial intelligence at work, appear to follow Los Angeles or London, depending on whether Paul Smith or Mary Quant or Vivienne Westwood is the celebrity designer of the time. Without local curation not many ripples flow out from this centre to influence centres elsewhere, because people assume that they are second best. Styles are the second best of international discourse, snaking through design in a pale imitation of ideas everywhere, in the flickering, indeed, of the pages of popular design magazines. As my hairdresser once said when I responded to his query as to whether I was going skiing that weekend by asking whether he was: 'No! I'd rather read a good magazine.' Yet we go to Padua to see what they made of the Renaissance, with as much pleasure as we go to Siena, Florence, Venice or Rome. These are not lesser experiences because apparently 'remote occasions' of the universal grappling with ideas that we now know to be unavoidable, because ideas well up everywhere at about the same time. Only empire past or present has the power to disable client communities with the belief that only what happens in the seat of power is real.

In Melbourne today a local culture has vigorously asserted itself in fashion, art and architecture. Melbourne has convincingly trans-cended this game of always regarding the local as a dim resonance of something better elsewhere. In art, as we shall see, the vigorous culture of this city depends on a group of ardent curators: Anna Schwarz and Jan Minchin in the inner ring of private galleries, Jenepher Duncan and Juliana Engberg in the inner ring of the public realm, Maudie Palmer in a new outer ring, with scant evidence of successors who go beyond their initiating curatorial visions. In fashion too the local is vigorously championed, through the prodigious density of tiny production houses all eying each others' works through the annual lens of the Melbourne Fashion Festival, itself created through a curatorial process to which Robert Buckingham was party. And in architecture that vibrancy is manifest in the growth of a tripolarity in the architectural culture, as showcased in my Melbourne Masters Architecture exhibition at TWMA (November 2004 to April 2005). The same is, alas, not true for industrial design, lacking as it does critique and patronage, and would also not hold true for furniture were it not for Kjell Grant and his Melbourne Movement and its regular manifestations in Milan. Architecture is at the apogee of Melbourne's claim to be a design city, thanks to a well-seeded field, strong curatorial ambitions and the beneficial circle of reflective practice and patronage that I initiated at RMIT in the late 1980s.

Crucial to a design city is an enduring curatorial intelligence devoted to each field of design. Melbourne has been lucky to import former Rhodesian Rob Adams as Director of Urban Design in 1985, and as we shall see his persistent care for the bones of the city infrastructure has been a crucial component in the reawakening of the city's sense of itself as a particular place worth living in. This is a big turnaround. In preparation for the 1956 Olympics Melbourne tore down the inner city verandahs and blanketed buildings in hessian in the attempt to appear to be a generic modern city, an attitude that persisted among the ruling elite until challenged by Adams in Urban Design, and by the construction programme of RMIT in architectural terms. Adams's vision has been sceptical of the importance of design, but, as we shall see in the concluding section of this book in an account of the QV complex, it complements my own insistence on the need for design ambition in

every instance. And this despite even Vincent Scully's apologetic notion that design is the friend of the building and the enemy of the city,[13] a notion that gets recycled by the Beverly Nichols of every generation (currently Alain de Botton, who has announced just this as the theme of his next book).

How is this focus on local design ambition and its realisation perceived in the media of the city? Melbourne just gets by in this regard: the local press hosts regular critiques by architect Norman Day, but otherwise is woefully unable to see what is going on under its nose in design, tackling it in the one bad meaning of that fine epithet 'provincial' – without overview. Aside from sport, only art is regularly and provocatively reviewed. The lack of a local poetry of quality seems to stem from a lack of curatorial or publishing interest in the city, puzzling when one realises that small reading groups persist and there is a vigorous tradition of political and critical writing, currently promoted by entrepreneur Morrie Schwartz, plus vigorous offshoots of international commercial publishers and two university presses focused on local production. Some argue that a quirk of migration has ensured that patronage in Melbourne is skewed to the visual arts, and to literature in Sydney. Here Antoni Jaques's tiny press tries hard and the unique Peter Lyssiotis persists with artists' books under his 'Masterthief' imprint.

Designers cannot do the job on their own. Their discourse soon collapses into gossip and sectional bipartisanship. The mind of a curator is the essential partner to the endeavours of designers. Without curation creativity flounders, attacks issues head on, cannot find ways through, fails. What is this curatorial intelligence that supports every design city? Critical intelligence can be acute but it has a tendency to be partisan, as has *Quaderns*[14] in its issue on manifestos in which three positions are described, but only one is argued for, the editors thus taking a side and creating straw men as opponents who can be easily dismissed. Or such intelligence can promote an artist or a school in the interests of a market position, as did Clement Greenberg with the Abstract Expressionists, actively denying space to any other school in the process. Watching Schwartz, Engberg, Buckingham and Grant one can see that curatorial intelligence situates itself differently in the world of its interest, like some Goliath wading through oceans on which float all possible endeavours in that field. From this vantage point this intelligence draws towards itself this or that raft of works, never losing interest in what lies in the flotillas beyond, ready always to pull into a close focus what currently sits on the edges of the ocean or in oceans beyond, what has just emerged into being, what has almost faded from memory. That at least is how I would like to see the task. Curatorial intelligence has an eye on what is being pulled into focus in other fields, in other oceans, but is always working out what needs to be brought into focus where it is at work if the full potential of the local culture is to be released. Curators play host to as many theatres of memory[15] as they can sustain, juggling them, juggling what is within each argument that forges a collective, cross referring, collecting and, as Susan Sontag argues, always remaining dissatisfied:

A complete set of something is not the completeness a collector craves. The entire production of some notable dead painter could conceivably, improbably, end up in someone's ... cellar ... (Every last canvas? Could you be sure there was not one more?) But even if you could be sure you had every last item, the satisfaction of having it all would eventually, inevitably, decay. A complete collection is a dead collection. After having built it, you would love it less each year. Before long you would want to sell or donate it, and embark on a new chase.[16]

So what is it that we contribute? Newspapers have been eager to have me attack works of architecture ever since I arrived in Melbourne. Vituperation sells, but it does nothing to grow the culture. It simply reinforces public mistrust of those engaged in a supremely difficult calling. I decided that I would only write to explain what was good about work, and how it had come so to be, and this I do extensively. In this I cast myself as the curator who is a connoisseur, collecting into arguments works that have caused intellectual change. To such curatorial intelligence, every new arrival or discovery shifts the balance of appreciation within an argument. As in ethics if there is no content, in design if there are no collections, there is no argument. And note that plural. Not one collection, but many, arranged around different criteria. If I had my way, there would never be singular design awards in any category, always three, allowing for the healthiest situation – that in which three positions are being argued out in design.

Today curators are interested in assembling collectives because the Modernist myth of individual creative originality has been discredited by research into mastery and innovation. This is what I was determined on when I arrived here, that I would find what was good in Melbourne and make it see how good it was, and then this city's culture would find its place in the world, and I mine with it. My mentor Peter Cook, whom I love dearly and whose significance for architecture I believe he cannot fully comprehend (can any of us see ourselves?), once alienated an entire room full of Asian architects by averring that they

Below: Group portrait of participating architects in the Melbourne Masters Architecture exhibition at TarraWarra Museum of Art, November 2004 to April 2005. (Standing) Tom Kovac, Kerstin Thompson, Shane Murray, Carey Lyon, Roger Wood, Ian McDougall, Peter Corrigan, Peter Elliott, Maggie Edmond, John Denton, John Wardle, Randal Marsh, Allan Powell, Maudie Palmer (Director of the Museum); (seated) Ivan Rijavec, Leon van Schaik (curator), Eli Giannini, Rob McBride, Debbie Ryan, Niki Kalms (research assistant to Leon van Schaik for exhibition)

were doomed to marginality because they were not working in London. And what a room! The faded splendour of the Eastern and Oriental Hotel in Penang in 1987, where they still served the original colonial menu, complete with Brown Windsor Soup! Not for the last time, a room caused the confusion, reeking as it did of the Empire. This is the confusion of empire – against which I have fought all my life – a confusion composed of a conflation of power and ideas. Power may well have been – may well be – metropolitan in the geographical sense, but ideas have never been metropolitan in origin even if developed with an eye on the centres of power. Even Cook has to be seen as from Bournemouth, rather than from London, if his true import is to be understood. Whether I was in Johannesburg or Timbuktu, I would have fought for what was there against what was dreamed of as being elsewhere. Once on a walk in Johannesburg, I attempted a count of the number of white gardens

palely reflecting Sissinghurst. And yet, who would go to South Africa to see Sissinghurst? I eschew this inbuilt kowtowing and embrace what can be done wherever we are, by being there.

Alan Powell puts it like this:

Until van Schaik opened up space in the discourse in Melbourne, that discourse was completely overshadowed by a bullyboy, beer-swilling, masculine camaraderie that made it impossible to talk about any but the most matter-of-fact design concerns. Opening that space meant that many of us who were at least metaphorically in the shadows of that 'boys' club' culture could fulfil our potential and emerge on to the field as players.

Kerstin Thompson has said the same in different words. I have to say that I did not see it thus; I was too engaged in trying to feel my way towards understanding

the different positions that I could at first faintly discern, though of course in that very plurality I can see that I was indeed opening doors to more than 'one true way', and for this I was attacked at the time by some of those I was seeking to support. Powell's is a sobering account of the duty of a curator. Far too few have the practical grounding to transcend the easy purisms of theoretical postures. And far too many still espouse a singular Modernism that the 20th century closed the doors on for all time, or so one devoutly hopes. To be a design city, a city must have curators who ensure that there are spaces in which all voices can be heard, not as a cacophony of every voice for itself, but rather in clusters of voices around arguments or theatres of discourse. As I showed in the exhibition Melbourne Masters Architecture (TWMA, 2004–5) such clustering is what makes for vital discourse in a culture. In design, as in any field or discipline, intellectual change is supported when three contrasting positions are strongly articulated. These clusters need to be re-framed as the culture

evolves; they are not immutable, even if at bedrock they seem to be about how people place emphasis on one or other of the trio that Vitruvius identified 2,000 years ago: commodity, firmness and delight.

In architecture, whether interior, landscape, urban or generic, discovery[17] takes place through design, but what has been discovered must be integrated into existing knowledge by critics and curators before others can apply what has been discovered and disseminate it further afield.

Applying a curatorial eye to this, the city of my adoption, as I stand on the extreme end of the extension into Docklands of the financial spine, on Collins Street, and see my Alpha Ville, what are 'the one or two things I know about her'? Behind me there is an apartment tower by Wood Marsh (2005), one of four brave experiments in the form, the first of which has a block seemingly stranded on top – perhaps the trigger for the ark that rides over this latest addition with its exoskeleton and zigzagging skin, all sitting on a dockside podium that is as urbane as anyone could hope for. Ahead of me to my right is Watergate, a series of apartment slabs by Elenberg Fraser with zigzagging balconies that burr on the local eidetic of the Capitol Theatre interior which, as we shall see, is one of the formative spaces on the civic spine of the city. Over to my far right is a series of dockside restaurants by Eli Giannini and pavilions by students from RMIT. As if a gas chromatograph, the vacuum of the Docklands has leached out of the city some of the deep archaeology of the design culture, those design ideas that every design intelligence operating in this city comes into contact with as a resistance that needs to be mastered before any innovation is possible. Even in this bleak, newly formed peripheral zone of this city, you do get the sense that something is up!

All of these curatorial efforts pose the question, what next? And all seek a new generation of curation if the vitality is to continue into the next generation. Is Melbourne a design city? My answer is, 'Yes, for the moment.' This coincidence of all of the possible strands of curatorial intelligence is a 'once and future thing'. Cities do not seem aware of the alchemy that is at work and in all probability, the next generation will misread the causes of success – as did Barcelona – and lapse too into quiescence, failing to put the arguments needed to maintain innovation.

1 Peter Rose, *The Rose Boys*, G Allen & Unwin (Melbourne), 2001.

2 Leon van Schaik, *Opere é progetti, Sean Godsell, Documeti di architteture*, Electa (Milan), 2004.

3 Brian J McLoughlin, *Shaping Melbourne's Future*, Cambridge University Press (Cambridge Melbourne New York), 1992.

4 Paul Fox, *Clearings: Six Colonial Gardeners and Their Landscapes*, Melbourne University Press (Melbourne), p139. 'Guilfoyle's trip to Europe in 1890 ... rather than creating a longing for Europe ... reaffirmed the colonial experience ... there was "no doubt that as the facility of communication with Europe and America" increased, the Australian colonies' "vast resources" would bear fruit ... Guilfoyle read "the colonial clearing as an intersection of cultivation, technology and nature ...".'

5 Rohan Storey, *Walking Melbourne. The National Trust Guide to the Historic and Architectural Landmarks of Central Melbourne*, National Trust of Australia (Victoria), 2004; Melbourne: St Pauls, pp 12–13, St Patricks, pp 84–5.

6 Richard Florida, *The Rise of the Creative Class and How It Is Transforming Work, Leisure, Community and Everyday Life*, Basic Books (New York), 2002.

7 Leon van Schaik, *Mastering Architecture*, Wiley-Academy (London), 2005.

8 Leon van Schaik (ed), *The Life Work of Guilford Bell 1912–1992*, Bookman Transition (Melbourne), 1999.

9 Leon van Schaik (exec ed), Nigel Bertram (ed Vols 1 and 2), Winsome Callister (ed Vol 3), *Building 8: Edmond and Corrigan at RMIT*, Schwartz Transition (Melbourne), 1996.

10 Raymond Williams, *The Country and the City*, Hogarth Press (London), 1973. Williams contrasts this with the French obverse.

11 Mary Beard, 'Half-Wrecked', *London Review of Books*, 17 February 2000, pp 24–5. Cf p 25 for the discussion of symbiosis between artist and architect, in which Soane began to work in the idiom that Gandy had established; Gandy, in other words, taught Soane what 'Soanian' architecture was to be.

12 Celeste Olalquiaga, *Megalopolis. Contemporary Cultural Sensibilities*, University of Minnesota Press (Minneapolis), 1992.

13 Vincent Scully, introduction to a book by a Mrs Dowling on the work of architect PT Shulze. It is dated and signed New Haven 1988 and was shown to the author as a photocopy by the doyen of Melbourne Modernists, architect Neil Clerehan (on whom a book is in preparation by RMIT).

14 Editorial, 'From Manifesto Activity to Radical Activity', *Quaderns*, Vol Q40, No 244, Collegi d'Arquitectes de Catalunya (Barcelona, 2005), pp 12–13

15 Frances A Yates, *The Art of Memory*, Pimlico (London), 1966.

16 Susan Sontag, *The Volcano Lover*, Jonathan Cape (London), 1992, p 72.

17 Discovery, integration, application and dissemination are the scholarships identified by Ernst Boyer as the defining activities of the professoriate in our universities, the institutions that should foster curatorial intelligence. Ernest L Boyer, *Scholarship Reconsidered. Priorities of the Professoriate*, Carnegie Foundation for the Advancement of Teaching (Princeton, NJ), 1990.

CIVIL MISSION OF THE CITY & INTERIORS

Civil Mission of the City & Interiors

This photo essay highlights the civil mission of Melbourne and the extraordinary heritage of interior spaces created to support it, from the world's largest surviving timber exhibition structure, through the interior of Burley Griffin's Capitol Theatre, to ARM's AMCOR Lounge, the Melbourne Museum and on to Federation Square.

Melbourne teems with dim resonances of designs from other places, untheorised, replicated as styles. Neo-Modernism, Minimalism – all the currencies of commercial normalcy from around the world play their way out here in interiors that could be placed in a journal and ascribed to any city in the world. Shiny surfaces, metal, glass and polished concrete all carefully composed in an orthogonal frame – the look is ubiquitous. You would not travel a long way to examine some such for yourself. Just like the editor of *Wallpaper* or any publication that aims to keep an eye on breaking innovations, you probably see these interiors and yawn.

What is interesting about Melbourne is not how well it too does these universal designs. What is interesting is the archaeology of spatial inventions that the city harbours, the discoveries about space that have been made here. These are the designs in Melbourne – just as there are other, very different designs in, say, Barcelona – that cannot be avoided by any designers who take the responsibility of aligning their horizons with those of their home culture. Many of the most radical of these can be found along Swanston Street, often described as the 'civic spine' of Melbourne. Others, like neo-Gothic banking halls, the Stock

Exchange and most corporate and banking head-quarters buildings, all rather more establishment in intention, are found on the transverse streets – especially Collins Street, the financial spine of the city, running at right angles to Swanston Street, one end of which has always been known as 'the Paris End'. While it is common to refer to these central city spines and the grid within which they sit as 'Melbourne', the city is in fact a city-state of about 4.5 million people in a region as large as England and Wales. And the process by which inventive designs come to lodge on these spines is a city region phenomenon, with most young designers doing their early experimental work on the city fringes or in the region before being invited to work on the spines. And many notable designers refresh their creativity with inventive, or self-critical works back in the fringes after a success in the centre. So it is important to bear in mind that around this central arena are set works that offer a critique to the prevailing experiments of the culture, those that have achieved full declarative potency by being situated on a spine and thus in the public eye. In this section of the book, we will journey quickly through these, with an emphasis on that archaeology which I mentioned at the beginning of this paragraph, seeking out the historical spaces that give Melbourne its unique spatial history. But in the background, out in the country, there are important works that mount a critique of those works we will encounter on this journey along the spines. Currently the most urgent of these are Sean Godsell's Woodleigh School Science Block, Allan Powell's TarraWarra Museum of Art and Kerstin Thompson's Black Swan House at Connewarre. In Melbourne – if one is to understand

Above: Allan Powell's TarraWarra Museum of Art (2004). There is a powerful lyricism innate in Powell's work, an emphasis on states of mind that invoke a dreamlike stance at odds with the more usual word-based approach to design

Below: Kerstin Thompson's Black Swan House at Connewarre (2003). This house argues for a much closer relationship between the vast flat surface of the continent and architecture than the design canon derived form that is commonly forged

Above: Looking across the arts precinct from Wood Marsh's Australian Centre for Contemporary Art (ACCA) (2002) towards the central city, one senses the critical polarity between the two. The red rust of the building evokes the arid reality of the continent, which the form of the city beyond defies

Left: Nicholas Grimshaw's Southern Cross Railway Station (2006) serves a similar purpose at a functional level, linking city and region to the national rail network

Above: The Exhibition Buildings, built for the 1881 international exposition, home to Australia's first federal parliament, were World Heritage listed in 2004

Opposite: Exhibition Buildings – the interior revealing the timber construction for which the building is noted as the largest timber construction in the Southern Hemisphere

the culture – one is always looking at the core with the periphery in mind. But later in the book we will find many more contemporary works that are part of the very particular curatorial engine created by dialogues between works on the fringe and in the region, and works on the spines.

What kind of spaces populate the spines? To understand the prevailing experiments that line the civic spine today, and the counter intelligences now on the periphery, one has to track back through some of the works that haunt the popular and professional imagination of the city. A great gift to the city is the discoveries of Marion Mahoney Griffin and Walter Burley Griffin, architects who met in Frank Lloyd Wright's office and who worked in Melbourne from 1915 to 1936, having arrived in 1914 to implement their winning plan for the Australian capital, Canberra. At that time the Australian Federal Parliament sat in the neo-Florentine basilica of the

Exhibition Buildings[1] constructed for the 1881 World Exposition (described as the largest timber building in the Southern Hemisphere and becoming in 2004 Australia's first World Heritage listed building). The earliest of the Griffins' Melbourne inventions is Newman College (1915–18). Peter Corrigan, architect to the recently completed Newman College Study Centre, itself an inescapable essay on humanity's fragile cultural project, describes the impact this has on the imaginations of students and architects alike: 'the strong evocation of a New World landscape, the extreme compression of space by the vaulted cloister, but most marked of all the perplexing power of the dining hall – a space with immense power, the source of which we cannot quite fathom.' The strength of the hall – in my view – stems from the way in which the dome that surmounts it, itself topped with a crown of pinnacles, springs from the base of the mezzanine balcony that rings the hall at just above door height. This pulls the dome down tightly over the space and around our heads, creating an atavistic, cave-like compression. While here the dome comes down on to a uniform shoulder, in another context and in another time Soane used the same compressive strategy to give his banking halls for the Bank of England their extraordinary tectonic power, but he brought the dome down into the space only in four pendentives formed by pulling the dome down over a cube,[3] thus

Above: Newman College (1915–18) by Walter Burley Griffin and Marion Mahoney – a college of Melbourne University, and a work that haunts the imagination of the city

Left: Newman College Study Centre, Edmond and Corrigan (2004). This spiralling interior pays homage to the spaces of the original Newman College

Below: Newman College, the vaulted cloister, an unusually compressed spatial experience from which you are released into the dome of the dining hall

Top: Newman College dining hall, showing how the dome is brought tightly down on to the balcony set at the height of the cloister outside

Above: Newman College. A crown of pinnacles surrounding the lantern on top of the dome

Left: Newman College. Close-up of the mezzanine balcony around the dining hall

Above: The domed State Library Reading Room (1913) resonates with the
Newman College dining hall, but on a grander scale

Opposite top: Wilson Hall (1956), a rare Modernist space on the
civic spine

Opposite bottom: South Lawn Underground Car Park (1972), Melbourne
University, a space used in the film *Mad Max*. This relatively unknown
space has a spare engineering beauty rare in this city, and it serves
therefore as a puritan critique of the city's more expressionist spatial
preferences

creating an effect of floating completely absent in the dining hall. The paradox of the Griffins' soaring arched form, the valencies of which are expressed in ribs that support the lantern, and the sheer pressure the dome exerts on the space create a tension that is unparalleled, and that haunts the imagination of citizen designers.

The domed State Library Reading Room (1913), locally believed to be just a little larger than the Reading Room at the British Museum in London, and the largest concrete dome in the world for a few months,[4] has – handsome as it is – little of the inventive impact of the much smaller dining hall. Being exceptional in the Southern Hemisphere has mattered to Melbourne as much as being Catalan has to Barcelona! Featured in the movie *Mad Max*, the South Lawn Underground Car Park[5] (1972), located under the central lawn of the university, its catenary curved columns forming earth bowls under the trees above, is a structure that evokes the yet-to-come elegance of Calatrava, and has similarly haunted artists and the popular imagination. And in the 1950s Wilson Hall (1956), fronting this lawn, laid claim to the avant-garde with a second but overtly Modernist public space.[6] Attacked by Robin Boyd as 'featurist' in the sense that

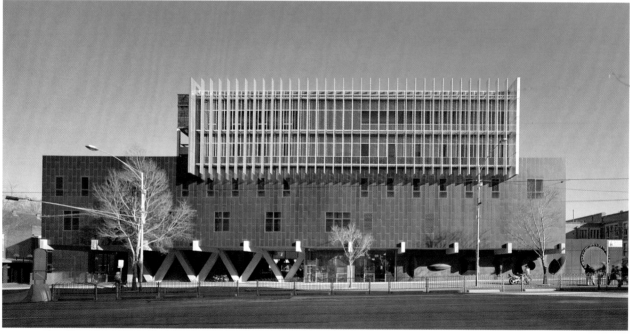

it is laden with what estate agents refer to as 'architectural features' (much as Coventry Cathedral was covered in works of craft), this hall with its long wall of glass facing east, a solid 'L' of ceiling and wall running from this down to a low level slot window all along the base of the west face, is the prototype of a rationalist space that has no other exemplar on the spines. It beckons towards Godsell's Woodleigh Science Block, in its dumb search for a successor. In the 1990s Melbourne University realised that it had lost its position as the patron of innovative architecture to RMIT, and began to respond, firstly with a series of commissions to Peter Elliott who inserted delicate Modernist embroideries on to existing buildings and a residence, and then two buildings by Nation Fender Katsalidis – the Potter Museum of Art (1998), and the Myer Asia Centre (2002) – for which Tasmanian Bob Nation was credited when the partnership split during design. The Potter Museum of Art houses a café, Brunetti's, an offshoot

Opposite top: Potter Museum of Art, Melbourne University (Nation Fender Katsalidis, 1998), somewhat in the Modernist genre

Opposite middle: Myer Asia Centre, Melbourne University (2002), also in a Modernist genre

Top left: Brunetti's at the Potter draws the Italian culture of nearby Lygon Street on to the spine. Lygon Street was one of the first neighbourhoods to embrace outdoor dining

Top right: Jimmy Watson's Wine Bar (1963) demonstrates Robin Boyd's eschewal of featurism, sitting undecorated at the end of a High Victorian street

Middle left: Jimmy Watson's in context on Lygon Street

of the Italian culture of nearby Lygon Street and the first manifestation of the city's postwar multi-culturism. On that street is Jimmy Watson's Wine Bar (1961–3), a double-cubed volume with mezzanine inside a white-painted, bagged-brick exterior that must have seemed very radical amid the Italianate High Victorian architecture of its surrounds when built, Jimmy Watson's Wine Bar is the only building by polemicist Robin Boyd that is in contention in the city centre.

Cross Victoria Parade and Swanston Street angles round to adjust to the orientation of the original city grid, and in the resulting triangle, there is the wonderful confection of the City Baths (1903–4), 'an exuberant and much loved Edwardian structure'[7] designed by EJ and JJ Clarke. This building is as close to a 'swimming pool library'[8] as Melbourne gets, a facility that brings people of every age, nationality and walk of life together. JJ Clark had designed the exceptional Treasury Buildings[9] at the head of the

Opposite and below: City Baths (1903–4; restored 1983). An exuberant
manifestation of public hygiene. The pool is a meeting place for people,
as baths have always been

financial spine of Collins Street 40 years earlier, when
only 19! (see Elenberg Fraser p 268)

Cross Franklin Street and we come to RMIT's
City Campus, where the current blooming of
Melbourne as a design city began with the series of
radical buildings[10] that, as described in the
introduction, I began to assemble for RMIT in the early
1990s. This campus has become the most intense
collection of inventive architecture in the city, and
these works are crucial to understanding what has
happened in the city since, as indeed they are to

understanding what has happened on increasing
numbers of university campuses around the country.
To get to these you have to pass the vast grey lump of
Buildings 14, 12 and 10, part of a 1970s' 'brave new
world' polytechnic design that turns its back on the
street and seems to assert a puritanical worthiness.
The baleful effect of these buildings on the civic spine
were a starting point for RMIT's determination to
change its attitude to the city. And they form the
context for the deliciously colourful Building 8 (1994)
placed provocatively over a low Modernist structure by
John Andrews, a 1970s' building perversely skewed to
the street and sunken into a half-basement. The first
building to be completed in the new system of
selection in which design ambition featured as a
criterion, Building 8 was designed by Edmond and
Corrigan.[11] This is the first centre-city demonstration
of their radical agenda for embracing Australian
'ugliness' in all of its manifestations, expressing in a
variety of narratives the salient elements of the civic
reality of the city. Why embrace 'ugliness'? What is
being argued is that the cities that Australians have
made have their own character, and that it is on that
character that architecture should be based, not on
ideals of beauty imported from elsewhere. The
building, as we shall see, sets out to speak in the
language of the citizens, using among other devices,
the colours of local football clubs to code its different
floors. Note what appear to be wind vanes on this
building. In fact they signal that this is a city block in
the original city grid, orientated northwest/southeast
parallel to the Yarra River, while back up Swanston
Street, beyond the City Baths, the street swings round
to true north. So the building apes nothing anywhere
else, but sets up an argument about being here, on
this site, in this city. All the buildings on the RMIT
campus have an argument to make. In Melbourne,

architecture was first taught at RMIT under Haddon, a radical Arts and Crafts architect in a period when architecture in Australia bloomed extensively, as is recognised as never before in a forthcoming book by Harriet Edquist, former Head of the School of Architecture and Design. Haddon's work, however, never made it on to centre stage. RMIT has long been set in opposition to Melbourne University (MU) through the pretensions of the profession that sought a home in the founding university of the city, not simply in its polytechnic, and established a finishing course in theory at MU many years later. This opposition continues to be a source of energy for the city. RMIT Storey Hall (1996) by ARM, which followed Building 8 in RMIT's reinvention of its relationship to the city, was the next product of the new process at RMIT, and it signals the reversal in the culture, with Architecture at RMIT taking over the intellectual high ground and working theory into practice. So radical was this design that the Minister for Planning at the time approved it on condition that it was built behind screens, because he believed that his colleagues would stop the work if they saw it under construction. We shall encounter this building many times, and

Top: Building 8 (1994). Startling to some when first built, this building sits almost reticently in the context of its equally exuberant neighbour up the civic spine – the City Baths – and it too asserts a civic narrative

Bottom: Lyons Architects' Sports Centre at RMIT – a powerfully experimental work that promised to add a new spatial experience to the spine

Below: Capitol Theatre (1924) brings Aladdin's cave to the civic spine. A space highly rational in its organisation, it was based on various, then current, theories about the nature of the universe

justifiably so, since it is perhaps Melbourne's most internationally famous new building. Most recently Lyons Architects, whose earth-shattering project for the Swanston A'Beckett Sports Centre at RMIT was thwarted at tender, have (as we shall see) added a Botany Building that brings their experimental position into play on the civic spine. Realised on the

spine is RMIT Storey Hall (1996), which I will discuss in the context of the Capitol Theatre.

Further down Swanston Street, opposite the City Hall, four years after the completion of the first phase of Newman College in 1918 (the chapel was completed in 1936 as the Griffins left for India) the Griffins designed the Capitol Theatre (1922–4). This Aladdin's cave of 'V'-shaped plaster elements backed with rows of red, blue and green light bulbs controlled by four dimmers 'produces an illusion of translucence giving the solid plaster the character of alabaster.'[12] Prosaically described as a response to a client suggestion that the theatre be 'built like a crystal cave'[13] Peter King has argued in his play Mahoney's Masques for a more profound emergence from the theosophical interests of the Griffins, and their consequent fascination with the crystalline and atomic forms of which the universe was thought to be formed. He also draws a line through Rudolph Steiner to Goethe's colour theories. The Theatre in full kaleidoscope of colour variations is still an experience of eidetic consequences even now, when – saved from destruction by RMIT – it is used as a lecture theatre during the day and hosts the Melbourne Film Festival and other events at night. What it must have seemed like when it opened with Cecil B de Mille's Ten Commandments on Saturday, 8 November 1924 one can only surmise. There is no doubt, however, that the space and what it signifies hangs in the spatial imaginations of generations of Melbournians. It is hard to imagine RMIT's Storey Hall (ARM 1992–6) cited by Charles Jencks[14] as the first built evidence of the influence of chaos theory on architecture without this seminal space by the Griffins. The impact of this new way of thinking about space is most evident in the interior, resheathed

Above: RMIT's Storey Hall (1996). Without referring to it overtly as a predecessor, it is as apparently complex and as actually simple as the Capitol Theatre, and draws on a wide range of contemporary research to achieve this

using a tiling arrangement discovered by Roger Penrose. In this sense it is an inverted Sydney Opera House, where discovering a tiling system for the outside of the shells exercised great minds. In this archaeological retrospection, Storey Hall sits on the shoulders of the Capitol Theatre, while its use of fractal geometry – the mathematics of chaos, increasingly appealing to architects because its nested repetitions at different scales allow for affordable complexity and decoration – foreshadows Federation Square.

Capitol House, the Chicago-inspired office building that houses the theatre, sits adjacent to some fine Art Deco office buildings close to Bourke Street. A block away, for some decades during the boom years of the 1880s, Melbourne vied with Chicago for the tallest building in the world.[15] Diagonally opposite, is Butterfield's cathedral, already discussed. Opposite this on the same side of Swanston Street is Federation Square (2003), the large tiled surfaces of which are a fractal pattern, and the glazed 'winter garden' of which has a fractal

configuration. Lab Architecture won an international competition to design Federation Square, and like the Griffins, Don Bates and Peter Davidson (the first from Texas, the second from Sydney who met in London, having studied with and worked for Daniel Libeskind) moved to Melbourne to undertake the design development of their winning design. The transmogrification of their initial Perspex fingers into the faceted wonder that sits over the railway tracks and reunites the city centre with the river bank was both a projection of their architectural ideals, learned in their choice of Daniel Libeskind as mentor, and an assimilation of what has been implanted in the city by previous generations.

Let's look at this from the perspective of an archaeologist again. The lineage, conscious or not, from the earliest of these different spaces to the latest is evident. The Capitol Theatre is an Aladdin's cave; RMIT Storey Hall reveals on the facade of the new annexe to the original 19th-century neo-classical assembly hall how Roger Penrose's non-periodic tiling system has been used to re-clothe the interior with a competing decorative effect; and while Federation Square covers its external surfaces with fractal forms, its Winter Garden is caged in a fractal lattice that is as organically decorative as the others, if at a grander scale.

Above: Capitol House (1924). The handsome elevation fits into an earlier tradition when Melbourne and Chicago vied with each other to build the world's tallest buildings

Below: Butterfield's St Paul's Cathedral (1878) seen across the forecourt of Federation Square. The sandstone disguises the radical red brick of the original design

Left: RMIT Storey Hall (1996). The tiling system used inside is revealed here in bronze castings on the entry face. Note the thin lozenge and the fat lozenge. When joined so that the line linking the two closest points is in an alignment that creates pentagons, these two tiles can cover any surface, a feat previously needing over 200 different shapes

Below: Federation Square (2003). The design's fractal planning strategically differentiates itself from the present central city layout, preserving the identity of the original city grid

Opposite: Flinders Street Station (1910). The great arch of the opening speaks of the class of spaces that includes Newman College dining hall, the State Library Reading Room and the National Gallery of Victoria

Continuing on down the spine, opposite Federation Square is Flinders Street Station (1899–1910),[16] its semicircular opening reminiscent of the Newman College dome and later reflected in the entry to the National Gallery of Victoria. This is the suburban commuter station terminal, baring its open-mouthed grin braced with clocks delineating the times of the next departures from its platforms towards the civic spine. This public space is indelibly fixed in the minds of commuters, as is the interior of the pub opposite, Young & Jacksons, host to the infamous nude portrait of Chloe. Along Flinders Street to the west, the city abuts its docklands, separated from them by the railway tracks that flank two sides of the city grid. Here, on the newly extended financial spine of the city, between Collins Street and Lonsdale Street, is Grimshaw's new railway station, an engineering structure that competes with Grounds' underground car park in terms of elegance and lyrical engineering grace. This space, resonant of London's great railway stations, curiously 19th century in scale and conception, is destined to burr on the popular imagination in a way that tilts the local culture away from Aladdin's cave towards techno-determinism.

A war of geometries continues to be waged on the other side of the Yarra River. The Victorian Arts Centre complex by Grounds Romberg and Boyd (1959–68)[17] seems to retreat from the Griffins' atomic and crystalline mysticism, but in asserting an older, Platonic geometry, it too subscribes to an ambition that has long linked architecture to our unfolding understanding of the universe.[18] The complex is an arrangement of cylinders (theatres and concert hall), three hollow cubes (the art gallery), a triangle (the art school) and a cone (the unifying foyer space). Much of the buildings are buried below grade. The use of Platonic solids is a muscular classicising comment on the incipient fractalism of the Griffins – visible on the exterior of Newman College as a set of flanged masonry fans over the windows. The semi-

Above: Grimshaw's Southern Cross Station (2006) has the same engineering logic and aesthetic as the South Lawn Car Park at Melbourne University

Below: Young & Jacksons, host to the infamous nude portrait of Chloe

Above: The semi-circular opening into the National Gallery of Victoria (1968) asserts the Platonic and the neo-classical

Right: The Victorian Arts Centre complex (Grounds Romberg and Boyd, 1968–96). A composition of Platonic geometric forms, but the illuminated spire melts into the night scene

Below: Newman College has sets of flanged masonry fans over the windows, an incipient fractal geometry in the contrasting atomic tradition that includes RMIT Storey Hall and Federation Square

circular opening into the gallery perhaps asserts HH Richardson's East Coast gravitas against the Prairie School frivolity of the Griffins. However, in a historical irony, embedded within the complex is an extraordinary Aladdin's cave by ARM: the AMCOR Lounge (1997), a set of reception rooms lined with a translucent wall of resin panels containing thousands of bits and pieces of consumer ephemera.

For a long time Grounds Romberg and Boyd's classicising Modernism was the side of the argument that was clearly visible on the civic spine. This assertion of the primacy of the Platonic solids (circle, square, triangle, sphere, cylinder, cube and cone) over the organic or the functional has a curious resonance with Aldo Rossi's search for a universal language of architecture. It is classicising because it promotes form above process in design, and the forms chosen for promotion relate to ancient Greek architectural motifs. But the fractal approach has been strongly reasserted in Minifie Nixon's Centre for Ideas (2004) at the Victorian College of the Arts around the corner, and ARM have undercut the Melbourne Shrine[19] with an acclaimed visitor centre (2004), that uses a mature consideration of their fractal approach to achieve access to this monument through the mound at its base with incisions that seem so right that they appear to predate the building which they serve. Curiously, this parallels the fractal lattice that Carlos Ferrater laced across the rubbish tips of Barcelona in designing the new Barcelona Botanical Gardens. As Robert Hughes remarks in his book *Barcelona*,[20] linking the painters who used to work in the '*plein air*' manner outside Melbourne to other artists doing the same outside Barcelona, there are times when province speaks unerringly to province, here far removed from the cutting edge in Paris.

Opposite: The AMCOR Lounge (ARM, 1997) is in the tradition of Aladdin's cave

Left: Centre for Ideas (Minifie Nixon, 2004). A virtuoso work in the new mathematics, at least on the outside

Below: Melbourne Shrine of Remembrance, red entry court to Visitor Centre (2004). ARM used a Boolean mathematical process, reinforcing the processes of the universe tradition even while creating forms that evoke 18th-century military engineering (in the inverse), while the colour is about blood and poppies

Bottom: ARM have undercut the Melbourne Shrine of Remembrance with the Visitors Centre (2004)

Opposite top: Old Observatory Visitor Centre (Peter Elliott, 1999). The lanterns of the new building subtly echo the forms of the small observatory buildings scattered around nearby

Opposite bottom left: Melbourne Shrine of Remembrance, Green Court (2004). This court contains plants that symbolise peace after victory

Opposite bottom right: Aerial view of the civic spine, looking over the Shrine of Remembrance towards the central city grid, through which Swanston Street cuts

Right: At what was once a closing node on a civic spine that stretched all the way to the destroyed St Kilda Junction, a spark of ambition is revealed in an enclosed rooftop swimming pool by Tom Kovac (2006)

As Swanston Street reaches Princes Bridge over the Yarra River, the city becomes the imperial Domain,[21] with Government House (its ballroom bigger than the one at Buckingham Palace and at least as crudely detailed) and the adjacent Observatory where Peter Elliott (1999) has played out his gentle amplification, constructing more pavilions among the redundant observatory domes and huts to form a visitor centre. The Botanical Gardens are on the northeast and the military barracks to the southwest, and the street becomes St Kilda Road, a boulevard that was originally a track skirting sea marshes as the route to the first seaside resort of the city. In the 1920s it was diverted to encompass the Melbourne Shrine on its mound. It came to be lined with the mansions of the rich, and then in the 1960s began a slow transformation into a commercial office-space tail stretching from the city. Until traffic engineers improved it into oblivion, the boulevard led to St Kilda Junction, a local Piccadilly Circus or Times Square in the popular imagination of the time. Here the main north–south arterial intersects with the tail of the civic spine. St Kilda Road continues up a steep incline to become the Nepean Highway setting out for the Elysian Fields of the Mornington Peninsula; the Queens Road sweeps around from the southwest of the city to emerge beyond as the Dandenong Road, heading for the centre of gravity of the population of the city, an hour to the southeast. The desire lingers to rebuild this once glorious urban hub as an urban place with all of its evident metropolitan congestion, with sporadic attempts at international competitions. As it is, a scattering of office and apartment towers is all that marks the underpass that has resolved the traffic conflicts at the cost of the urbanity. On one of the apartment blocks, construction of one of the largest manifestations of the current avant-garde is about to commence: an enclosed rooftop swimming pool by Tom Kovac.

Underlying the Aladdin's cave strand of spatial design on the civic spine (Capitol, Theatre, Storey Hall, Federation Square, AMCOR Lounge) is another and

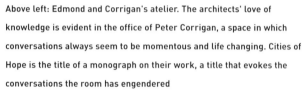

Above left: Edmond and Corrigan's atelier. The architects' love of knowledge is evident in the office of Peter Corrigan, a space in which conversations always seem to be momentous and life changing. Cities of Hope is the title of a monograph on their work, a title that evokes the conversations the room has engendered

Above right: RMIT Building 8 Library (Edmond and Corrigan, 1994). The architects' concern for the popular imaginary includes a love of libraries as repositories of the knowledge that imagination generates

allied line of argument, Edmond and Corrigan's assertion of the popular imaginary. RMIT's Building 8 (1990–4) was the commission that opened the CAD to the new generation of architects whose work had been formed on the periphery during the 1970s and 1980s. It is a manifesto of populist civic legibility, but it also contains a space of immense reverential power – the university library, in Corrigan's mind the repository of human knowledge, a knowledge that is applied and built upon in every city in its own way. This broad, flat plate library, designed for access by many thousands of students every day, contains a number of enclosed cells, studiolos for scholarship set amid the sea of computers that is the contemporary face of the library. His own atelier, in Little La Trobe Street opposite Building 8, houses in one such space, behind tiered shelves with locked mesh fronts, one of those extraordinary collections of architectural and theatrical books that sits in the consciousness of every thinking design professional everywhere. This is

a space in which conversations always seem to be momentous and life changing. Cities of Hope is the title of a monograph on Edmond and Corrigan's work, a title that encapsulates the tenor of these conversations.[22] A sofa and a table laden with open books attest to Corrigan's own active scholarly pursuits, a series of lectures on modern architecture that are delivered as weekly marathons in the main lecture theatre in Building 8, a two-tiered curving space that is derived from sections pioneered by the Finnish architect Alvar Aalto. At Newman College, Edmond and Corrigan have completed a Study Centre (2004) that contains one of the finest library spaces in the city, a double-storey space with mezzanine. Here both the hope that knowledge inspires and the certainty of our ephemerality are played out in a lozenge-shaped lacuna of space that seems to be wrested from contingent reality.

Corrigan is not alone in this fascination with the library. A little further away in Queen Street, Peter Elliott, that quiet master of careful listening and looking and enhancing has wrought another of his amplifications on a classical base, with a two-storey law library in his Law School for Victoria University (2004) that is arranged almost as a double cube layered with a mezzanine. This too is a space that haunts the civil memory of the city, in a gentle generosity that, over and again in this architect's work, seeks out what spaces and places would want to be if

Above: The main lecture theatre in RMIT Building 8 showing evidence of the architect's love of Alvo Aalto's work. Here Corrigan lectures on modern architecture

Below: Newman College Study Centre (2004) from the chapel

Right: Newman College Study Centre Library (2004) at mezzanine level – showing the organic sensibility Corrigan shares with Aalto

Top left: Law Library for Victoria University (Peter Elliott, 2004). The library rises concertina-like from the stone base of the old archive. The courtyard between is both a meeting place and a pedestrian short cut

Bottom: The new Law Library sits on an existing base alongside the refurbished building

Top right: A stair runs between the two levels of the Law Library alongside a glazed wall that unites the space of library and courtyard. This is as close as contemporary Melbourne gets to a Modernist space in the centre

Top left: Swanston Street was rescued in the late 1980s and has become a street happily occupied all year round

Top right: Swanston Street looking towards RMIT across the State Library forecourt

Middle left: Swanston Street looking past the front of the Town Hall

they were to realise their fullest potential as aids to humanity. Aligned but in contrast to the theatrical populism that inspires Corrigan, this is a sensibility that ennobles what has been contingent and reveals how it may be important to citizens. In this strategy, Elliott is accompanied by Shane Murray, an architect whose works – still all on the periphery – have pursued the architectural order that may be innate to the vernacular, but that is seldom acknowledged and embraced in a global milieu that seeks out the seemingly 'original'.

This, then, is the argument that the civic spine holds up to debate. There is a sense in which the

hidden structure of the spine, the laterals and the periphery, is – as Churchill said of the House of Commons – a physical form that gives rise to a certain way of debating.[23] No one has worked so hard to maintain this underlying structure as Rob Adams. Thanks to his vision since 1983 as manager and then Director of Urban Design and projects for the City of Melbourne, in the late 1980s Swanston Street was rescued from terminal decay. By emphasising its public transport and pedestrian functions Adams has ensured that it has become a focus of urban regeneration, giving rise to the QV complex that is the subject of the concluding chapter of this book. It was Rob Adams's understanding of the infrastructural heritage of the city grid and his grasp of the basics – ensuring that streets are not deadened by closed walls – that have preserved for Melbourne a variety of events and venues in the centre that in turn have ensured the city's resurgence as a hub of activity for the 3.5 million people who live in the surrounding 7,500 square kilometre urban sprawl.[24] In this context, it was Adams who appreciated the layout of its major thoroughfares, divided laterally by minor roads (Flinders Street and Flinders Lane, Collins Street and Little Collins Street, Bourke Street and Little Bourke Street, Lonsdale and Little Lonsdale Street, La Trobe Street and Little La Trobe Street) and linked in the other direction by arcades; and it was Adams who understood the importance of the often elm-lined boulevards leading across the parks around the central grid into the inner suburbs. Only recently however, as we shall see in the account of the QV development, has he come to accept the need to work with the level of curatorial action that concerns design.

From Newman College to St Kilda Junction the civic spine exerts a curatorial ambition that has been a magnet for innovative design in this city from its outset. In functioning thus it is one part of a net of urban elements that the city has been able to sustain through the destructive years of the 1970s when this spine itself was the subject of numerous utopian Modernist schemes. One such scheme flattened the fabric of the city down one side of the street and replaced it with a series of slab blocks riding above a podium along the full length from RMIT (where the vision was partially realised) down to the river, where the cathedral was separated from the river by the only other slab blocks to be built (they were demolished to make way for Federation Square). In this, Swanston Street was true to its role as the attractor of radical thinking, a role it has achieved largely because in establishment thinking the mindset runs on the cross-lateral streets. To bankers and civil servants alike, Collins Street takes prime position in the mental map of the city; Swanston Street has merely been a way of getting into the city. Around this central polarity the city extends in rings of development valorised to the southeast – pretty country where everyone wants to live. These rings of development are complicated by a secondary wave of denser development that flows across them after the first generation of settlers has passed on. At those times when the establishment mentality of Collins Street is dominant and there is little room for emergent local experiment, it pops up across this terrain and in the hills beyond, up to the Great Dividing Range and down to the oceans. And when Swanston Street radicalism is operating, and some aspect of the local culture has its day, critiques of this local skewing of the canon emerge in these same zones.

The earliest works of architects are usually villas and seaside holiday homes. The works of architects questioning the dominant paradigms of the centre – the currently lauded works on the civic or financial spines – are smaller institutional buildings, schools (Norman Day), clinics (Ian McDougall) and colleges of technical and further education (Carey Lyon and Lyons). Thus even in the 1970s and 1980s when those commissioning buildings cravenly believed that only international 'names' could deliver, architects – as if in Franco-dominated Barcelona – worked on their ideas in the academies (Deakin, Melbourne University and RMIT) and built smaller experimental buildings many miles away from the centre. And when in this generation, RMIT opened the way for them to build their experiments in narrative expressionism on the civic spine, a critique of this work has developed around the periphery, in Godsell's Woodleigh Science Block, in Powell's TarraWarra Museum of Art and in Thompson's Black Swan House. So when Melbourne is recognised around the world as a design city, what is being recognised is an argument about design being waged up and down the civic spine and conservatively in the cross-lateral streets, while on the periphery new alternatives are being researched in small experiments and the city is 'all the way alive'[25] with its discourse.

1 Rohan Storey, *Walking Melbourne, The National Trust Guide to the Historic and Architectural Landmarks of Central Melbourne*, National Trust of Australia (Victoria), 2004, p 99.
2 Jeff Turnbull and Peter Navaretti, *The Griffins in Australia and India*, Melbourne University Press (Melbourne), 1988, pp 122–7.
3 Leon van Schaik, 'Walls, Toys and the Ideal Room, an Analysis of the Architecture of Sir John Soane', in Mary Wall (ed), *AA Files # 9*, Architectural Association (London), pp 45–53.
4 Storey, *Walking Melbourne*, pp 92–3.

5 Philip Goad, *A Guide to Melbourne Architecture*, Watermark Press (Sydney), 1999, p 202.

6 Ibid, p 164.

7 Storey, *Walking Melbourne*, pp 94–5.

8 Alan Hollinghurst, *The Swimming Pool Library*, Penguin (London), 1988.

9 Goad, *A Guide to Melbourne Architecture*, p 89.

10 *Belle* magazine, in its 1999 (Belle, No 152, April/May 1999, pp 30–48) survey 'Design Visionaries in Australia' described it thus: 'Professor Leon van Schaik has ... earned Melbourne's RMIT the reputation of being one of the world's top educators. Committed to hauling the institution's building stock up to world standard, this ... expatriate has both turned the top of Swanston Street into one of the most important groupings of modern architecture in this country, and finally given us a credible voice in the international design debate.'

11 Leon van Schaik et al, Foreword, *Building 8: The Appointment Process*', in Leon van Schaik (exec ed), Nigel Bertram (ed Vol 1 and 2), Winsome Callister (ed Vol 3) *Building 8: Edmond and Corrigan at RMIT*, Schwartz Transition (Melbourne), 1996, pp 1, 2 and 3, 8–12, 92–6.

12 Turnbull and Navaretti, *The Griffins in Australia and India*, p 190.

13 Ibid, p 189.

14 Charles Jencks, *Fractal Architecture – New Paradigms in Architecture: The Language of Post Modernism*, Yale University Press (New Haven and London), 2002, pp 240–1.

15 Unpublished RMIT masters thesis by Rohan Storey; and with Helen Stuckey, 'Gone but not Forgotten – The Sweet Sentiment of Remembrance; A Short History of the Urban Form of "the City"', in *Transition*, No 47 (Melbourne, 1995), pp 75–81.

16 Storey, *Walking Melbourne*, pp 12–13.

17 Goad, *A Guide to Melbourne Architecture*, p 184.

18 WR Lethaby, *Architecture, Nature and Magic*, Gerald Chatsworth (London), 1956.

19 Goad, *A Guide to Melbourne Architecture*, p 124.

20 Robert Hughes, *Barcelona*, Harper Collins (London), 1992.

21 Nigel Westbrook, 'Phantom Grids and Master Views: The Melbourne Domain – Emergence of an Urban Park', *Transition*, No 47 (Melbourne, 1995) pp 6–19.

22 Conrad Hamann, *Cities of Hope – Australian Architecture & Design by Edmond and Corrigan*, Oxford University Press (Oxford/Auckland/New York), 1993.

23 The same case can be made for landscape architecture, with the Botanical Gardens in the Domain as the original official horticultural library-garden transformed in a generation into a picturesque but polarising centre, and works of critique on the periphery, only recently drawn into the centre with the new park around Federation Square. However, given its own history of patronage, the periphery often contains the most conservative of ventures, designs for the establishment such as Crudens farm, home of Lady Murdoch, and Bolobek and the grounds of the Nicholas House in the Dandenong Ranges. Some peripheral houses, like the Grimshaw house by Desbrowe Annear were, however, surrounded by innovative plantings of aromatics in an attempt to become self-sufficient. Many wonderful new designs for pocket parks by RMIT graduates crowd the periphery in what promises to be a flowering in the centre sooner rather than later.

24 Drawing on Kathy Greening's research into the activities in the city's streets from 1956–86, completed under my supervision.

25 Macdonald, *The Instant Enemy*, c1970: 'I had to admit I lived for nights like these, moving across the city's great broken body, making connections among its millions of cells. I had a crazy notion that some day before I died, if I made all the right connections, the city would come all the way alive, like the Bride of Frankenstein.'

MODES OF CULTURAL PRODUCTION

Opposite: Ideogram E by Leon van Schaik. Melbourne, the southernmost city of any size, is perched on the stage facing a southern ocean. The theatre curtains list some of the conditions for creative innovation: intellectual, political and demographic. The drops list a cascade of past achievements and ambitions. The flats contrast liveability with the melancholy of distance captured in *On the Beach*, Neville Shute's novel about the nuclear holocaust that was set in Melbourne, a perfect city for making a movie about the end of the world, said Ava Gardner in 1958. Piled up on the front stage and bannered across it are names of artists who have struggled to find the soul of the city-region

Modes of Cultural Production

ARCHITECTURE AND ART IN THE
DESIGN CITY (with Jan van Schaik)

There is a strong nexus between art and architecture in Melbourne. The first public showing of the work of many architects of the last two decades has been in group shows, curated by the directors of art galleries, in which artists and architects have collaborated in making projects. Almost all of the architects whose work has ultimately found a place on the civic spine had their first public exposure in this way, as we see in the case of Greg Burgess. The interplay can be seen in the reception desk designed by Howard Raggatt and built by (then) craftsman John Cherrey. This is a quarter full-scale model of a house in Alphington, brought into the public arena through an exhibition and then acquired by me for the RMIT architecture collection in 1993, where it became the Dean's desk – a deliberate assertion of the need to celebrate our material culture. The quarter full-scale model is a procedure that was appropriated from 19th-century engineering practice and it haunts art practice today through the works of Callum Morton. After a period making full-scale replicas of everyday components of roads like *The Strip* (1997), a group of works that ghosts architect Allan Powell's work, Morton now makes models of Modernist icons like his *International Style* (2002) of the Farnsworth House, subtly undermining them with acoustic and lighting effects that, in this instance, situate an increasingly wild party in the house, a party that is stilled by a

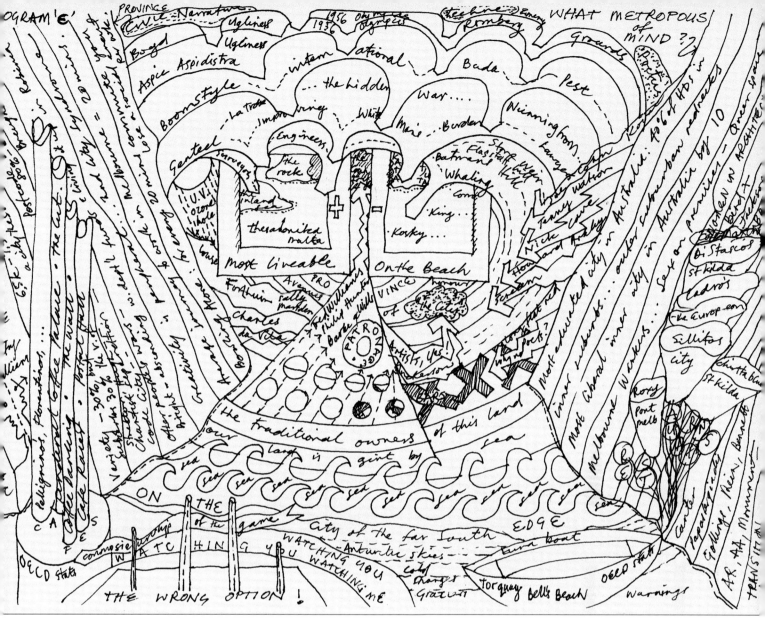

single gunshot. The scaled model links art, architecture and engineering. The suspension bridge over the Thames at Marlow, where I went to school, is a quarter full-scale model for the suspension bridge later built to link Buda and Pest, and the Tyne Bridge linking Newcastle (where I studied Fine Art under Richard Hamilton) and Gateshead is a quarter full-scale model for the Sydney Harbour Bridge, Australia's major built icon prior to Danish architect Utzon's Sydney Opera House.

The striking nexus between art and architecture in Melbourne is clearly evident in the work of Allan Powell or Wood Marsh, who often seem to design spaces with a work by Bill Henson or a Dale Frank in mind. That they do this speaks of an intimacy between these practices that is quite unusual. Peter Corrigan has an intense interest in Phillip Hunter's work and here there is a shared passion for Australian Rules Football as well.[1] Sculptor Robert Owen has collaborated with DCM on the Webb Bridge in Docklands[2] and with Perry Lethlean and others on the Craigieburn Bypass,[3] and worked in many other such partnerships. Artist Stephen Bram has sought out architects as collaborators, working on his obsessions with the translation from two-dimensional depictions of three-dimensional objects or spaces into three-

Top left: Callum Morton's *International Style*, Anna Schwartz Gallery (2002). This animated model of the Farnsworth House extended the artist's critique of the made world into an initially genial interrogation of modern architecture's icons

Top right: Callum Morton's *The Strip*, Anna Schwartz Gallery (1997). For this work a full-scale replica of a sleeping policeman was constructed inside the gallery

Bottom left: Maudie Palmer, Director of TarraWarra Museum of Art, at the museum

Bottom right: The Dean's desk at RMIT, was a quarter-scale model of the Alphington House by Howard Raggatt, in front of which it is picture here. The desk was a collaboration between the architect and John Cherrey, who subsequently studied architecture at RMIT

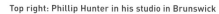

Top left: A Bill Henson on the wall at Cafe Di Stasio by Allan Powell

Top right: Phillip Hunter in his studio in Brunswick

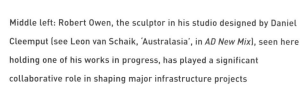

Middle left: Robert Owen, the sculptor in his studio designed by Daniel Cleemput (see Leon van Schaik, 'Australasia', in *AD New Mix*), seen here holding one of his works in progress, has played a significant collaborative role in shaping major infrastructure projects

Bottom: The Webb Bridge (2003) in Docklands on which Robert Owen worked with Denton Corker Marshall (DCM)

Above: The immense LED display on the Craigieburn Bypass (2005) on which
Robert Owen worked with Taylor Cullity Lethlean and Tonkin Zuleika Greer,
is based to a considerable extent on his work *Cascade: A Short Span of Time*

dimensional spaces.[4] His paintings of dissolved spaces emerged at the same time as ARM's spatial envelope defying Storey Hall was constructed, though both architects and artist deny any direct connection, His work in the foyer spaces of Elenberg Fraser's Watergate (see Elenberg Fraser, p268) is an extension of his gallery work in Munich[5] and his collaborations with other architects, most recently with James Brearly in Shanghai. The foyer work at Watergate has been orchestrated by Anna Schwartz, who has worked closely with architects Powell, Wood Marsh and DCM in building up relationships with artists in her stable, while Jan Minchin has worked closely with Corbert Lyon of Lyons on building up a relationship with another significant cluster of artists.

Among these is Louise Forthun. Few Melbourne artists are as collected by architects in the city as is Louise Forthun, who has an interest in architectural or urban subjects. Her interest turns on the difference between a painter's approach to cities and architecture, and that of an architect or designer. Her early work abstracted from the Eiffel Tower can be seen as research into its cellular structure, rather like the

Above: Stephen Bram in his studio in North Carlton

Top right: Stephen Bram's dissolved spaces have had an influence on Melbourne's persistent interest in the deconstruction of space: three paintings in the collection of Leon van Schaik are seen here, with Andrée van Schaik, between a Phillip Hunter landscape and a Robert Owen sculpture. His work in Elenberg Fraser's foyer at Watergate (see Elenberg Fraser, p268) demonstrates one strand of his interest in space

particle studies of artists such as Yayoi Kusama, whom she met in Tokyo in 1992. She spent her initial four months in Tokyo immersed in building sites that could be viewed from her studio in the city. Her use of airbrush caused people initially to bracket her work with that of Howard Arkley, who was also among those artists showcased and encouraged by the Tolarno Galleries. They did share an aversion to the dominant earthy outback art that was then the prevailing mode.

Forthun observes mentorship cycles at work around her, the ongoing encouragement given by James Mollison, the visionary (former) director of the National Gallery in Canberra (who sticks so closely to his mission that he once famously refused to comment on a work of architecture, arguing that it was not his field) to generation after generation of artists, currently Ben Armstrong and Bradd Westmoreland. Forthun herself admires Tony

Clark's work, and enjoys inspiring conversations with him, even though their work lies in different directions. These conversations are important in the making of an artistic community, as such interaction (fellow feeling?) is important in a lonely profession like painting. Forthun values regular exchanges with her peers, Angela Brennan, Kristin Headlam and Cathy Blanchflower.

Like many in her generation, Forthun has been a practitioner academic in art and enjoys the links this sustains with the younger generation of artists. Now, as local critic Ashley Crawford observes, if it is true that you can 'knit' anything into a work of art, the curatorial role of the key public gallery directors is crucial. Max Delany (Heide, Gertrude Street and then Monash), Juliana Engberg (ACCA) and Chris McAuliffe (Potter at Melbourne University) now exert the auteurial power of a film director in the manner in which they assemble their shows. The role of the curator seems more important than ever in mediating between work and the popular imagination, though artists like Forthun and the others mentioned here continue to project their own distinctive auteurial practices.

There are many close relationships between artists and architects such as that between Phillip Hunter and Peter Corrigan. Phillip Hunter is one of

Australia's foremost painters of landscape, concentrating on small areas for long periods of time, during which he becomes familiar with microclimates, the shifting values of light through the day and from season to season. He draws his way into these works at night, after days in the field, and he expands to medium sized canvases, and then to large, all in evidence here. Peter Corrigan is drawn to this work that has some of the theatricality exposed by his own designs for theatre. Corrigan's competition entry for the Melbourne Museum has featured in a series of Hunter paintings. Hunter's partner Vera Müller's work is three-dimensional and she accepts that as a consequence of their living and working together it could be seen as modelling the whorls and flecks that

Phillip uses to depict force fields in the landscape. In the illustration (opposite, top) Andrew Keen, who is Head of Visual and Performing Arts at Charles Sturt University in New South Wales, not far from Hunter's current research site, is persuading the others to do a workshop at his school. The talk is energetic, weaving through theatre, media, architecture and art; shaped by hand gestures, building local knowledge.

Theoretician, writer and artist Paul Carter, Professorial Fellow at Melbourne University, has helped to shape the intellectual climate within which Melbourne has come into bloom as a design city. As a migrant to Australia, he exploited his curiosity about how the place came to be what it is in his seminal book

Opposite: Juliana Engberg, artistic director of ACCA, one of the most important curators in the city. Her Melbourne Biennale – like most such ambitious projects in the city, it only happened once – was an internationally acclaimed event in which Australian artists and their peers from other countries were displayed without any sense of a 'cultural cringe'. Her shows at ACCA are building a new audience for innovative art

Above: Peter Corrigan in Phillip Hunter's Brunswick studio talking to Andrew Keen (left) and Vera Müller (right)

Left: Paul Carter in the restaurant at TarraWarra Museum of Art

The Road to Botany Bay: an Essay in Spatial History (Faber and Faber, 1987). He designed some of the earliest sound works in Australia. Profoundly interested in the surface that we encounter when we first land in a place, Carter's work carved into the surface of the stones that pave the amphitheatre at Federation Square is a tribute to the first verbal exchanges between Australia's indigenous peoples and the first settlers. His focus on ephemerality in the architectural environment has inspired the research of a generation of design research students at RMIT, where he is an Adjunct Professor. Carter's recent book, *Material Thinking: The Theory and Practice of Creative Research* (Melbourne University Press, 2004), explores the pleasures and pains of collaborative work.

The work of many artists admired by architects can be seen in the galleries that line Flinders Lane in Melbourne – especially at the Anna Schwartz Gallery, Tolarno Galleries, ARC and William Mora Galleries (now in Richmond) – as well as from time to time in the Ian Potter Centre of the National Gallery of Victoria (NGV) at Federation Square, at the Australian Centre for Contemporary Art (ACCA) and in many of the buildings described in these pages. While galleries off the spine like Charles Nodrum, Niagara, Sutton and Nellie Castens are also important, the existence of this Flinders cluster is a major curatorial process in the cultural production of Melbourne, a constellation not equalled in any other Australian or Southeast Asian city. Artists and

Top: Peter Lyssiotis in his workshop in East Burwood, beyond the outer limits of the tram system. Perhaps it is appropriate that the artist who deals with the political realities of the distributed city with such intense connections to the imagery of the world at large should live and work where most Australians live – in the outer suburbs of our city-states

Bottom left: Louise Forthun, *Eiffel Tower* (1989), in the collection of Cath Stutterheim, landscape architect, who is pictured here with the painting in her St Kilda home

Bottom right: Emily Floyd's *Signature Work* (2004)

Top left: Gallery opening. There are dozens of openings in Melbourne every week. A group of supporters gathers to honour Susan Cohn in Ross Madigan's home base, centre of a chain of stores retailing high design

Top right: Louise Forthun with Shane Murray at their home and studio (designed by Shane Murray) in Brunswick

Right: Jenepher Duncan, now at the Art Gallery of Western Australia, with architect Allan Powell at an opening at ACCA

Bottom: A work by Dale Frank in the Docklands Foyer by Wood Marsh (2005)

Opposite: Paul Carter, a notable collaborator with artists and architects as well as one of Australia's most important writers on space and our habitation of it, designed the inscribed paving at Federation Square (2004). These are some of the first words used in exchanges between settlers and the indigenous peoples of Melbourne

Above: Anna Schwartz Gallery (1991), entrance. The gallery, designed by DCM, is an uncompromising white shoebox lit by fluorescents. It takes on a different character with every show, making it a chameleon among galleries

architects wander through these galleries checking up on what is happening. Most rigorous in its pursuit of the locally new is the Anna Schwartz Gallery, a pursuit shared with Tolarno Galleries, ARC and Sutton Gallery.

Directors of galleries have been significant patrons of architecture. Without Jenepher Duncan's entrepreneurial initiatives – in which she involved me among many others – there would be no Australian Centre for Contemporary Art (ACCA). Without Francis Lindsay, now director of the Ian Potter Centre at the National Gallery of Victoria, there would be no Potter Museum at Melbourne University – or rather there would be no architecture of distinction associated with the project.

Another director who has had a major impact on the development of the city's architectural culture is Maudie Palmer, formerly Director of Heidi Museum of Modern Art in the northeastern suburb of Heidelberg, once the home of the Reeds, important patrons of modern art in the mid 20th century. The gallery was formed around their second house, a virtuoso design by McGlashan Everest, inspired by the New York Five, and built adjacent to the original clapboard homestead on a site that was once outside the city. Maudie is acknowledged to be a director of outstanding vision in art, but the procurement process for the gallery extension was bedevilled by the belief of the board that there were no architects capable of designing a gallery in Melbourne – the common perception among the commissioning class in the city in the 1980s. Moved by the criticism that the indifferent result attracted, Maudie acted purposively to support the patronage of innovative architecture. She convened a small committee (including Daniel Besen and myself) and drafted the brief that persuaded the state government to run an international competition for Federation Square. The Ian Potter Centre at Federation Square now accommodates the NGV's Australian Collection – arguably one of the most important new architectural housings of art anywhere. For the TarraWarra Museum of Art (TMWA) she guided

Top: Ron Robertson Swann's *Vault* at ACCA where it was relocated in 2004, after many years of exile on the banks of the Yarra River

Middle left: Alexander Knox's *Nolan Tower Screens*

Bottom: DCM's *Vault Yellow* – the City Gateway to the Freeway and the airport

Opposite top: RMIT's Storey Hall by ARM incorporates a vault yellow folded plate as a stair

Opposite bottom right: *Overlogo* tram ticket installation by Jan van Schaik and Lou Weiss (2003) was located on a laneway called AC/DC Lane

Opposite middle left: Simon Perry's *Public Purse* (1994) in Bourke Street Mall

Opposite bottom left: John Meade's *Mean Yellow* (2000)

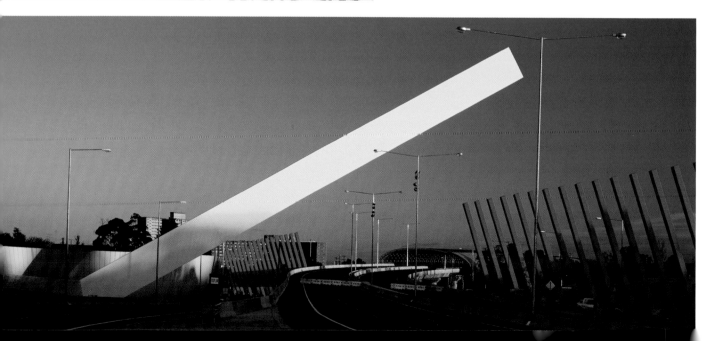

Above: Ian Potter Centre (2003) at Federation Square. Anything but a white cube, Lab Architecture's design continues to challenge Modernist perceptions that art can only be exhibited in neutral space

Opposite: Ian Potter Centre at Federation Square. The gallery consists of a number of handsome rooms linked enfilade, and capable of becoming vessels charged with the power of the works – here by artist John Nixon

the Besen family through an exemplary limited competition that resulted in the commissioning of the Allan Powell design that has won widespread public acclaim.

Outside the galleries the interaction between art and urban space has been hotly contested in Melbourne. Art and architecture have been intertwined in the design of public spaces, beginning in 1980 when the exile by the City Council of *Vault* by Ron Robertson Swann from the City Square designed by DCM created a legend that has been in play ever since. The architects adopted its colour as their leitmotif, using it all over the city on columns notably in the City Gateway on the Tullamarine Freeway between the airport and the centre city. A homage to the artwork was incorporated inside RMIT's Storey Hall by ARM as a stair. The dialogue has never stopped, with many artists practising primarily as 'public artists' thanks to Public Art in Laneways programmes run by the Melbourne City Council Public Art Committee. Such art is represented by pieces like *Overlogo*, the tram ticket installation by Jan van Schaik and Lou Weiss (2003); by

the Visual Arts programme of the Melbourne International Arts Festival that has included John Meade's *Mean Yellow* (2000) and Sean Godsell's *Bus Shelter* (see Godsell, p182); by events like Fiona Abicare's installation *FitOut* (2002) in the window of Le Louvre, the couture house in Collins Street's 'Paris End' that was associated with the Fashion Festival; and by a programme in the Docklands initiated by Maudie Palmer. Some of the results of these programmes are frankly populist like Simon Perry's *Public Purse* (1994) or Emily Floyd's *Signature Work* (2004). Others like the *Webb Bridge* (2004) in the Docklands programme are more abstract; collaborations in art, architecture and engineering between architects DCM and sculptor Robert Owen, who also collaborated with Taylor Cullity Lethlean and Tonkin Zuleika on the Craigiburn Bypass (2005). Alexander Knox's golden car park screens and Dani Marti's windscreens created with architect Dale Jones-Evans,[6] both in the Docklands programme, are further examples of the close relationships that permeate the culture, as we shall see with the several artists who participate in Elenberg Fraser's work and with David Noonan in Paul Morgan's work.

Ever since my initiation into popular art under Richard Hamilton at Newcastle-upon-Tyne, with David Sweetman as tutor, Stephen Buckley as mentor and Bryan Ferry as fellow student and housemate for those four intense years, I have dreamed of the kinds of collaborations that have come to seem second nature here in Melbourne. In my own case, the most significant

of these collabrorations has been achieved in a series of projects conducted with the artist and publisher Peter Lyssiotis through his 'Masterthief' imprint of artists' books. Our major opus to date, a work on the poetics of space, has yet to be published. A fragment of this work was unveiled in *The Poetics of Architecture* (2002) in which monograph Lyssiotis's haunting images of possible and improbable cities divide the different sections.[7]

Our joint work, an illustrated poem called 'Paris', was launched in September 2005. Peter's work is always intensely but humorously sensitive to the political undercurrents of our existence. It is conducted through a mental network that connects the ancient library of Alexandria to people who produce books and develop the material cultures of their cities through words and imagery. If Paul Carter's insight holds true – that the migrant inhabits a surface world, denied access to detail and depth by their recent arrival in any place – then Lyssiotis's world of plausible images imperceptibly collaged together is emblematic of the culture of Melbourne, because around 40 per cent of the city's inhabitants have been born somewhere else. The desire to express this popular imaginary stems from this glissade between us and our memories of there and here, and it drives our architecture into expressing much that others do not feel architecture can express. Hence, in a city that has never had access to the certainties of power that go with being first cities, our warring approaches:

those seeking the commons of Platonic solids, those engaging with the fractal chaos of existence, and those determined to tell and retell our stories.

1 Justin Clemens, 'Sentiments of Intent: Art and Architecture', in Leon van Schaik (ed), *Poetics in Architecture*, AD, Vol 72, No 2 (March, 2002), pp 86–91; and for a discussion of connoisseurship in sport and architecture, see Leon van Schaik, Foreword, in Leon van Schaik (Exec ed), Nigel Bertram (ed Vols 1 and 2), Winsome Callister (ed Vol 3), *Building 8: Edmond and Corrigan at RMIT*, Schwartz Transition (Melbourne), 1996, Vol 1, pp 8–12.

2 Leon van Schaik, article in 'Webb Bridge', forthcoming.

3 Leon van Schaik, 'Craigieburn Bypass', in Justine Clark (ed), *Architecture Australia* (July/August 2005), Vol 94, No 4, pp 60–7.

4 Project with James Brearly in Prahran: see Leon van Schaik, 'Divine Detail', *Monument*, No 31, (August/September 1999), pp 44–7.

5 Leon van Schaik, 'Light', *AD*, Vol 74, No 1 (January/February 2004), pp 126–7.

6 Leon van Schaik, 'Practice Profile Dale Jones-Evans', Emergence: Morphogenetic Design Strategies, in *AD*, Vol 74, No 3 (May/June 2004), pp 106–14.

7 Leon van Schaik (ed), *Poetics in Architecture*.

Opposite: Ian Mowbray, *The Wall* (1999). Mowbray's miniature sculptures are often exhibited as a wall, stacked one upon another

ARCHITECTURE AND CRAFT
IN THE DESIGN CITY

Jewellery that is innovative in Melbourne is architecture writ small, or industrial design domesticated. Quite literally in the case of Sally Marsland, who studied architecture at RMIT. Her work, and that of most of those engaged in radical design in this field, can be seen in Funaki, a tiny shop in Crossley Street, a lane between Little Bourke and Bourke Streets, on the latter corner of which is Pellegrini's, the early espresso bar. Also in this street is Art Salon, a tiny bookshop specialising in unusual books on architecture, art and design founded by Allan Powell's wife Gail and run today by his sister Louise Green.Now, in case you imagine that this is a discrete area of endeavour in Melbourne, Sally Marsland is married to artist Stephen Bram, whose family owns a large and traditional jewellery emporium on Swanston Street itself. And further to this, the space for radical design was opened up by Susan Cohn, doyenne of contemporary craft in Melbourne, designer of the classical Alessi fruit bowl made of two layers of mesh that create a moiré effect. And Susan Cohn, most of whose oeuvre seems to have emerged from a miniaturised metalwork factory working in new alloys, is the partner of John Denton. Cohn's work includes lapel pins made of rolled anodised aluminium clamped to a spring steel arm, and stamped with a date. Cohn's bracelets made of aluminium mesh are classics; one made for Sand Helsel, Associate

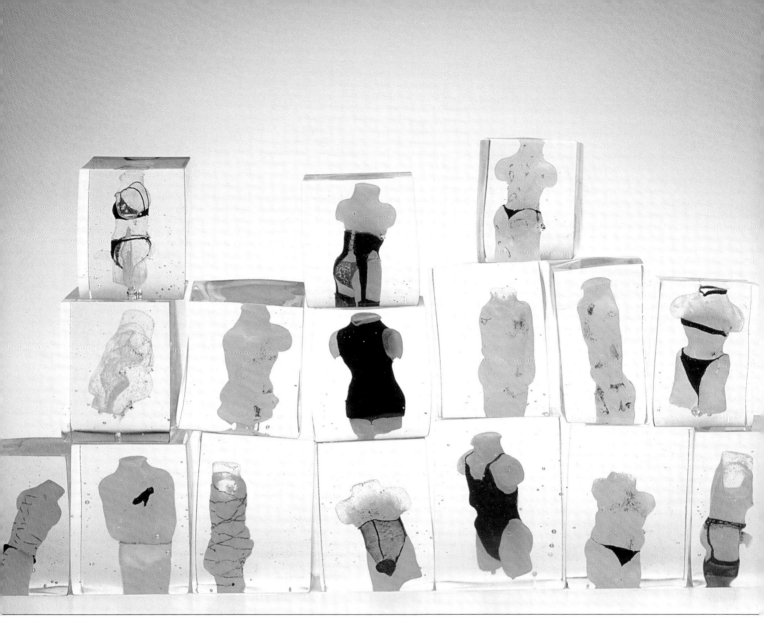

Professor of Architecture at RMIT, contains the ashes of Helsel's favourite cat, a cat that migrated with her to Melbourne from London. An advocate of decluttering, Cohn offers to crush into a tiny cube any metal memorabilia that are crowding the jewellery boxes of her clients. She is also a social activist, designing at the height of the HIV Aids campaigns in Australia, and adopted also by Alessi, a range of containers that held a condom.

Cohn is passionate about modern craft, strongly supporting the shift of focus from ancient crafts towards new experimentations with a technical base. Along with Suzie Attiwill, the curator who completed the reorientation of Craft Victoria towards an engagement with new technologies and now Director of Interior Design at RMIT, Cohn has been unstinting in her support for Ian Mowbray's glassworks. Mowbray creates homoerotic figurines that are first formed in coloured glass, then thrust into molten blocks of glass that are then cooled, flash heated and polished, revealing in one case out of 20 an outcome of breathtaking beauty. Mowbray was awarded an Australia Council 'New Works' grant for October 2005 to May 2006 to complete a new series of glass sculptures, benefiting from a system in Australia that supports the arts but not architecture and design.

Top left: Susan Cohn in her studio in central Melbourne

Top right: Helsel and her bracelet by Susan Cohn

Opposite top left: Suzie Attiwell in her studio in central Melbourne

Opposite top right: Buda (1861), Castlemaine. The north face is designed to let in the low winter sun, but excludes it in summer

Opposite bottom: Buda (1861), Castlemaine. The hedge to the south protects the green parts of the garden from hot northerly winds in summer

Gold- and silversmithery have a long tradition in the city, getting a head start with the Gold Rush, during which a fortune earned by a jeweller from Hungary bankrolled the construction of a fascinatingly inventive house called Buda in the former mining city of Castlemaine (open to the public Wednesday to Saturday from 12 noon to 5 pm, and Sundays from 10 am to 5 pm). Set on a hill above the city and an early precursor of the cross section that Kerstin Thompson has perfected in her work (see Kerstin Thompson, p 236), this bungalow faces north with verandahs that admit the low rays of the winter sun and clerestory widows that allow reflected light to penetrate, while its main windows face south into a thick hedge through which an opening leads to a soft, green garden protected from the hot northerly winds of summer. Traditional jewellery is often about creating settings for gems and this garden has a Central European attitude to lawn, confining it to an oval in the midst of gravel like an emerald in a setting – an invention that is in striking contrast to that of its anglophile peers. This historical link cements in place the connection between the two domains, in which an unembarrassed and frank embrace of mundane materials in a search for a move that will transfigure them into a desirable object seems often to be the driving force of design. In 2002 at the final year show in Gold and Silversmithery at RMIT there was an infinitely desirable set of rings consisting of two silver bands in-filled with fine concrete. Irresistible, at least for an architect! These looping connections between people, institutions and practices are always present when a city blooms in design.

ARCHITECTURE AND FASHION
IN THE DESIGN CITY

When you walk into the alleyways of the QV complex on Swanston Street, immediately south of the State Library, you encounter a series of fashion stores. This is the first manifestation on the civic spine of Melbourne's emergence as an internationally rated fashion powerhouse. Understanding how this has come about leads us into a history of visionary curatorial activity centred now on a thread of interactions that link Robert Buckingham to numerous designers and innovators. It also takes us to the inner suburb of Prahran, which is the engine house of this phenomenon, prevalent in Australia and especially in Melbourne, in which designers establish their own retail outlets, selling to the community of design-interested professionals who have made inner Melbourne their home, rather than concentrating on running wholesale businesses.

The mode of production and the clientele that it serves have had a mutually reinforcing origin in the activities of a small group of people who came together in the early 1980s to pursue an art and performance led agenda in fashion and design. Robert Buckingham, recent graduate in Arts Law from Melbourne University, and Kate Durham, jeweller and artist and then partner of architect Dale Jones-Evans, joined graphic designer Robert Pearce (d 1989) in a series of ventures that explored the interconnectivity

between art, performance, music, design and fashion. Jones-Evans was then a member in the seminal Biltmoderne partnership with Randal Marsh and Roger Wood, both regularly cited as the best dressed men in Melbourne, while Wood's partner Shelley Lasica was and is a prime force in performative movement in Melbourne. In a sense their project was driven by a conscious desire to look at life through 'the body' – an area of investigation in which Melbourne academics, Elizabeth Grosz in particular,[1] were beginning to make an internationally recognised contribution. Robert Buckingham acknowledges an unconscious parallel with developments in the UK documented in the book *Excess*,[2] and recalls the

influence of alternative lifestyle magazines like *ID* and *The Face*. A radio show, 'Party Architecture', broadcast of community network 3RRR during the early 1980s, developed the idea for a fashion event featuring young fashion designers and artists interested in expressing their ideas through fashion. Robert Pearce designed the programme and the set, Robert Buckingham assisted with the choreography and Kate Durham, who has a nose for publicity, helped promote it. Artists and fashion designers involved in this fashion event included Roslyn Piggot, Maureen Fitzgerald, Jenny Bannister, Clarence Chai, Kara Baker, Ian Russell, Sarah Thorn, Bruce Slorrach, Vanessa Leyenhelm and Jane Joyce. Many of these names are synonymous

Below: Material By-Product design partners Susan Dimasi and Chantal McDondald's workroom in Prahran. Susan Dimasi is working on a novel international practice between Melbourne, Milan and Paris

from FilmVic, then supporting films that were making waves around the world, and commission Melbourne-based filmmaking group Rich Kids to make a film.

This history is important because it reveals that the notion of staging a fashion show was not the end in itself, more the framework for an event that brought unusual combinations of people together. Building on this idea, and encouraged by Peter Corrigan whose own work flowed seamlessly between architecture and theatre set design, the trio founded the Fashion Design Council of Australia (FDC), a membership organisation bringing together all of these collaborators and would-be collaborators. Corrigan, then a mentor to Dale Jones-Evans and Robert Pearce, says that he acted as adviser for the Fashion Design Council of Australia so as to add weight to the concept. FDC, with Robert Buckingham as director, applied for funds from Arts Victoria and received a small grant. From 1984 to 1989 it mounted an annual fashion event (missing a year in 1986), organised exhibitions, professional development and networking, and issued a regular newsletter while Buckingham supplemented his income by working in bars and restaurants and Pearce and Durham pursued their respective design careers. At the same time Jane Joyce and Michael Trudgeon started a style magazine called *Crowd*. Trudgeon continues to practise as a designer of spatial futures under this name, with a notable set of film pods in the Australian Centre for the Moving Image in Federation Square just off the civic spine. All of these initiatives were run out of studios in Stallbridge Chambers, a building on the corner of Bank Place and Little Collins, then teeming with milliners, hairdressers and designers – rather as the Nicholas Building on Swanston Street does today. In between the events of the FDC, members of the

with Australian fashion today. Martin Grant became involved at the age of 16, showed his work in 1984 and has become established in Paris.[3] In recognition of his international significance, the National Gallery of Victoria in St Kilda Road, the foremost such institution in the state, mounted an exhibition of his work in late 2005. Back in 1983, organisers Buckingham, Durham and Pearce pooled a few thousand dollars each and filmed Fashion '83 for a future documentary. The three-night event held in the Seaview Ballroom at the George in St Kilda, a venue known for presenting punk and new wave bands, was an enormous success. The trio, uncertain as to where the future of their collaboration lay, considered how to capitalise on this triumph, thinking at first that they should raise money

group were involved in staging events for the newly emerging nightclub scene in the city. The Hardware Club in Hardware Lane, a traditional business club with a 24-hour licence, was colonised by young entrepreneurs at a time when 1 o'clock closing was the norm. Inflation nightclub, completely redesigned by Biltmoderne in 1984, became a popular venue for fashion shows and related events. Meanwhile the annual FDC fashion shows, Fashion '84, '85, '87, '88 and '89, showcased the work of as many as 40 artist-designers selected by the organisers from proposals submitted in advance by members of the FDC, in huge theatre-like productions over two to three-night sessions in front of a large and enthusiastic paying audience. Participating designers included Fiona Scanlan, Bettina Liano, Peter Morrisey, Leona Edmiston, Dinasour Design and Rebecca Patterson. Fashion was sponsored, and support by Nestlé led to the event being mounted in two cities, Melbourne and Sydney. (The FDC had always had members from Sydney, and the same studio/retail phenomenon, somewhat smaller in scale, evolved in Sydney in parallel to Prahran, as discussed below.) The audience grew with 6,000 people viewing the show in the Tennis Centre in 1989!

The audience began to ask where they could buy the clothes and in 1988/9 FDC set up an outlet in Collins Street, where it was conventionally thought designer fashion should be. The store struggled, partly

This page: Collins Street, the financial spine of the city, was conventionally thought to be the ideal place to sell designer fashion but it struggles to compete with the likes of Chapel Street. Fiona Abicare's installation *FitOut* (2002), in La Louvre, the premier fashion shop in Collins Street

because rent was high and Collins Street was in the throes of a construction boom, which in turn was followed by a steep downturn in the economy. But mainly the shop could not compete with the artist-designers who set up their own studio/retail outlets (so-called 'vertical integration' of design, production and retail) all along Chapel Street in South Yarra/Prahran – selling directly to the market the FDC had created through its events. This they continue to do, and the street is a fascinating exhibition of emerging talent, with the newer designers located at the Windsor end and the most established at the SouthYarra/Toorak Road end. The FDC, shop and council, closed in 1992.

Robert Buckingham worked on the establishment of the WR Johnston Museum, a private decorative arts museum in East Melbourne, then between 1992 and 1996 reinvented Craft Victoria as a nimble NGO supporting innovative craft and design. In 1996 he was recruited to run the Melbourne Fashion Festival (MFF), an annual public event that used similar concepts to the groundbreaking FDC but aimed to involve the traditional fashion industry in an innovation spiral alongside the art-designer culture that had been created by the FDC. State supported, but still modestly, Robert Buckingham's role as, first, creative director and then festival director, was to generate enough support from the industry to make this an event with an international dimension, with the resources to invite admired designers, retailers, academics, models and photographers from around the world to see for themselves what had emerged. Robert Buckingham left MFF in 2003 to set up his own consultancy and MFF continues now under the directorship of Karen Webster, Head of Fashion at RMIT (cited by *Wallpaper* as one of the world's top six fashion schools).

The outcomes of this beneficial interaction between curatorship and lean management are very evident today in the QV complex and in a walk up and down Chapel Street in Prahran. Musing on this, Robert Buckingham compares Melbourne to Antwerp, where the same combinations of people in professional roles in art, design, fashion and education have created a similar local market for designer fashion, but where really substantial state and industry support has bolstered this into international success for Dries Van Noten and so many others.

1 Elizabeth Grosz, *Volatile Bodies – Towards a Corporeal Feminism*, G Allen & Unwin (St Leonards, NSW), 1994; E Grosz, Anne Bermann, D Agrest and others. 'ANY Architecture New York', in Cynthia C Davidson, Laura Bourland (eds), *Architecture and the Feminine – Mop up Work*, Anyone Corporation (New York), 1994.

2 Maria Luisa Frisa and Stefano Tonchi (eds), *Excess: Fashion and the Underground in the 1980s*, Edizioni Charta (Milan), 2004.

3 www.martingrantparis.com

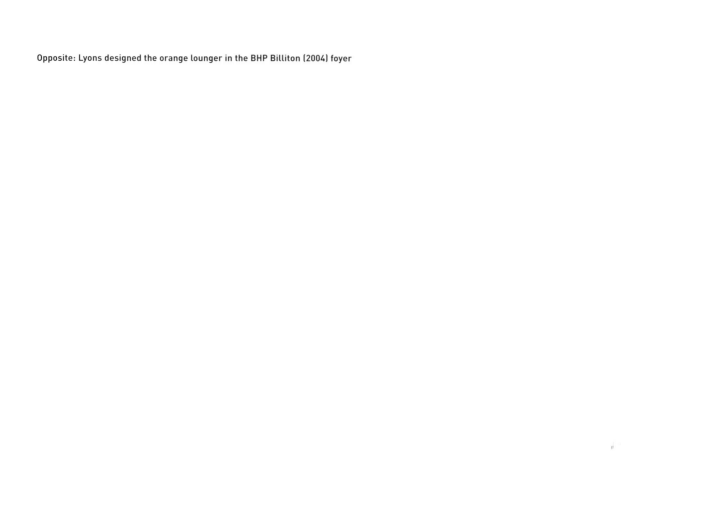

ARCHITECTURE AND FURNITURE
IN THE DESIGN CITY

Recently Giulio Cappellini visited Melbourne. He is the design director of a suite of furniture houses in northern Italy and adjacent Europe. In a sense he is their curator, selecting designers and defining projects and ensuring that these houses have a pre-eminent position in the marketplace. He spoke for an hour and half, including taking questions, openly and simply talking about how he does this, confounding many in the audience with his failure to refer to theoreticians from other fields. At one point he averred that he was not interested in the concept of 'Italian Design', and went on to elaborate on how this notion limited his curatorial project because he worked with designers from all over the world, choosing them because he saw something in their way of working that appealed to him, and then setting up projects with them, and sticking with them over the years that it takes to realise a good project, understanding that his companies' intellectual property lay not in the look of the products but in the technical solutions that brought them to fruition. Cappellini understands that a product has a long life and may sit on the shelves for years until its time comes, or sells in one place and not another, and that it is the role of curators to stick with the ideas that they believe in, and bide their time. He understands too that success also has to be curated, so that when something is selling fast, you restrict access by

making it only in blue one year, only in orange the next, thus prolonging its success. He revealed many of the measures of his curatorial experience, among them how Castiglione designed only 158 projects in 50 years of practice, but every one of them was a winner. The curator, he said, must work on bigger landscapes than the individual product, tell stories, 'take time, travel to be contaminated [sic] by other cultures...'

And then he bemoaned the way in which all cities were becoming the same, their downtowns devoted to duty-free emporiums. The following day I took him on a tour of a few of the buildings on the civic spine, and he acknowledged that there was something going on in Melbourne with respect to architecture that is simply not happening in Italy, or elsewhere, today. But he left me wondering about the difference between architecture and furniture, because the story I tell about cities is about how architecture comes from being there, and cannot be flown in. Architects in Melbourne are great clients of Cappellini, although Lyons designed the orange lounger in the BHP Billiton foyer (see Lyons, p 194) and Wood Marsh design as much furniture as any client will allow (see Wood Marsh, p 254). It is hard to resent moveables originating from the great design culture of the world, as long as we are contributing. Melbourne does not have a design director like Cappellini, and it suffers from this

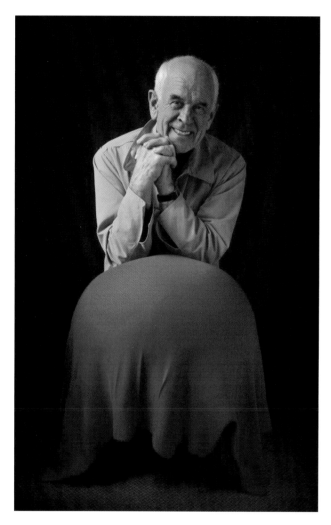

lack. But it does have one of the doyens of international design, someone who has devoted the latter stages of his career to curating on to the world stage a designer presence from Melbourne. This is Kjell Grant.

Kjell offers to his students and his colleagues one of those irreplaceable lineages in design. Born near Stirling in Scotland, he studied at the Royal College of Art in London and won a scholarship to the Illinois Institute of Technology (IIT), attracted there because as a musician he had played a Bach duet with Moholy Nagy in Ulm, who invited him to apply to IIT. There he studied architecture under Mies van der Rohe, developing a passion for hard edge corners and black in the process, then studying industrial design and taking as his first job on graduation a position with Raymond Loewy, working on porcelain dinnerware of which he is still proud. A keen yachtsman, he took his breaks sailing to Bermuda, became embroiled through the skipper of a yacht with a firm of architects working in Casablanca, where he found himself out of work and in love with a woman who had returned home to Australia. He bought a yacht confiscated from a diamond smuggler, sailed to Durban and worked there earning the money to refit the boat before sailing single-handed to Sydney and into the arms of his first Australian wife. His second wife took him to Melbourne. 'We fell in love in those days,' he observes. The architect Roy Grounds commissioned his first iconic furniture design, the Montreal chair and tables for the Australian pavilion at the Montreal Expo '67, and these went on to be displayed at the Australian pavilion in Osaka in 1969. Then in the 1970s, Roy Grounds commissioned the ceremonial academic furniture for the Great Hall at the new Monash University campus. In the 1980s, for Fred Ashton, founder of the newly opened Mitchelton Winery[1] he designed a tubular chair, but not in the manner of Breuer. Roy Grounds also commissioned furniture for the International Room at Stanford University.

With the success of these designs, Grant was catapulted into the Australian avant-garde and on to the world stage as a 'signature' designer. He worked for years with Ford at Geelong, involved in the new technologies that have transformed ideas about upholstery. Many chairs arose from this translation of technologies. His 'Alto' chair (2003) is a design of which he remains proud. In the 1990s he designed a chair 'ecco' that became a best seller. At a birthday party held for him in Tokyo, Toyo Kogei, chairman of the company producing this chair, took him on to a platform and drew red velvet curtains apart to reveal one of these chairs, announcing that it was number 6 million! Off and on for 26 years Kjell Grant has taught at RMIT, seeing now that his failure to continue to produce 'icons' himself has undermined his curatorial position – perhaps this is the problem when you lead from within as a designer, rather than from without as a 'design director'? Looking back, he feels that of the thousand designs he has created, 70 per cent are from the middle of taste periods, constrained by market expectations. The times when he could break out were when one fashion trend was fading and the new paradigm was not yet entrenched. It was at those cusp periods that his iconic works emerged. Melbourne is currently in one of those periods, and Kjell is hard at work on a prototype of a new chair that he hopes will inspire a new generation of students.

Consciously pursuing a curatorial position, Kjell founded the Melbourne Movement in 1998, mounting an exhibition in the foyer of 101 Collins Street. The exhibition became the platform that brought him to Milan at the invitation of internationally renowned designer Marra Griffin. He has taken a team to the Milan International Furniture Fair every year since 2000, and there they have established a reputation for Melbourne that is unrivalled. But to do this he has had to struggle for funding – Australia does not support design curation. Nonetheless, from his latest group, Lisa Vincitorio's Fruit Loop fruit container has been taken on by Alessi, making this the fifth design in the Alessi stable that originates in Melbourne, the first and second being Susan Cohn's fruit bowl and condom container, the third and fourth being DCM and Kovac's Tea and Coffee Plaza sets.

There is much to be learned from the story of furniture in Melbourne, so dependent on the city's initial welcome for an innovator, yet undercut by the city's later indifference to the financial plight of the pioneer who has created an internationally respected curatorial position from within design, unlike Cappellini who has created an international stable of designers through his commissions.

1 Wineries have been consistent clients of inventive architecture, and the international acceptance of Australian wines is built on the same 'we can do it' spirit that is currently abroad in Melbourne's architectural community. See S Stanwick and L Fowlow, *Wine by Design*, Wiley-Academy (London), 2005, which includes several architecturally innovative Australian wineries, among them Prince Wine Store in Melbourne.

ARCHITECTURE AND GRAPHICS
IN THE DESIGN CITY

Years ago Bryan Ferry said to me that architecture was an impossibly risky business with a high unit cost, low turnover structure that exposed players to every likelihood of misfortune. Far safer to invest in practices where a high volume of products pay minuscule dividends. Graphic design could be seen to be such a practice, and in Melbourne there is a notable tendency for such designers to play architecture-lite, as it were, leveraging off the necessarily more cumbrous ambitions of architects.

Garry Emery is the doyen of Melbourne graphic designers. His practice is international and it has pioneered design as an essential tool of communication in many new territories, especially graphic identities for creative industry firms and signage in large building complexes. Leading with the enthusiasm of an autodidact, he has opened up this new terrain for successive generations of designers to explore. For a long time this was a lonely position, and his own self-avowedly Modernist approach arose in the context of a close friendship with the partners in DCM, who designed his office in a South Melbourne warehouse. Here he famously answered a question from a visiting Domus Academician, who asked how many people worked in the office, with the riposte: 'About half'. DCM have also designed a country house for him, recently

completing – to his and his partner Pam's delight – a new wing. Their townhouse is an apartment in Melbourne Terrace by Nonda Katsalidis. Indeed, some observers regard Garry as part of a Modernist push launched by that practice and supported by John Gollings in what was for some years in the 1970s and early 1980s an oasis of design ambition in the city. A vigorous self-curator, he has theorised his experience in a succession of critical monographs[1] and an exhibition curated by Suzie Attiwill, feeling an increasing need to drive the work from a theoretical rather than stylistic perpective. Sometimes it feels as if he has had to haul the idea of graphic design up a slippery slope, so readily does it slide back into

an anti-intellectual pursuit of a 'look', with conversations to match. Emery aims to practise not as a packager of any client's content, but rather as a curator of their enterprise. This makes him as concerned about the stories that are to be told, as is Giulio Cappellini about every product in his range, seeing the job of design director as one of finding the persuasive story for every piece included. Garry is increasingly preoccupied with the possibilities of applying these curatorial skills to the urban environment, talking of 'editing the urban flux'. The jobs that excite at the moment are ones involving large complexes like sports stadia, where an environment can be shaped by graphic surfaces.

Below: Garry Emery with Akio Makigawa sculpture on the rear outdoor deck at his South Melbourne office (designed by DCM)

Opposite: Graphics solutions inside the Melbourne Exhibition Centre by DCM

Riding in his slipstream, so to speak, have been the designers in Fabio Ongarato, an Australian design firm specialising in graphic design and corporate identity. Among them is Ronnen Goren, a graduate of RMIT Architecture, who led the firm's work on the monograph on Guilford Bell[2] (published by Morrie Schwartz under his Bookman Transition imprint, which book Ronnen also project-managed), and on the Daniel Libeskind catalogue[3] for the exhibition at Melbourne's Jewish Museum that won the ISTD (International Society of Typographical Designers) London Major Award 2001 and a distinction from the AGDA (Australian Graphic Design Association) Publication 2002. Elly Bloom, a graduate of Melbourne University Architecture, project managed this exhibition and has been seduced into the museum world by the experience, working now at ACMI (Australian Centre for the Moving Image). So sensitively attuned to their subjects are these designs

that they seem to have been generated by the minds of these self-same subjects. This projective intelligence supports the firm's major work in corporate identity, much of it conducted in Sydney. Ronnen, who is driven by a sense that life needs to be lived in depth, has taken a partial sabbatical to concentrate on holistic health studies – which has led him into a family business, SMXL, that sells health-food lunches in a brightly hued, designer ambience. He can be found minding this shop between flights north, turning design to account in a series of high turnover, low unit cost ventures.

Some 20 years or more ago Garry Emery initiated a period of near silence in graphic design after the excesses of super-graphics, with his penchant for minute characters. Now, Fabio Ongarato issue an annual party invitation with wording consisting of so small a line of text concealed in the fold of a piece of paper that many do not find it until holding the invitation up to a powerful light. Each generation in this field of design seems intent on outdoing the self-effacement of its mentors, a strategy that certainly divides the under-42s from their elders.

Juli Jame bridges disciplines in another way, regularly exhibiting drawings that capture the nature of the hills and vineyards around Melbourne. Her work, including wine labels, has a determinedly crafted character, a hands-on approach that defies the almost ascetic Minimalism of much graphic work. She is married to triathlete and architect Tony Styant Browne, whose practice is increasingly involved in intricate community work. Jen Rippon, who is one of those architects whose skills have brought so many significant projects to fruition, is now in Styant Browne's office, currently working on a centre for

the Aboriginal community at Lake Tyers. She earlier played a role in the documentation of the ground-breaking RMIT Storey Hall by ARM.

3Deep (www.3deep.publishing.com.au) is the latest innovative design intelligence to emerge on the local scene, not it seems tempted to outdo Ongarato in this respect, but adopting an interesting curatorial approach with a bold publishing strategy supported by advisory committees made up of the more ambitious of their peers in architecture and the arts. This firm is an unusual combination of advertising, graphic design and architectural expertise and its high profile within the profession is evidenced in that other design firms currently see 3Deep as the designers of choice for their stationery and brochures. 3Deep's books repay the

compliment by having an almost architectural materiality about them. Australia is a vast continent with the population of the Netherlands, and distribution is always an issue for a small publisher. Peta Carlin, a graduate of RMIT Architecture, has a devotee's interest in architectural books. She has researched the book-shops of the world that support architecture and, unusually and promisingly, has sought out allies in distribution from the bottom up. She acts as a consultant to 3Deep on its publications, nurturing alliances with other niche publishers and developing local projects germane to the artist's book terrain.

Younger yet again is Simon Clancy-Hikage, a designer who is an architect manqué and sports Le Corbusier framed spectacles that enable him at least

Below: Simon Clancy-Hikage's design of the catalogue for the 2004
'Paul Knight Photographs' exhibition at the Centre for Contemporary
Photography, Fitzroy, Melbourne

to continue the pursuit of the invisible in communication in that he can read small text! His passion for a classical approach to photographing buildings has led him to promote the work of German photographer Jan Bitter, an exhibition of whose cool-school pictures of an admittedly cool-school Neo-Modernist or Minimalist subject matter he is planning to mount in Melbourne, surrounding it with a forum on the roles of photography in disseminating architectural discovery. The earnest intellectuality of this designer is reflected in the almost severe rationality of his designs, which one can imagine being pared down over and again while black coffee is consumed in an atelier in the current Paris End of the city, a vision that is reinforced by the knowledge that his partner in life and work is an ascetic Japanese.

1 Leon van Schaik, 'Editing the Urban Flux' in Jackie Cooper (ed), *Garry Emery Inside Outside In*, Images Publishing (Melbourne), 2002, pp 42–50. This monograph served as catalogue to the exhibition at the Potter Museum, Melbourne University, curated by Suzie Attiwill. See also Jackie Cooper, 'Emery Vincent Design' in Jackie Cooper and Julian Dahl (eds), *Emery Vincent Design*, Images Publishing (Melbourne), 1999.

2 Leon van Schaik (ed), *The Life Work of Guilford Bell 1912–1992*, Bookman Transition (Melbourne), 1999.

3 Leon van Schaik (ed), *Lineage: The Architecture of Daniel Libeskind*, Jewish Museum/RMIT (Melbourne), 2000.

4 Clancy-Hikage has arranged an exhibition of Jan Bitter's photographs of works of Sauerbruch Hutton and Peter Eisenman, and of Daniel Libeskind's new project in Denver at the Centre for Contemporary Photography, Sept/Oct 2006, Fitzroy, Melbourne.

ARCHITECTURE AND INFRASTRUCTURE
IN THE DESIGN CITY

If Melbourne is a city of rooms, as 18th-century London was a city of rooms that epitomised its institutions,[1] and it is my contention that the civic and financial spines marshal a series of rooms that is a contemporary compendium of a culture that thrives on meetings in rooms, then the relationship of this companionable culture to the great Australian outdoors is left somewhat in question. Melbourne sits on a vast mud and clay plain ringed at a considerable distance by ranges of hills and divided from the drama of the Southern Ocean by a 60-kilometre diameter bay. A romantic contrast between city and wilderness is difficult to force, just as – in their contrastingly dramatic geographies – such a contrast sits at the forefront of the mind in Hobart or Sydney. On Melbourne's mildly differentiated tabula rasa, settlers of a romantic cast of mind – settlers being divided between those who sought to recreate the Europe whence they came and those who sought to find a new instrumentality with which to create a new world[2] – have been constrained to create their vision of the natural in parks surrounded by the city's remorselessly expanding suburbs. These tamed wildernesses are, in a sense, interiors – rooms in the city. Chief among them are the Botanical Gardens in the governmental Domain, but the grid of the city on the commercial side of the river is ringed with parks planted in High Victorian style, like the Treasury Gardens, crisscrossed

with avenues of elms, interrupted with moist shrubberies and covered in rolling lawns. Landscape architects such as Edna Walling seized on the notion of the urban room in the 1930s, working with the sunken cricket oval surrounded by London plane trees in Victoria Gardens in Prahran to create a pergola room where today elderly European migrants can be seen deep in conversation. The sunken oval ringed with trees and a pathway for evening passagiatos has been replicated a few blocks away in the pocket park, Princes Gardens.

Birrarung Marr, adjacent to Federation Square, is a determined contemporary extension of the parks that surround the central city grid, complete with its axial structure (see pp 12–13). Here, however, it is complemented with a gravel plain like a hard standing area in a French urban park, capable of accommodating events both formal and informal, from boules to a circus, and a counter axis that replicates a screed riverbed lined with river red gums, a new *parti* in the use of indigenous plants in the city, which have tended to be scattered about mindlessly as if that was what it takes to replicate nature. This is a further achievement of Rob Adams's vision for maintaining and extending the bones of the city. Yet the idea of the landscape room is present across the wider city. On Sydney Road, Cath Stutterheim has

devised a churchyard garden that offers a paved floor, furniture and a canopy of shade, an urban room that is cherished by the locals. Leanne O'Shea, landscape architect to Moreland City Council, in partnership with Patrick Franklyn (both graduates from RMIT Landscape Architecture) have created two urban rooms of particular strength that promise well for the future development of the type: Randazzo Reserve and Bain Reserve. In both of these, and with increasing confidence, one can see a distributed architecture at work, with decks integrated with level changes to form seating, an approach that eschews the usual urban design furniture clutter. Boundaries real and psychological are defined wittily at Randazzo with large balls incised with single letters – rolled here at the end of a game of bowls seemingly played by giants – that light up with the name of the reserve. At Bain Reserve a plain of land between ailing shops and the railway station has been lined with a deck that has transformed public perception and therefore use of the space, bringing new life to the neighbourhood.

The malleable plain on the other hand conceals an infrastructural heritage of outfall sewers that – while in need of renewal – is nevertheless a hidden treasure, protecting the bay from the worst exports of human consumption, and offering a potential for water recycling that may well allow the urban rooms of the city to flourish even as the climate dries. Although, alas, the Yarra River itself has come as close to being canalised as is possible without concrete in a replication of that misguided intervention prompted by the puzzlement with which early engineers confronted Australian waterways, those braided chains of ponds that simply did not flow like proper rivers and which they dynamited into conformity with the European or American ideal in one of the direst of partnerships

between romance and instrumentality. Over this plain, the same engineering intelligence that gave us the sewers has strung necklaces of freeways. In the 1970s there were attempts to drive these into the heart of the city, but these were defeated by massive citizen protests and the structural difficulties of dealing with 50 or so municipalities. It is a quirk of Melbourne's governance that the City of Melbourne is an entity confined to the inner city. This administrative complexity has saved the city from many decisions that were easily reached everywhere else in Australia: Melbourne's trams owe their survival to the determination of outer municipalities not to dispense with them when it was the received wisdom that they impeded traffic. Nonetheless, as I have written in a tribute to the landscape architects of the state's highway authority, VicRoads: 'Cities build or un-build their cultures by embracing virtuous or vicious circles of public behaviour.'[4] This division of the state's highway authority has been responsible for the commissioning of, or has contributed to, a series of major works on the highways of the city that can be seen as spatial containers, both of drivers, their passengers and their cars, and of the noise which they produce. Notable among these is the City Gateway by DCM on the freeway out of the city that includes a wonderful ovoid tube through which the freeway is conducted as it passes a high-rise residential complex. DCM's pedestrian and bicycle bridge, the Webb Bridge,[5] in the Docklands, a collaboration with sculptor Robert Owen, is a virtuoso work of spatial containment of linear movement at an appropriately smaller scale.

Wood Marsh have turned the Eastern Freeway into a landscape experience of which Robert Moses would have been envious. On other freeways Kerstin Thompson and Lyons[6] have also been involved in

Top left: Rob Adams, Director of Design and Culture at Melbourne City Council, with a sculpture by Akio Akigawa, one of the foremost sculptors to be based in Melbourne. He is pictured in front of L'Incontre, a cafe on Swanston Street that was an early insertion of street life in the long history of the rejuvenation of the street. Behind him is Council House 2, a pioneering new office building for the city council that is designed to be a six-star Green Building that creates new precedents for sustainable design

Middle left: St Ambrose Cloister Garden (2000) off Sydney Road in Brunswick, an inner suburb of Melbourne. This is a highly structured urban space. Cath Stutterheim, now a sole practitioner in landscape architecture, designed this pocket park while a partner in Rush Wright Stutterheim (RWS); Rush Wright Associates (RWA) did the construction management. The pocket park off Sydney Road is intensively used by locals

Below: Leanne O'Shea, landscape architect for Moreland City Council, with Patrick Franklin, landscape architect, designed the Randazzo Reserve (2001), a pocket park in Brunswick, an inner suburb to the north of central Melbourne. The space is sculpted with grass terraces, boardwalks, timber-topped concrete beam seating and lights

Above: DCM – internal view of the acoustic tube that protects high rise residential blocks from the noise of the Tullamarine Freeway (1999)

Below: Webb Bridge (2003) pedestrian and cycle bridge across the Yarra River at Docklands, a collaboration between DCM and sculptor Robert Owen

Above: Contrasting concrete and steel-framed sound walls on Wood Marsh's Eastern Freeway (1997)

Opposite: DCM's Tullamarine Freeway gateway (1998)

making sound barriers into scenographic architecture. Most recently the Craigieburn Bypass has upped the ante for future curators of these works with an extraordinarily dramatic and yet fitting design combining a rusted steel sound wall that turns on its side and snakes across the freeway to form an access and emergency vehicle bridge, while at the same time framing the first view of the city afforded a driver arriving from the north. Following this the sound wall's dark-blue vertical blades twist on their axes and finally spill over as the bypass joins the ring road. The blades lead to Perspex screens etched in a pattern reminiscent of the lace curtains in the suburb they protect, and a long wall of LED lights that makes the experience of driving into the city at night gently momentous.

Given the complicated governance of the city, a crucial resistance to perceived wisdom that either builds or unbuilds the culture, thinking about the city region as a system is mostly in the hands of our engineers, who have often been visionary. But, together with planners, they have regarded the built fabric of the city as beyond rational investigation, a force to be channelled as far as possible. The city grows through 3 million individual decisions made every year.[7] The 38 South programme at RMIT is the only programme in Australia that attempts to speculate on how the pixilated ownership patterns of the city region might be influenced into a higher architectonic order, embracing and enhancing the new beauty that its citizens are forging. These studies[8] unflinchingly scrutinise urban strips and wonder, in a homage to Mario Gandelsonas, Colin Rowe and Fred Koetter, to Venturi and Scott Brown, how these could be, as Louis Kahn might have argued, more what they want to be. This design in the interstices looks for ways in which surface alignments in vast shopping-mall car parks, garbage collection subdivisions and a perma-culture for a sustainable future could spread through the yards of the suburbs. These are searches for new urban rooms in a world created by individual transit, a search for the new beauty that lies within this ugliness.[9]

One part of this search lies in uncovering and encouraging new public behaviours, the ephemeral architectures of the new city. Paul Carter has been the

Above and below: Craigieburn Bypass (2005) – the framing is followed immediately with a slow curve of blue blades; these give way to a Perspex screen etched to flare in a lace curtain pattern at night

Opposite: One of Sue Anne Ware's ephemeral memorials – The Heroin Memorial, the Esplanade, St Kilda (2001) with text on each victim stencilled on to the pavement

mentor to this process that involves a cohort of researchers at RMIT. Sue Anne Ware, a landscape architect, has pursued her investigations to a conclusion with a temporary street memorial to people who have died of heroin overdoses (Melbourne Festival 2001, St Kilda) and a memorial to young people who have died on a country road (2003 ongoing, Gippsland). Both of these investigations build on the ways in which people spontaneously mark sites of tragedy and, in surfacing these individual gestures in a municipally approved communal event with a specific duration, both provide a neighbourly context for these lonely griefs and bring them to a cathartic closure. Design is both material and performative. These projects that take years to gestate are the companions to their physical neighbours in spatial design and they reveal, in all their raw unvarnished detail, the web of communications out of which any human construct is created. Without this countervailing investigation, conducted here for a decade in the researches of Sand Helsel and with generations of undergraduate students, and now joined by the research of Mel Dodd, an associate of 'muf', the London-based art and design cooperative that has similar concerns, the merely physical would cloy.

1 Thomas Rowlandson, *August Pugin: Weltstadt London* [The Microcosm of London] von 1808-1810, Harenberg (Dortmund), 1981.

2 Paul Fox, *Clearings: Six Colonial Gardeners and their Landscapes*, Melbourne University Press (Melbourne), 2004.

3 Rob Adams's career at the Melbourne City Council has progressed through a number of position descriptions: Manager, Urban Design (1983–5); Manager, Urban Design and Architecture (1986–95); Director, City Projects (1995–2001); Director, City Projects, Arts and Culture (2002–4); Director, Design and Culture (2004–).

4 Leon van Schaik, 'Craigieburn Bypass: Taylor Cullity Lethlean, Tonkin Zulaika Greer and Robert Owen', *Architecture Australia*, Vol 94, No 4 (July/August 2005) pp 60–7.

5 Leon van Schaik, 'Webb Bridge', forthcoming.

6 See van Schaik 'Craigieburn Bypass', pp 60–7.

7 Brian J McLoughlin, *Shaping Melbourne's Future*, Cambridge University Press (Cambridge Melbourne NY), 1992.

8 Various chapters in each of the following: Leon van Schaik and Paul Morgan (eds), *38 South*, RMIT (Melbourne), 1991; Shane Murray and Leon van Schaik, *38 South* (II), RMIT (Melbourne), 2000; Shane Murray and Nigel Bertram (eds), *Urban Architecture Laboratory, 2002–2004*, RMIT University Press (Melbourne), 2005.

9 Mark Cousins, 'The Ugly/1', in *AA Files* No 28, ed Mary Wall, Architectural Association (London), 1995, pp 61–5.

ARCHITECTURE AND ITS INTELLIGENTSIA IN
THE DESIGN CITY Critics, theorists and media

When I arrived in Melbourne in the late 1980s, it seemed necessary to assert that architecture was a public, intellectual activity. Internationally the artist/architect phenomenon was in the ascendant, a reaction against the decades of reconstruction after the Second World War in which a Modernist social compact between the state and architecture had prevailed. Bright colours and exotic shapes were emerging against the grey concrete backdrop of those years of technocratic service.[1] An attempt at theorising this shift was being made, using the term 'Deconstruction'.[2] To me it seemed that this shift was a revolution in the sense that it simply turned everything mindlessly on its head. Hence, I argued in South Melbourne Town Hall in a lecture series organised by Norman Day for the Royal Australian Institute of Architects (RAIA), Victorian Chapter, that it was time to return to rebellion – that mode of critical engagement with specific issues espoused by Camus. 'And what,' I asked, 'is the locus for such a rebellion? 'It is your own city,' I answered, but your own city as the province of your endeavour, in conversation with the world as the metropolis of ethical and intellectual argument.'[3] I laid down a three-fold challenge for the practice of architecture in Melbourne: What does this city teach architects? What is the autonomous body of knowledge that architects can derive, as those pioneers of reading

the city, the Situationists, would have put it?[4] And how can that knowledge be used to help this society?

There is a sense that this book is an account of what has since transpired in the conscious building up of a local culture of architecture, something which I discuss in some depth in *Mastering Architecture*.[5] Much of our effort has lain in bringing practitioners who have established a body of work that demonstrates mastery back into the critical frame of the academy where they examine the nature of the mastery thus established with their peers – local and international – and speculate through their ongoing work about the direction of their future practice. But

all of this begins with a relationship between architects and their critics: through professional reviews of their work in the professional journals, and in the context of a climate of critique that is built by social commentators. For a country as small in population as Australia, there are a large number of professional journals dedicated to architecture – for 20 million people as opposed to one for 360 million people in the USA, for example. These are *Architecture Australia*, which functions like the *Architectural Record* in the USA as the journal of record for the Institute of Architects, and two independent journals, *Architectural Review Australia* and *Monument*. These journals rely on the work of a small group of photographers (John Gollings, Trevor Mein and Peter Bennett chief among them) who seek to convey the ideas of buildings through their representations, and a group of reviewers, academics in the main, who explain and situate works of architecture in their local and international context. Among these last are Anna Johnson, Brent Allpress and Doug Evans of RMIT, Philip Goad and Sandra Kaji O'Grady (now at University of Technology Sydney) of Melbourne University, Conrad Hamann of Monash University and Stuart Harrison of RMIT who joins a line of radio commentators on architecture in the weekly 3RRR 'Burning Down the House programme' that has included architects Peter Brew and Peter Raisbeck.

The editors of these journals have played a crucial role in building the critical climate. Ian McDougall (see ARM, p 140) took up my challenge with a vengeance, alienating architects from the more conservative Sydney. Davina Jackson succeeded him, continuing his quest for argument with a gusto that also created a backlash against her, chiefly again from architects in her home city, Sydney. Justine Clark, recent arrival to Australia and a Melbourne-based editor, has built on this and concentrated on extending the range of critics writing in the journal. Helen Kaiser, a RMIT-educated interior designer, built a critical edge for *Architectural Review Australia* with a strong curatorial intent that made this the journal with a strong theoretical basis to its critique, a tradition that Andrew McKenzie, the present editor, has underscored by building issues around themes of current moment. *Monument* was founded by Graham Jahn in Sydney, but after two near collapses has risen phoenix-like under the editorship of Fleur Watson and Martyn Hook of RMIT, both originally from Perth. In terms of content this is the most international of the three publications, and the most widely distributed in Australia. The reviewers in these journals often engage in a debate about the strength of their critiques, but the focus is very healthily on what the works under review add to discourse. None of the journals is in any sense specific to Melbourne and for those interested in architecture as a creation of the culture of every city (Modernists remain in denial of this provincial specificity), they feed the competition between the city-states of Australia. This critique surfaces in the Melbourne press through the weekly column of Norman Day, Adjunct Professor at RMIT (see Norman Day, p 152) and the occasional writings of Dimity Reed, formerly Professor of Urban Design at RMIT, and champion of women in architecture.

Crucial to the critique is the work of the historians, Philip Goad at Melbourne University, Conrad Hamann at Monash University and Harriet Edquist at RMIT. Their work brings to the surface and re-examines the record of what has been achieved by the generations since settlement. Their research students reveal previously little understood aspects of the cultural capital that has been established. Edquist's work on Desbrowe-Annear[6] has brought an

Opposite top: Dimity Reed, Randal Marsh and Conrad Hamann choosing works for inclusion in a publication on the history of architecture awards in Melbourne and Victoria

Opposite bottom left: William Lim receiving his honorary doctorate in architecture from RMIT, seen here in Storey Hall in his doctoral gown with the author

Opposite bottom right: Paul Fox at citi espresso, opposite RMIT Storey Hall, a lunchtime meeting place on the route from Museum Station to RMIT and Melbourne University

Below: Nikos Papastergiadis. The wandering scholar, pictured here in Greece, land of his forbears

social commentators in the city. Paul Carter has already been mentioned (see Architecture and Art, p 74), but it is impossible to overestimate the impact of his writings on being in Australia[10] given the enormous impact of migration on the culture of Melbourne, which – like Sydney but unlike other Australian cities – has a population of whom 40 per cent were born outside Australia (the national average is 25 per cent, making Australia the country with the highest proportion of overseas-born citizens in the world). Carter's concern for the ephemeral in architecture is a constant goad to the discourse.

Another Melbourne theorist of migrant culture is Nikos Papastergiadis, Melbourne-born in what is the third largest Greek city in the world. He completed his education in Cambridge and is currently a research fellow of Manchester University in the UK, but is based at the Australia Centre at Melbourne University. His work on collectives and on para-functional space is having a growing impact.[11] Critics working in associated areas of interest who engage with our material culture include Chris Healy and Scott McQuire of Melbourne University and Justin Clemens of Deakin University.

almost forgotten era back into focus, and her next book, on the Arts and Crafts Movement in Australia, uncovers architecture of extraordinary achievement that has gone unremarked through the Modernist period. Philip Goad[7] has a catholic interest in architecture and a dispassionate interest in establishing an accurate record of achievement. Conrad Hamann[8] has written on Edmond and Corrigan and, as a forthcoming book will demonstrate, has an unparalleled understanding of how early Australian architecture dovetails with the architecture of the New World USA. In addition, Doug Evans, more theoretician than historian, has documented new architecture in Melbourne through the publication *Aardvark*.[9]

The critique delivered by the Melbourne reviewers in these journals draws on an intellectual climate that is constantly being developed by the

Paul Fox, landscape architect, is our foremost scholar of the city in its landscape and of what our cultural attitudes have done to that landscape.[12] He works through the photographic record of settlement, and has unearthed the origins of crucial ongoing debates about the nature and future of settlement on this arid continent. Over and over again, in a process that is crucial to architecture in the city, he reveals how mindsets determine physical outcomes. An underlying struggle between attitudes that focus on the New World ideas of post-colonial situations and an

Old World focus on the higher qualities of life is increasingly compounded by a contemporary discourse on being an Asian country, deeply dependent on China and India – as indeed Australia was in colonial days, as Fox points out, when it provided horses and food for the British imperial forces.

International visitors play their part in this critique too, most importantly in my view RMIT Adjunct Professors William Lim and Ranulph Glanville. Lim has been a pioneer of the movement that is engaging Australia with its geographical region, insisting that Australian architecture be considered as a phenomenon of its region. His books address the crucial ethical issues of Asia, and they draw us into the debates that are shaping our region.[13] Glanville has helped Australians establish an understanding of second order modernity, and together with Paul Carter and Nikos Papastergiadis, he has assisted me in establishing the doctoral practice-based research programme that promises to deliver the next wave of innovation in the architecture of Melbourne.

1 Leon van Schaik, 'Practice Tendencies', paper delivered to AASA conference, Sept 2003.

2 The argument was best formulated in Aaron Betsky, *Violated Perfection*, Rizzoli (New York), 1990.

3 Leon van Schaik, 'Province and Metropolis', in Robin Middleton (ed), *Architectural Associations: The Idea of the City*, Architectural Association (London), 1996, pp 156–78. Leon van Schaik, 'Province and Metropolis', in *AA Files* No 14, ed Mary Wall, Architectural Association (London), 1987, pp 48–54. Leon van Schaik, 'Architecture in Asia: Province and Metropolis', in Tan Kok Meng (ed), *Asian Architects*, Select Books (Singapore), Vol 1, pp 15–31.

4 Simon Salder, *The Situationist City*, MIT Press (Cambridge, Mass), 1998.

5 Leon van Schaik, *Mastering Architecture: Becoming a Creative Innovator in Practice*, Wiley-Academy (London), 2005.

6 Harriet Edquist et al, 'Knowledge and/or/of Experience', In John Macarthur (ed), *The Theory of Space in Art and Architecture*, Institute of Modern Art (Brisbane), 1993; Harriet Edquist and Frederick Romberg, *The Architecture of Migration 1938–1975*, RMIT (Melbourne), 2000. Harriet Edquist, Harold Desbrowe-Annea, *A Life in Architecture*, Melbourne University Press (Melbourne), 2004.

7 Philip Goad, *A Guide to Melbourne Architecture*, Watermark Press (Sydney), 1999; Philip Goad, Patrick Bingham-Hall, *New Directions in Australian Architecture*, Pesaro (Sydney), 2001.

8 Conrad Hamann, *Cities of Hope – Australian Architecture and Design by Edmond and Corrigan*, Oxford University Press (Oxford/Auckland/New York), 1993

9 Doug Evans (ed), *Aardvark: Architecture of Melbourne*, RMIT, Department of Architecture (Melbourne), 1990, 1993 and 1998.

10 Paul Carter, *The Road to Botany Bay. An Essay in Spatial History*, Faber and Faber (London and Boston), 1987; Paul Carter, *Living in a New Country – History, Travelling and Language*, Faber and Faber (London and Boston), 1992; Paul Carter, *The Lie of the Land*, Faber and Faber (London and Boston), 1996; Paul Carter, *Material Thinking. The Theory and Practice of Creative Research*, Melbourne University Press (Melbourne), 2004.

11 Nikos Papastergiadis, *Dialogues in the Diasporas*, Rivers, Oram (London), 1998; Nikos Papastergiadis and Heather Rogers, 'Parafunctional Spaces', *AD: Art and Design – Art and the City: a dream of urbanity*, Academy Group (London), 1996, No 50, pp 76–8; Nikos Papastergiadis, *The Turbulence of Exile*, Polity Press (Cambridge), 2000; Nikos Papastergiadis, *Metaphor and Tension. On Collaboration and its Discontents*, Artspace Australia (Sydney), 2004.

12 Paul Fox, 'Sweet Damper and Gossip', in Paul Fox (curator) and Jennifer Phipps (ed), *Colonial Sightings from the Goulbern*, Benalla Art Gallery (Benalla, Australia), 1994; Paul Fox, *Clearings: Six Colonial Gardeners and their landscapes*, Melbourne University Press (Melbourne), 2004.

13 William SW Lim, *Asian New Urbanism*, Select Books (Singapore), 1998; William SW Lim, *Alternatives in Transition. The Postmodern, Locality and Social Justice*, Select Book (Singapore), 2001; William SW Lim, *Architecture, Art, Identity in Singapore. Is There Life after Tabula Rasa?* Asian Urban Lab (Singapore), 2004; William SW Lim, *Asian Ethical Urbanism: A Radical Postmodern Perspective*, World Scientific Publishing (Singapore), 2005.

Opposite: The giant door of Double Happiness opens, releasing patrons into the street

ARCHITECTURE AND BARS IN THE
DESIGN CITY Reviewed by Jan van Schaik

Melbourne's first drinking establishments were rudimentary hotels. Horses could be stabled and rooms were available for the night. Early Australian colonial life was rough and drinking was a large part of existence. Hotels were such drinking holes that their role as places of stabling and accommodation became defunct. They are still called hotels and until the 1960s they were the main model for drinking establishments. Hotels of this type still exist in Melbourne, sad dinosaurs of a romanticised past. Young & Jackson's and the Waterside Hotel, both on Flinders Street, are just beginning to struggle over the line of dark, sticky carpeted sleaze into the land of full historicism. Young & Jackson's was famous for a portrait of scantily

naked Chloe in the upper bar. Known affectionately as the Mona Lisa of Melbourne, her breasts were reputed to follow you around the room. Young & Jackson's has been dragged kicking and screaming into contemporary Melbourne by the Federation Square project, which is diagonally opposite it.

The Waterside Hotel maintained its murky reputation by hiding behind an early 1960s' overpass between the business district and the river. The Waterside looked out on to a large concrete wall over an underused laneway running off Melbourne's main traffic sewer, a view it shares with the only remaining legal brothel in the inner-city colonial grid. At the time

of writing the overpass is being demolished and the Waterside and the brothel now appear uncomfortably naked and out of place in their newly prominent spot, with a new view of the river and its populated banks.

Pubs from this era are characterised by tiled facades at street level. Until 1964 liquor licences allowed service until six o'clock and no later. Patrons would order chains of drinks at the call for last orders, and down them in a race that led to polite customers being transformed into a loud drunken rabble that was turned out on to the street, where they would relieve themselves. To prepare for this saturated end to the evening entertainment the facades of hotels were clad in the very same way as the interior of the urinals: with tiles.

In contrast to these there were elite clubs with strict membership policies that exercised the right to refuse entry to define a drinking environment that was specifically designed to exist outside the catchment demographic of hotels. A small clique of these still persists in the city today such as the Melbourne Club, notorious for its heavily restrictive membership policy and an insistence, enforced by ejection, that a jacket and tie be worn at all times. Only in the last 20 years have women been allowed in at all, let alone permitted to hold membership. The club has an oasis-like

garden surrounded by high walls, ironically overlooked by the Lyceum Club, for women. The Kelvin Club, the Savage Club and the Athenaeum Club, members of the very same elite family, can only be visited at the invitation of a member.

Postwar, returned servicemen's leagues opened in force. The sadness of the war-ravaged psyches of the returned soldier drowning his sorrow is eschewed by the lush time capsule of the Duckboard Club and the heroic hovering box on concrete arches over the red-brick and green-painted steel entry gate of the Naval & Military Club.

Italian immigration to Australia boomed in the 1950s and with this came relief from the English culinary straitjacket. Pellegrini's, the first coffee house to open, is still under the same old management. Immediately north of the city grid is the suburb of

Carlton, home to working-class Italian immigrants during this era. This invasion of foreign cultural habits, rituals and practices was not ghettoised in Melbourne, but permeated with ease across the city. Carlton is home to a plethora of Italian restaurants such as Tiamo's and Brunetti's, but this introduction of European cuisine to Melbourne affected everything. An exemplar of this broadening of culinary culture is Jimmy Watson's Wine Bar, by Robin Boyd, an early example of Modern architecture in Melbourne. Ironically, Robin Boyd, a very vocal promoter of architecture in the late 1950s and 1960s, bemoaned the tackiness and decoration that appeared to define working-class continental immigrant taste. The cosmopolitan explosion bloomed into and crossed over the student fallout area of Melbourne University and is such a clear stomping ground of the cafe intellectual that a restaurant can be found that has taken the name: the University Cafe, with green brass decor and its

Below: Robert Simeoni at Jimmy Watson's Wine Bar, telling his audience about the crypt he is designing for his family in Italy

brass and glass cake cabinet beneath a highly polished timber banister stair. It is not for the decor, but its patrons stay far longer than the time it takes to drink the tea they are served in double stainless steel pots.

From here cafe-bar culture mushroomed into the city by way of our working college, now the Royal Melbourne Institute of Technology, and headed straight for the Lounge, Melbourne's first pool hall/restaurant/bar/nightclub combo. This emerging-adult, sticky-floor, dance-hall cum meat market, cum soap box and movie house is an institution. Its timber floors have weathered the trampling of thousands of dateless revellers and have suffered the occasional re-sealing. The walls are a rich burgundy of high build paint, applied with the delicacy of a spade. The Lounge's rough finishings are a canvas to an array of projections emanating from never-tiring analogue slide projectors. Its place in our history of venues is cemented by the fact

that it was the only venue in the central business district worth patronising until the 1990s. Its type was unique until recently when it was joined by Ding Dong, once the International Bar, and Cookie.

Cookie's dark stair entry belies its monumental cut and paste interior of magazine-clipping wallpaper and faux ornate columns. All this is corralled around a kitchen concealed behind a thousand timber slats, the products of which are worth risking the decibel levels for. The bar staff are barricaded from the patrons by a statuesque, veined-marble bar whose ice-encrusted beer taps drip suggestively on to well-oiled stainless steel drainage traps. The serving of beer is nothing but performance, beginning with the elaborate rinsing of glasses on a high-tech pressure operated rinsing rig and ending in the beer being placed atop the stacks of upturned fresh glasses stored on the bar. Its yawning volume is deftly offset by a bar within a bar: the Cookie back bar, with soft dark brown wall panels etched with discrete white antlers, is a nook for the discreet and shy and littered with children's books of a decade ago. The return bar that services this cranny is the workstation where staff retire to concoct cocktails that take longer to make than to drink. All attempts to attract the attention of workers on this production line are fruitless and fuel a sense of invisibility in patrons that is perfect for the back bar's key anonymity.

Prior to the commercial crash of the 1980s the central business district of Melbourne was a wasteland by day, and worse by night. With another commercial boom some distance beyond the event horizon, a revitalisation plan was hatched by the city called Postcode 3000. The plan, implemented in 1992, relaxed development and licensing laws and fees. The two years following the changes should be described

as a heady time, fuelled by a new bar opening every month, with all ears to the ground listening for news of the latest. A bar three months old was a bar out of date, and attendance there became unbearable due to the crush of thirsty office workers, their information on the latest happening venue lagging somewhat behind that of their cooler counterparts. Many of the bars of this crash and burn era have faded away like one day wonders, but those that survived are now the genetic blueprint of the city's drinking habits.

The Myers Place Bar, as it is known, was one of the first to open in this new environment. Interestingly it has no sign and no official name, anonymity being a key to its success and its only advertising is word of mouth. It pokes its concrete bar out in to the street, pushing aside an airport window and a stained-glass door in the process. Its walls and floors are recycled plywood, and the ceiling is carpet, yes carpet. The folks behind the bar are, and always have been, the coolest dudes in town. A coiled roller shutter door hangs Damocles-like over the entry, behind which the whole arrangement is concealed after closing.

Rue Bebelons, aka the Red Bar, is named after its address, Little Lonsdale being equivalent to Baby Lonsdale which truncates to Bebe Lons. It is a tiny South American-operated bar, whose owners discuss nothing but soccer while playing the same music night after night. The walls are painted a rich red and glow on the patrons in a most flattering manner. They sit endlessly chatting on the eclectic collection of rickety timber chairs at particle-board tables half-heartedly disguised with cloth. A stained timber bar top with an aluminium edge cuts the plan diagonally in half – staff are allowed an equal amount of room behind the bar as are the patrons in front of it. This equity is a guide to how best enjoy this bar: as a regular, such that you might get invited to the other side. A necklace of dried roses hangs from the ceiling suggestively as mistletoe, and has done so since 1991. In 2004, one of the paintings changed on the wall. Apart from that, time stands still at Rue Bebelons.

Sadie's, on the other hand, died a horrible death. Its Japanese washed-pebble, bamboo water garden, tiered floor levels and light-weight, black-stained timber screens with a discreetly hidden doorway to a dance level were too cool for its clientele, who wanted topless bar staff.

The Croft Institute is one little laneway away, however it is separated from Sadie's by a huge psychological distance. The laneway is so dark and dingy and littered with restaurant refuse that a journey to the front door risks a mugging or two. A risk worth taking as the Croft Institute is a vodka brewery on display. The science-lab aesthetic of this contemporary distillery infects the entire establishment; the bar and benches have Bunsen burner taps and deep trough ceramic sinks. Your liver is the subject of a controlled laboratory experiment. Hose-down flooring, curved up at the walls, and glass cabinets of Petri dishes and curious burnt-orange rubber-hose-attached glass-beaker derivatives drive the story home. Might you drink enough to miss the theme, you are pulled back in by the white coat worn by the scientist concocting your next drink.

Phoenix was the *Herald Sun* newspaper's local pub for many years, and managed not to register on the consciousness of all but those from longstanding drinking families. Its location opposite the no-man's-land of the Flinders Street rail line meant that its arrival on the palate of a more general public came to it late in life. This arrival was due, just like Young & Jackson's, to the construction of the Federation Square project. Its history lingers in its interior as the new owners had the presence of mind to keep its terrible vinyl chairs, tables and crazy early 1960s' splatter stucco walls in which they've spliced a pendulous black steel stair and a constellation of stalactite lights. Somewhere in its bowels is concealed a kitchen that serves the best bar food around, and the music is reliably infectious.

The Victoria Hotel Back Bar is associated with a 1970s' inner-city-hotel, and its public bar, buried in the back of the hotel, is an exquisite archaeological find. The bar has been saved from under-new-management-ism by its association with the hotel and the hotel operators. Cigarettes linger in ashtrays over sticky timber-look laminate tables. Wall-mounted televisions blare over a raised felt of cigarette burns passing for pool tables. The televisions are a badly disguised blessing as the carpet is unwatchable, but the handsome dark timber beams and panelling of the ceiling can capture the attention should the night's sports programming fail to entertain. The very pejorative callings that might steer you away from this bar are its charm.

Robot is run by a very dedicated Japan-ophile. Melbourne's most compact bar, it is littered with a hailstorm of trinkets from contemporary Japan. He only hires Japanese staff, and the 6 feet he reaches when standing full height behind the bar puts you in mind of Swift's Gulliver. The bar is famous for its Australian saké and after enough of it you start to forget that your legs don't fit under the matchbox tables any better than do those of the owner. The high dark timber bench and the glass sushi cabinet, over which the staff strain to see, barely fit under the intricately constructed black painted steel mezzanine. Its lofty heights are accessible via a timber stair whose rake tests the limits of our building code. Upon it teeter even smaller tables than below. The bathrooms, which are seemingly planned by the good folks at the Rubik's Cube factory, have walls of timber veneer applied to thin air.

Below: The Gin Palace

and the lighting is exact. A red wash, submarine dive glow coats the red, white and black inscribed wall panels. The bar turns its face away from the street with a bench backed against the front window. The red entry vestibule is dotted with portholes, and the door itself is a steel fire door with a cylindrical counterweight that takes both hands to open. Should a light source afflict your eye or the lighting level offend your complexion, simply raise it with the owner/barman and he will consult his mixing desk of dimmers and make the slightest adjustment with endearing care.

The Gin Palace has a martini-oriented menu, and waistcoated floor and bar staff. The owner, Vernon Chalker, used to manage Claridges in London, and it shows. The Gin Palace has the perfect air of invisible professionalism that materialises your every wish the moment you imagine it. That everything has been considered before it catches your eye is manifest also in the fixtures, which are the cornerstone for this monumental atmosphere. The flock walls and ornately framed art collection are second only to the decorative fabric upholstered chairs in radiating that weighty yet subtle sense of 'family heirloom'. It seems fair to assume there must be a floor finish, but the sense of floating across it denies its discovery.

Troika or 'Perestroika' as it is affectionately known, was initially opened by an unfortunate couple with the Midas touch. Unfortunate in that its owners opened the bar intending to run it as part of a peaceful retirement, but the place took off like hotcakes and they had to sell it to retain the sanity they had hoped it would bring them. Ironically, the outer suburb where they relocated for their retirement has become the latest in which to be seen, and not least because of their presence. Its current owner is a photographer,

The end of the fast bar craze was marked by the opening of Double Happiness whose doors, to the chagrin of the owners, opened to a noticeable absence of crazed patrons hungry for a new bar. Double Happiness was almost empty, even on a Friday night. It seemed doomed. But the saturation of latest bar-ism was not an end, instead it was the beginning of a new solid period of carefully considered establishments whose patrons were able to commit for more than a month. And commitment pays dividends in this bar, behind which a timber rack stores personalised bottles of your poison of choice. Swinging arms of lucky cats, communist propaganda posters and the giant Chinese character that adorn its agriculturally detailed grey steel front door make Double Happiness at home with its fortune cookie name. For the obstinately coldhearted who cannot be warmed by the angelic staff or their potions there is a fireplace at the rear.

St Jerome's is a barely renovated dilapidated Swiss sandwich shop in a long ignored laneway. The premise of this bar seems to be 'open for business, then renovate'. After a day of trading, the owners purchase a new chair. Piece by piece the bar takes shape. The clientele revels in its resulting unself-consciously unpretentious shanty town image. The chairs and tables have been salvaged from temporary primary school class rooms. The floor is a rocky road of paint flecked concrete, timber deck and bitumen with more types to be added after the upcoming months trading. The toilets are graffitied beyond recognition, and on busy nights a rickety white vinyl temporary bar is set up in the back yard. St Jerome's is not so much a bar as a party in a war-ravaged student house, but what a party!

A crossover business type for the bar, as the city matures with empty nesters and baby boomers and drinks less during daylight hours, is the cafe with its roots, as mentioned earlier, in the immigration-driven population boom of 50 years ago. Most bars serve food and coffee during the day, and some even dare to at night. Both Rue Bebelons and St Jerome's are coffee houses by day. A strong strain of cafe-only establishments is densely peppered across the city, crammed into commercial office lobbies, clothes stores and hole-in-the-wall tenancies big enough only for a coffee machine and its pilot. This type has no ascertainable geographical boundary, and word-of-mouth research quickly reveals that everyone has a distinct favourite. The godfather of Melbourne's cafe world is Daniel Colls who is responsible for the conception of Café Racer, Postal Hall and Federal Coffee Palace, all characterised by exact service, perfect food, clever furniture solutions and gregarious staff.

Hitherto resistant to the thriving bar and cafe culture is Melbourne's financial district, which now too is turning and is being raised from the grey by SMXL. Allona and Ronnen Gorens' to-die-for-sandwich/melts are displayed like jewels under glass-topped benches in front of a lowered serving area set in a raw concrete box on to which ash timber and white can lights are directly stuck. The crockery and cutlery have the healthy weight of quality. Their outdoor tables are primary colour painted steel boxes with an array of the letters S, M, X and L cut into them. Rather than as cafes, the SMXL stores present themselves as diagrams in a how-to book for savvy industrial designers and graphic artists.

Thus a complex demographic is arrayed across an eclectic range of bars, from polished to tarnished, from designed to laissez-faire, from entrenched to fleeting, from gargantuan to minuscule, from colonial to cutting edge and from industrial to domestic. With these images, any good in-flight magazine could illustrate a glossy culinary city, but off the record they are a plexus in the design conversation that is integral to an understanding of Melbourne as a design city.

Opposite: Murray Forthun Extension, Brunswick, Melbourne (1996). The frame to the rear of the existing Edwardian villa has been much imitated by the next generation of architects making their way through alterations and addition

ARCHITECTURE AND THE PRACTITIONER ACADEMICS IN THE DESIGN CITY

A city does not become a design city without regenerating its modes of creating mastery in design. When Alvin Boyarsky bemoaned the fact that London in the 1970s was an architectural desert, it was in support of his practitioner/academic educational model, which he began to implement at the Architectural Association School of Architecture in London in 1971. In 1986 when I was appointed to head Architecture at RMIT I began to implement this model in Melbourne. In a small way, since the half-time appointment of Peter Corrigan in 1976, RMIT had involved practitioners in its architecture programme. However, as a strategy the approach required that practitioners be invited to conduct their research as part of the programme by running studios, and that both practitioners and academic staff undertook higher degrees based on their practices. I was determined that we would conduct research in the medium of architecture itself – spatial intelligence. The argument is that while research about architecture – sociological, historical and environmental – is useful, without research in the medium of architecture itself, there is nothing that furthers architecture itself. Boyarsky deliberately employed the graduates from his own school whom he thought had the most potential to become practitioners who would make a difference. He argued that making them take full responsibility for a group of students, a 'unit', while

developing their own practices was the only way to continue the research into design that most graduates are commencing as they complete their studies. They need to be supported in that research in the early years of their practice by a flow of income and also by a flow of research, both provided through interactions with students. The beneficiaries, including Alsop, Koolhaas, Wilson and Hadid, have led a renaissance in British and European architecture.

At RMIT, Peter Corrigan remains the doyen of this group, running intensive early years undergraduate studios that no ambitious students feel they can afford to miss. The first generation of practitioner/academics that I appointed in the widened model included Howard Raggatt and Ian McDougall, Carey Lyon and Peter Elliott. The second generation included Sean Godsell, Lindsay Holland and Kerstin Thompson. Currently, we can see that Sand Helsel and Shane Murray, members of that second generation, are assisting in the mentoring of a third generation through the school around the theoretical positions of the Urban Architecture Laboratory: Mauro Baracco, Nigel Bertram, Martyn Hook and Richard Black; while Pia Ednie-Brown and Vivian Mitsogianni are clustered around Tom Kovac and Paul Minifie in Mark Burry's Spatial Information Architecture Laboratory. Meanwhile

Michael Trudgeon is working on the regeneration of industrial design as a discipline in the post-industrial milieu.

It is impossible to overestimate the importance of this educational model in the culture of the city. The traditional universities strive for a scholastic respectability that removes them from close engagement with practice, and entire national architectural cultures, as Boyarsky argued of the USA, can be crippled by the abstract verbal theorising that results. The practitioner/academic model not only intensifies the connections between practice and theory, it involves students in the ligaments of those connections from the outset of their education, thus pre-empting the widespread cynicism that arises when graduates emerge from a theory hothouse and confront the world of practice for the first time, finding it seemingly indifferent to their intellectual interests. We encounter many of these architects in our passagiata down the civic spine. The influence of those we do not encounter (architects like Peter Bickle and Hamish Lyon who are acknowledged in the civil mission) is critical to the creation of the depth and passion of the architectural culture.

Shane Murray's practice exemplifies the benefits of setting up feedback loops within a city's own culture, learning what the city can teach us rather than palely imitating through the canon what other cities have taught. Working initially in the '38 South' (the latitude of Melbourne) programmewith the writer, Murray then recruited Nigel Bertram to join him in developing this total city and latterly city-region-wide approach in the Urban Architecture Laboratory. Murray is building on his initial interest in the 'laconic' coastal beach houses of Australia, a vernacular self-build Modernism based on frame construction with fibro-panel cladding and skillion roofs. Searching for the iconic form hidden within, he reversed the usual theory/practice loop, going from the shadow of the ideal towards the ideal that it dimly resonated and then constructing that ideal. His early Byron Bay beach house pair, the subject of his research in the invitational programme at RMIT,[1] exemplified the approach and in 2005 came full circle in the popular imagination by being raffled by Coca Cola as the archetypal beach house.

Becoming aware that his search for what the beach house 'wanted to be' had generated within him a series of formal preferences, Murray was driven to examine the compositional matrix that his designs and built projects reveal, arguing that this research provided a theory of architecture grounded in practice as

Above: Murray Forthun Extension (1996). The studio is also an iconic invention – it resembles a caravan, the symbol of 1950s' family holidays

opposed to the more usual projection of intellectual ideas – usually borrowed from other discourses – onto form. Murray positions himself in a school that searches for the simplest strategy to achieve the wide range of outcomes that a project demands.

His much imitated house extension and studio for himself and his artist partner Louis Forthun in the inner suburb of Brunswick is an exemplar of this approach. The rear of a double-fronted Edwardian villa is given a new face with a corrugated iron frame, detailed like origami, and encapsulating in one gesture the turning around of the house plan to face the private open space at the rear. It provides a sun-screening overhang to protect against summer sun, and controls the view to and from neighbouring properties. The studio facing this along the back fence of the yard is a matching metal-fold origami, caravan-like form, launching itself upwards in a lean-to that runs at right angles to the usual skillions at the rear of suburban houses, and forming a backdrop to a venerable fig tree. In doing this it presents as a conscious contemplation of the qualities of the backyard, ennobling the situation through that implied conversation. A platform sits above the ground between these two forms, big enough to dine on, but also raised so to allow for more informal occupation by larger numbers of people. It also refers to the couple's extended visits to and enjoyment of Japan, its culture and cuisine.

Murray's search for the single gesture that resolves the diverse needs of the programme found its most expressive form in his competition design for

Above and below: Shane Murray's Negri Callcott Pavilion, Brunswick,
Melbourne (2003)

Above: Baracco Wright's George Murphy house (2004) in Kew. An inclined plane drawn up along the frontage provides a multitude of opportunities, sheltering and masking an external terrace, and incorporating a garage and utility room, while maintaining the fiction that the original house is a pavilion set in a landscape

Federation Square in Melbourne. For this he solved the issues of a site without ground (it is situated over the railway yards of the main suburban terminal), a site falling towards the cold southeast, open to the wet weather from the southwest, and a site that most felt needed to be strongly differentiated from the city grid that it abutted, by providing a ground plane that rose away from that grid, creating a tiered open space giving grandstand views to the city and accommodating the programme to a facade along the river. This use of a contoured plane then found its way into a competition design for the Brisbane Art Gallery, and was realised in humbler projects like the Negri House in which it becomes a wall at the rear of a west-facing extension, protecting it against afternoon sun, and opening up to the yard in the evening.

Currently Murray is completing research into the housing needs of soon to retire 'baby-boomers'. This is a more abstract research than would be ideal for a practitioner, but it should lead to commissions in the area. He sees that the focus on analytical research leads to a reaction against 'the significant object' in architecture, and is concerned that the focus on commodity and firmness that comes from reductive approaches may be working against the delight that sometimes emerged from the pursuit of the significant object. The ongoing search for the laconic-iconic characterises Murray's work, and his theorising of his practice makes him a vital mentor to his colleagues. Bertram's work we have encountered on the spine. Baracco Wright, the practice of Mauro Baracco and Louise Wright, is exemplified by their work on the Murphy house in Kew. Here they have sought a simple planar form that shelters the inhabitants of the existing house from the gaze of passersby while not divorcing it from the street and accommodating a new garage and utility room. The house has been edited back and then supplemented forward through joinery insertions to

Top: Harrison and Crist's St Leonards Corner House (2002). A house in a newly developing fringe suburb is – with its clear critique of Venturi Scott Browne's position on Las Vegas – exactly the kind of peripheral experiment with the new reality of the edge that eventually finds its way on to the civic spine

Middle: Innocent Bystander Winery by Irene Pedersen (2006). This highly sophisticated winery has such massive concrete walls and roofs that it simulates the conditions of a cave, needing no cooling or heating. Attached to the massive construction is a feather-light wine sales area

Bottom: Lindsay Holland's St Kilda House (2000). The architect used steel frame construction for this house in a dense inner suburban area winning free-flowing space from the clear spans

Opposite: Harrison and Crist's Tunnel House, Edmanson Avenue, Brighton (2003). This project, quite literally in the interstices of the suburb, demonstrates how second order modernity releases architects from the purism of the 20th century, while allowing a new rigour in form-making

process the most rewarding space – working to the sensibilities of his partner Fleur Watson, editor of *Monument*, one Australia's most important design journals. This is the kind of work that could give accountancy a good name! The Hook Winery at Healesville in the foothills of the Great Dividing Range can also be visited. This too is a strikingly pragmatic work, with no evidence of any desire for an overarching formal expression, but with an intense poetic derived from pushing the programme requirements to their logical limits. The clear span, concrete, constant-temperature production room, 62 metres long by 14 metres wide and 11 metres high, is one of the handsomest rooms in the region. Hook teaches with Richard Black, whose practice is more paper-based than that of his colleagues in this tradition, but whose rigorous production of project after project exploring the vastness and flatness of Australia takes the approach into a geographical scale.

Lindsay Holland, another of the second generation and whose work is exemplified by his Steel House in St Kilda, a virtuoso exercise in the principle of parsimony, is engaged in an exploration of urbanism in China, a process that has brought him back into the academy to study landscape architecture.

Another practitioner/academic whose projects are unrealised as often as they are built is Tom Kovac, who is a pioneer in non-standard work in Melbourne. Realised in restaurants, bars and houses, his work looms across every major development site in Melbourne, from his Digital Architecture Gallery under Victoria Street, a proposal that linked the Carlton United Brewery site at the cusp of lower Swanston Street and upper Swanston Street to his proposals for the Palace Triangle on the beach at St Kilda, and edges ever closer

become more what it 'wanted to be'. The existing garage at the rear has been similarly converted into a studio flat. Baracco Wright are working on the reverse archaeology of a 1960s house by Robin Boyd, a project that runs parallel to Baracco's doctoral research on rehabilitating the theoretical work of that architect.

Martyn Hook, part of the triumvirate Iredale, Pedersen, Hook, can be seen in his work to partake in a similar discourse of pragmatic reverse engineering, though in his case the driver is more construction based. His own house in Port Melbourne results from a painstaking research into the least effort needed to create from the pervasive tilt-slab construction

Opposite: Tom Kovac's 2005 suite of designs for the Marina in St Kilda, a sheet typical of his design approach and providing evidence of the lyricism that imbues it

Below: Tom Kovac's 2005 design for a roof top swimming pool at St Kilda Junction

to a major manifestation of a new mode of architectural production that the world is racing to perfect. In the final stages of design is a swimming pool on top of an apartment block at what was once the southern end of the civic spine: St Kilda Junction. Vivian Mitsogianni has an aligned interest in surface architecture, and has guided undergraduate students to completing a number of award-winning projects on the quayside in Docklands. Pia Ednie-Brown is the theorist in this group, furthering her practice through a regular flow of installations that explore surface and containment.

In the next generation there are encouraging signs of a continuing pluralism. Graham Crist and Stuart Harrison are investigating the civic narrative expressionism originally identified by Peter Corrigan as a way of dealing with the reality of the suburban city. In this they are somewhat aligned with Cassandra Fahey (see Cassandra Complex p 262) who is certain

that environmental sustainability will be more and more at the forefront of the public imagination. This is an investigation that is potentially transformed by the new technologies now available, and it may lead to architectures that are not in thrall to digital processes, but cloaked in them. If this promise is delivered, then the consequences for the future are exciting – a debate between the bare sculptural forms of the Kovac non-standard, the new mathematics of Minifie Nixon (See Minifie Nixonp 206), Pia Ednie-Brown and an interactive civic architecture in the tradition of Corrigan and Lyon leavened with the compositional strategies of Murray and his colleagues promises a future far from the tiresome solipsisms of the Neo-Modern.

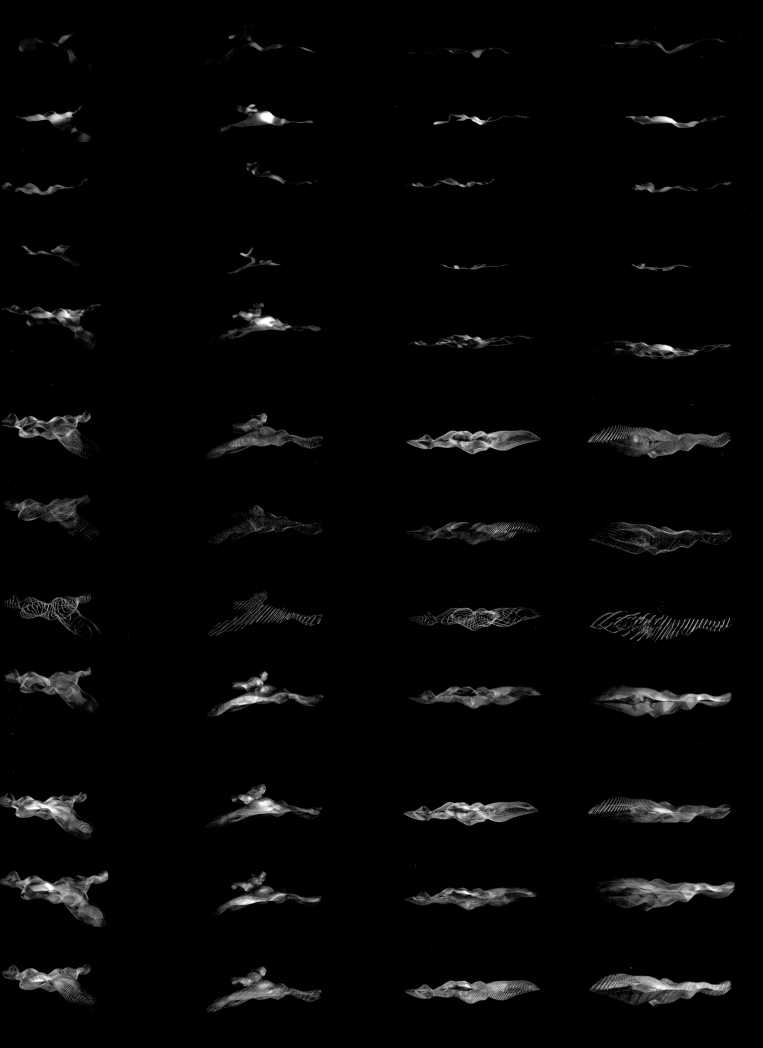

PASSEGGIATA DOWN THE CIVIC SPINE

Passeggiata Down the Civic Spine

ASHTON RAGGATT McDOUGALL (ARM)

Storey Hall (Tappin, Gilbert and Dennehy, 1887; and Ashton Raggatt McDougall, 1996), next door to Building 8 on Swanston Street, was RMIT's second commission under the curatorial approach to appointing architects that I initiated in the late 1980s, and it brought Melbourne's civic spine firmly into the heart of the international avant-garde in architecture. Internationally renowned critic and populist Charles Jencks cites this building as the first in the world to make use of the new fractal mathematics of Chaos Theory,[1] marvelling that this should have come about in Melbourne before bursting on the scene in New York, London or Tokyo. Howard Raggatt, who had graduated from Melbourne University and was teaching a studio at RMIT, conducted the research

leading to the use of the mathematics of topology in this design when invited to examine his mastery in my by-invitation postgraduate research programme at RMIT. The design is a lateral invasion of an existing Victorian building modelled on an 18th-century assembly hall and it created the university's only public building, the only named building on the city campus. His partner Ian McDougall, a graduate of RMIT, also teaching at RMIT, proposed in the same postgraduate research programme that buildings should engage with the popular imaginary if architecture is to matter in the culture.[2] An early example was the remodelling of the St Kilda Library (1992–4) into a giant book. Ian McDougall's belief that buildings should be designed so that they quite

naturally become souvenirs combines powerfully with the developments of the more arcane world of new mathematics to create an approach that makes ARM's buildings increasingly appealing to a wide public.

The assembly hall, formerly the Hibernian Hall, later home to an early women's movement, which was bought for RMIT in 1954 by the Storey family in memory of a son who was a student, had been gutted in the 1960s. ARM won the project with a design that provided lateral access to the 700-seat hall situated over the university gallery, providing substantial additional space – a 300-seat lecture theatre below grade and seminar rooms on the top floor. The design involved relining the interior of the hall to provide an acoustic environment suitable for lectures and the accommodation of air-conditioning ducts. As indicated above, Howard Raggatt had spent much of his time in the first cohort to participate in the by-invitation postgraduate programme at RMIT exploring the stretching of form[3] and had encountered Roger Penrose's non-periodical tiling system in the process. This tiling system using two tiles, a fat lozenge and a thin lozenge in a specified arrangement, is capable of covering all surfaces, convex and concave. These tiles are applied in differing scales, and in enlargements as through a distorting lens, to create the interior. They are then manifested as bronze castings on the outside. While the building is an astounding accomplishment in its own right, refreshing the civic legends of the

original is just as important as the unexpected use of fractal tiling – an invention the mathematician himself, as he admitted in an inaugural lecture in the hall, had thought to have no practical application.

Fronting on to Swanston Street, RMIT Storey Hall has a prime position on the Civic Spine and its location here alongside RMIT Building 8 has substantially reinforced the spine's role as a declarative armature, a site on which architectural positions about space and design are strongly argued. The dazzling new interior of Storey Hall becomes a companion space to the Mahoney and Burley Griffin Capitol Theatre a few blocks down, reinforcing the arguments for an engagement with the science of complexity. Lab Architecture's BMW Edge at Federation Square can only be seen as a recent member of the same family, furthering the same argument and contrasting with the Platonic geometrical basis of the chief opposing idea of spatial and formal generation that is espoused in the Newman College dining hall, the State Library and the Arts Centre.

RMIT Storey Hall is echoed in ARM's St Kilda Town Hall (1992–4) in the burnt out remains of which the architects wrought a space of rare elegance and wit. At the rear, up Carlisle Street, to this hall – one of those serving the 50 or so civic entities of which Melbourne at one time consisted (now reduced to around 25) – a suite of civic offices has been added. Strongly influenced by Finnish architect Alvar Aalto, whose peripheral position relative to Modernism appeals strongly to architects in Australia who feel very much on the periphery 'down under', this has a warm, engaging interior supportive of egalitarian concepts of micro-democracy that make the use of Aalto as mentor seem

appropriate, even if in Melbourne the issue is forging an identity rather than serving an existing homogeneity.

In the heart of the Victorian Arts Centre (1968) ARM were invited to design a reception centre for the major corporate, AMCOR (1997). Located on St Kilda Road (the name that the Swanston Street takes on as it crosses the Yarra River into the government Domain), the complex was developed by architects Grounds, Romberg and Boyd in the 1950s and 1960s, the last time Melbourne peaked as a design city – that time stimulated by the 1956 Olympic Games. Much of this complex is situated underground and the spaces involved have no access to daylight. Here, in a leap of the imagination, ARM created a lining of resin panels for the rooms, panels filled with engaging ephemera gleaned from around the city. This was foreshadowed in Storey Hall – look for an apple encased in resin in the foyer that serves as the foundation stone! These rooms are lit from behind these panels. The effect is

light-hearted and joyful – the antithesis of the underground slab of space that the architects confronted when called in to make the design. This wonderful set of rooms confirms and consolidates the lineage of the Capitol Theatre and Storey Hall and foreshadows the atrium at Federation Square, setting an ineradicably argumentative stamp on the curatorial influence of the civic spine.

ARM have made major contributions to the architecture of Canberra, the national capital, through their National Museum, and to Adelaide in the Marion Centre, before returning to the civic spine in Melbourne with the very delicate commission to add a visitor centre to the Melbourne Shrine (2004), the war memorial that sits astride the civic spine. Australian sensitivity to the two world wars is difficult to understand until you visit the towns in the country and discover the avenues of honour that line their approaches. Australia lost proportionally more of its

young men in the First World War than did the European powers, and its countrymen's experience of extreme cruelty in Japanese prisoner of war camps during the Second World War casts a long shadow over the generations. The need for a visitor centre was to serve this consciousness, but also to build a consciousness appropriate to the now heterogeneous society of cosmopolitan post-1985 Melbourne. The strategy adopted to address this involved undercutting the existing shrine[4] using a tool derived again from the new mathematics, creating an undercroft reached through two courts, a red entry space and a green contemplative space. The red space is to do with poppies and blood, and the wall is inscribed in bold handwriting: 'Lest we Forget'. The green space contains the paradoxical plant symbols of war and peace: bay, olive and oak.

ARM have moved into the commercial realm and their revamp of Melbourne Central brings them on to the civic spine with a multistorey timber representation of an opening box, facade to a new cinema complex on the corner diagonally opposite Storey Hall. The box is caught in the act of opening, so to speak, reasserting ARM's interest in process and procedure rather than form. This redesign of a city block carves out of the original department store complex a series of laneways that link the complex back into the arcades of the retail spine that run parallel to Swanston Street from La Trobe to Flinders Street, extending for eight city blocks. This reverse-engineering reasserts the city's own original patterning over the maze that was built around the failed Dimaru Department Store in obeisance to the shibboleths of North American retail consultants, shibboleths that have proven irrelevant to Melbourne.

When ARM's RMIT Storey Hall was built, it was concealed behind a screen at the behest of the then Minister of Planning, who said that while he was approving the building, he did not want any of his colleagues to see it before it was finished, as he was sure it would cause an uproar in parliament. And indeed it did cause heated debate when it was unveiled, not so

much in parliament as in the letters pages of the *Age* newspaper. Most of the complaints were academics who use the tram up Swanston Street to reach Melbourne University. ARM's National Museum has drawn the wrath of conservative politicians because it uses Libeskind's Jewish Museum plan as a footprint for its Aboriginal section. But this is the most visited building in Australia. And the excavation of space under the Shrine has brought nothing but accolades to the architects. These are signs of an increasing sophistication about architecture in the popular imagination, and an increasing enjoyment of and respect for the fact that it has something to say.

ARM return within the shadow of the civic spine with their design for the Melbourne Theatre Company and a series of recital halls, with construction due to commence on site in the Arts Precinct shortly. Here a series of virtuoso interiors, some as cool and empathetic as at St Kilda Town Hall, some as expressive as Storey Hall, are held together in a large frame, the ridges and folds of which are painted in a fluorescent paint that catches every glow of the city at night. ARM return to sit adjacent again to a work by Edmond and Corrigan, in this instance the much smaller School of Drama at the Victorian College of the Arts (VCA). The curatorial processes of the city have somehow mirrored themselves here, almost two decades after the current wave of conscious city-building began to be implemented at RMIT.

1 Charles Jencks, *Fractal Architecture, New Paradigms in Architecture: The Language of Post Modernism,* Yale University Press (New Haven and London), 2002, pp 240–1.

2 Ian McDougall, 'The Autistic Ogler', in Leon van Schaik (ed), *Transfiguring the Ordinary,* Printed Books (Melbourne), 1995, pages unnumbered.

3 Howard Raggatt, 'Notness: Operations and Strategies for the Fringe', in Leon van Schaik (ed), *Fin de Siècle and the Twenty-first Century: Architectures of Melbourne,* RMIT A+D (Melbourne), 1993, pp 113–172.

4 Leon van Schaik, 'The Shrine of Rememberance' [ARM], *Architecture Review Australia,* No 091, 2004.

GREG BURGESS

Atypically for a Melbourne architect, Greg Burgess is best known for his work in the remote areas of Australia. Like Sean Godsell, a former Australian Rules Football player, Burgess's interest in organic form led him to a symbiotic relationship with the elders of indigenous communities in the Grampian National Park (Gariwerd), a few hours' drive to the west of Melbourne. Here he designed the Brambuk Aboriginal Cultural Centre (1990) creating forms that came to represent Aboriginality in architecture, a period that culminated in the Uluru-Kata Tjuta Cultural Centre (1995). This building sits in possibly the most sensitive site in Australian mythology, in view of Ayer's Rock, an outcrop of red sandstone with a footprint the same size as that of the central grid of Melbourne. For settlers, the common name 'The Rock' signifies a core of national identity with a rather masculine oneness, a singularity belied by Uluru's close spatial relationship to Kata Tjuta, common name 'The Olgas', another equally large but more complex and perhaps more feminine outcrop 40 kilometres away. The two outcrops are so close that the one can be seen through the windscreen of a car while the other fills the rearview mirror. A visitor who takes the time to observe these as a pair discovers that they are engaged in a perpetual dance with the one turning red as the other turns navy blue: dawn and dusk. Externally, the Uluru-Kata Tjuta Cultural Centre seems to marry these two colour states. In both of these cases Burgess's clients responded strongly to

his use of natural materials and sinuous lines approximating to drawings in sand. The interior at Brambuk focuses on a fireplace and chimney with a looping mezzanine, a daring multicultural mixture of hobbit-like country pub comfort and a songline made manifest. The interior at Uluru-Kata Tjuta spirals inwards around the outer shell until you reach the central space, telling a story as well as functioning as a museum for artefacts from the culture of the local guardians of the national park.

Greg Burgess's work first appears on the civic spine in 2004 with *Cathedral*, an installation on the St Kilda Road forecourt of the Arts Centre named after a Raymond Carver short story about a blind man who guides a friend through the process of drawing a cathedral with his eyes shut so that he could experience something of his friend's blindness. Somehow it is characteristic of Burgess that he finds a spiritual message in a work of popular fiction, a direct connection between the public imagination and the profound that seems to come easily to someone who has excelled in both sport and high culture (Burgess was awarded the Royal Australian Institute of Architects Gold Medal in 2005).

This piece was part of an exhibition in support of the late Fred Hollow's work with glaucoma sufferers in Third World countries. Burgess worked with artist Domenico de Clario on the piece – such

Opposite: Uluru-Kata Tjuta Cultural Centre (1995). The power of the approach is evident from the air, from where this cultural centre seems to be as much a part of the landscape as Uluru beyond

Above: Brambuk Aboriginal Cultural Centre (1990) focuses on a fireplace and chimney

Left: Uluru-Kata Tjuta Cultural Centre (1995). A tree form focuses the central space, a form that is surprisingly appropriate as the desert here is dotted with large 'desert oaks' – Casuarinas

Below: Studios at RMIT Bundoora (1989). Another experiment into the rigours of organic structure created a complex space suffused with light and with volumes that are difficult to discern at one glance

Left and above: Catholic University (1999). Proof that Burgess is able to create the same embracing spaces in the heart of the city as he does in the country

Below: Memorial for John and Sunday Reed (Heidi Rose Pavilion 1991). Burgess's pursuit of organic form is not idle, but is driven through many experiments such as this

Opposite: Greg Burgess in his atelier in the inner-city suburb of Richmond, Melbourne

architect-artist collaboration is a consistent part of the local culture over more than three decades, in shows that have often been the first curated appearance of work by architects now well known. Made from donated materials, including borrowed gym weights to hold it down, the two wings of the piece resonate with other Burgess experiments in roofs, like the Rose Pavilion at Heidi Museum of Modern Art (1991) and the painting studios at RMIT Bundoora (1989). Burgess's description of the installation, from which this account is drawn, concludes: 'This was a restorative fragment – a seed capable of transformation.' This sentence encapsulates the ambitions of his work, which is part of a wider spiritual quest and includes much

concern for the grounding in the universe that could flow if everyone was in touch with cosmic spirals and energy flows.

Burgess's major inner-city project is a building for the Catholic University off Victoria Parade (1999). The exterior reveals a commanding exploration of Fibonacci series-like growth, while the interior features a twin-winged, lantern that has the same twin-wing seed-like form as *Cathedral*.

NORMAN DAY

Norman Day would be represented on the civic spine from mid 2005 courtesy of RMIT, were its South Saigon campus contiguous to its city campus, but of course it is not. At RMIT Vietnam, Norman has completed the first stage of the university's complex in the delta south of Ho Chi Minh City. As a current member of RMIT's chancellery remarks, it is unmistakably a RMIT building. A Mengers Cube wall screens several floors of malleable space, readily reconfigured to meet the changing needs of learning environments as information technology evolves. Out of this super-crate project extraneous programme elements – the major lecture theatre, security checkpoint, loading bays, plant rooms and entry canopies. Within its compass and beneath it lie large social spaces, where street vendors sell food, and where motorbikes can be secured.

In a postscript to this building, which at least in a virtual sense forms part of the RMIT collection on the civic spine, Norman and RMIT have been busy with the design of a number of learning resource centres (LRC) and the construction of the Cantho University LRC in southern Vietnam. Evolved from branch libraries, these are key focal points in the distributed learning networks that are being built around the internet. They are places where learning communities can find themselves face to face between periods of remote interaction, in crucial physical engagements that militate against the loneliness of internet-based

study, a loneliness that worldwide – even within the training programmes of large corporations – causes 80 per cent of those who are not properly linked to some of their peers to drop out, dispirited.

Norman is passionate about this work, drawn to it through his involvement in post independence East Timor, where in a *pro bono* initiative he helped the government to establish its institutions in a number of lightly restored buildings. He and his team (Enza Angelucci, Ms Hoa Bach, Ms Hang, and his architect/wife Kirsten Day) have taken to working in Vietnam with zest, an interesting innovation for a practice with a home base in St Kilda. Norman was an *enfant terrible* in his early years, perhaps

to differentiate himself from his more diplomatic brother, an architect who has made his career within the politesse of reflected Toorak/Tuscany. A certain irreverence remains, making Norman's column in the *Age*, the local broadsheet newspaper, an often disconcerting read. It also makes his column well read and no other writer has kept architecture in the public gaze this consistently in the past decades. He cannot resist taking the overtly successful down a peg or two, but makes up for this by often supporting work that has otherwise been overlooked. Still, like Clive James, he cannot resist a good phrase. His somewhat pugnacious defence of the underdog brings him under the spotlight of the gossip column in his own paper at times. His underlying seriousness is

Left: On the civic spine (by proxy) RMIT Vietnam (2005). View of the entry to the university's South Saigon Campus Building

Above: Cantho Learning Resource Centre (2006). Day is introducing a refreshing sprightliness to architecture in Vietnam, which has suffered from much high-seriousness in architecture in the decades of Russian influence

Below: RMIT Vietnam (2005) at night, aerial render by the architect. 'Unmistakably a RMIT building!', remarked a Pro-Vice Chancellor proudly, noting its experimental air

Above and bottom right: Infill House for the Housing Commission (1983). Norman Day's irreverence and wit enabled him to deal with Postmodernism as if he always knew it was a dead end, avoiding the pitfalls of failed seriousness, and finding an enduring edginess. The breezy nonchalance worked inside too

Bottom left: Norman Day holding Leo, Sheila Teo, Enza Angelucci and Kirsten Hulley

evident in his postgraduate research at RMIT, which also featured a suite of his large canvases.[1]

However, when in his stride he is more interesting as a designer than as a critic. A string of early houses for the Housing Commission, constructed in the early 1980s, show him tussling with Post-modernism, and winning from that engagement a quirky style that sits unremarkably today with its neighbours, clearly having more to do with them than with the style itself, or rather winning from the eclectic porosity of the approach that which is of the genre itself, as epitomised in a house in Fitzroy. The interiors have the same chirpy, now period, ease. This is a very knowing charm. Day has produced a book on modern houses of Melbourne,[2] and this is precisely but irreverently located in that lineage.

Two other projects give a clue to the more serious grounding of Day's work. The Burford House, originally a 1920s' Federation building, is a very entertaining romp through the history of Melbourne's 1960s' avant-garde, complete with a pergola screen that is a projection of the house on to a picture plane well removed from the house itself. The most haunting part of this ensemble is the cylindrical bay under a square plane. While established by reference to the corner towers of Federation architecture (1910s–20s), itself sprung from American Freestyle, the bay resonates with the geometrical obsessions of the previous generation, as seen in Kevin Borland's extension to the Grollo House in Thornbury (see Simeoni, p 274) and in Roy Grounds' compositions, whether houses or the Arts Centre with its triangle, cylinder, cone and double square. At Melton Mowbray School to the west of Melbourne, during the period 1980-98 Norman was architect to a campus that today is in need of refreshment, but where he created some wonderful miniature developments from Le Corbusier's last work in Zurich, the Heidi Weber pavilion.

Below: Norman Day and staff in the office in Ho Chi Minh City

In mid 2001 Norman commissioned a review of his work from me, and in this I wrote of his architectural laboratory and its experiments:

[A] strand that seems to me to be well developed is that of the wilful adoption of forms from Le Corbusier's oeuvre, especially the vernacular trawlings. At Melton Mowbray and in the houses these moments are delicious, because again something toy-like has taken place.[3] The elements are transferred from concrete mono-colour into smooth dry-construction self-coloured materials. Reassembled they are smaller scale commentaries on the best or most intimate moments of that austere master's work. They humanise it, suburbanise it, wittily. The references are clear, humble and funny. One laughs with delight, and finds that the spaces are supportive and scaled to the 'little life' that Bergman intuits is the best we can achieve. This is what democratic architecture should be about, I feel. Pavilions like the Art School at Melton Mowbray give meaning to

the term 'human scale', and they connect our emotions to our intellectual history. At a larger scale, the sketches for the ANZ College of Anaesthetists reveal that Day can manipulate larger scale toy blocks as Le Corbusier did at La Tourette, or in the Rio Education Ministry Building.

At RMIT Vietnam, four years later, this larger scale promise has been fulfilled.

1 Norman Day, 'Particular Architecture', in Leon van Schaik (ed), *Fin de Siècle and the Twenty-first Century: Architectures of Melbourne*, RMIT A+D (Melbourne), 1993, pp 17–40.

2 Norman Day, *Modern Houses: Melbourne*, Brian Zouch (Armadale), 1976; updated as *Heroic Melbourne*, RMIT (Melbourne), 1995.

3 Leon van Schaik, 'A Wide Palette of Architectural Elements – The Work of Norman Day', *Monument*, Sydney, No 13 (June 1996), p 52.

Opposite: On the civic spine – City Square original design (1980). Ron Robertson Swann's *Vault* (nicknamed the 'Yellow Peril' by the press) in the position for which it was designed

DENTON CORKER MARSHALL (DCM)

Along Swanston Street and across Collins Street from the Town Hall, running to Flinders Lane and the back of St Paul's Cathedral is an open space called 'City Square'. This space is an unremarkable urban square, similar in scale to the open space in front of the State Library further to the north, but not anchored to any building in the way that that apron of lawn is an integral part of the design of the entry face of the library with its large portico and symmetrical cascades of steps. City Square has a highly contested history that reveals much about the idea of the city in the minds of its governing elites. The Town Hall makes its mark on the civic spine with a large portico that projects to the street edge over the pavement, giving the upper floor loggia a commanding view up and down Swanston Street. The building does not address City Square. Indeed, City Square is a recent phenomenon, created in the early 1980s in the belief – held by the city fathers – that a real city must have a square. The colonial government laid out the city grid on this side of the Yarra as an exclusively commercial venture – government was confined to the Domain on the other side of the river[1] – and only the Eastern Market (formerly located between Little Collins and Bourke Street, fronting on to Exhibition Street) and the Town Hall asserted a public role in the city. A half block of the city was purchased and demolished, and there are those who can recount in loving detail every building and shop that was lost in the process.

It was with their winning design for this site that DCM launched their brilliant and largely international career, commencing unusually on the civic spine. Their design, which featured a waterfall behind which were located shops, cafes and tourist information offices, was demolished to make way for the Westin Hotel and the truncated space that we see today. The site has a baleful influence on innovative design. Melbourne's most famous public art work, Ron Robertson Swann's *Vault* was commissioned for the first City Square, its acid yellow setting off the grey-blue of the stone (known as bluestone and used as the pavement in the city), standing near where today the statue to Burke and Wills is situated. The abstract form of this work, immediately labelled the 'Yellow

Peril' by the popular press, was too much for the city fathers and they had it removed to a then remote site on the banks of the Yarra River, from whence it has recently been moved to grace the forecourt of the Australian Centre for Contemporary Art (ACCA) (see Wood Marsh, p 254).

DCM then won the commission for the Australian Embassy in Beijing and they have continued to work abroad with great success, most recently winning the competition for the Stonehenge Visitor Centre in England. Their next Melbourne commission of note was the Adelphi Hotel, up Flinders Lane from City Square. Designed in the mid 1980s, this conversion of one of a pair of loft buildings

Below: Adelphi Hotel (1991). Even today people crane their necks to see the lap pool, one end of which is cantilevered over the street

Opposite: Adelphi Hotel. The rooms were a very advanced design for their time, and sadly are being refurnished in 2005–6

on each side of a small lane at right angles to Flinders Lane, became known all over the world for its roof level, glass-bottomed lap pool, cantilevered over the street. It is still probable that you will find people on the pavement craning their necks to look up into the water. This entrepreneurial venture by the architects – they held a controlling share in the development – was one of the world's first 'designer hotels' and its pool-

deck bar with a view through the spires of St Paul's Cathedral was the site of many an important design business encounter.

In an increasingly recognised phenomenon known as 'morphic resonance'[2] ideas tend to be generated around the world at the same time, and credit goes to those with the best publicity. DCM have repeatedly anticipated in built form what has become avant-garde paper architecture elsewhere only later. Being pioneers, however, has not been easy. On the Collins Street commercial spine of the city, they were the first Melbourne architects to break the stranglehold of interstate or overseas architects on major commissions in the city, designing 101 Collins Street (1987–90). Without doubt the most architectonic high-rise building in the street, unfortunately the enlightened client who commissioned the building sold it on during construction and the new owners fell back into the prevailing 'cultural cringe'. In the belief that nothing local could be as good as something from elsewhere, they flew in Philip Johnson's partner John Burgee to redesign the foyer, which in DCM's design was an astonishing open space created by transferring the load of the building via transverse beams on to perimeter walls. Perversely, this effect in Burgee's design is cancelled out by placing massive columns under the beams. DCM were not favoured with a public building in the city until there was a change of state government after which they were commissioned to design the Exhibition Centre on the Yarra River in the partly constructed shell of what the previous government had commissioned as a museum. This long exhibition hall projects an extreme cantilever towards the river and is known as 'Jeff's Shed' after the premier who changed the brief, and the architect. Political transitions in Melbourne tend to have a visible

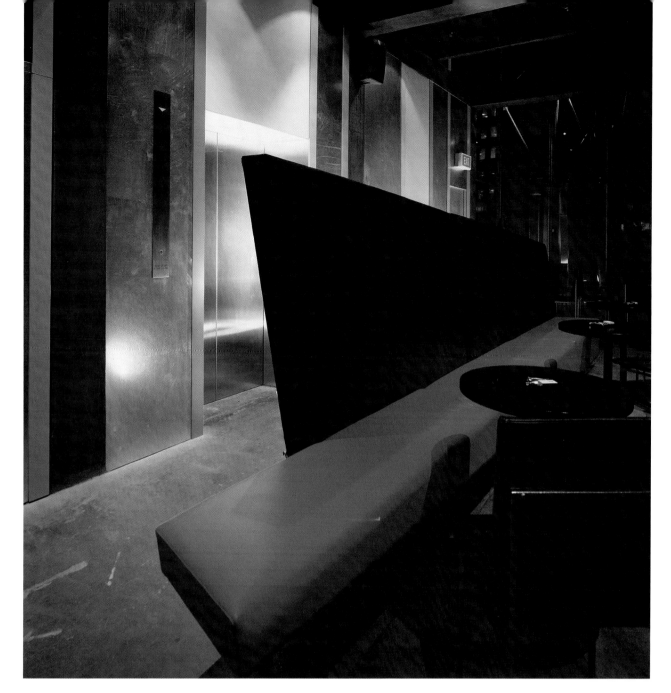

consequence – when Jeff Kennett lost power during the construction of Federation Square, his victorious opponents cut several storeys off the 'shard' that stands in front of St Paul's, so ruining its function as a signal to the civic spine like that of the Town Hall *porte-cochère*. This political competition to create and shape large institutional facilities is a feature of the curatorial culture of the city, but it is not often well handled. The large casino complex which was let as a government tender, typically confused finance and design. The complex and indeed the entire south bank of the Yarra, even as reclaimed for the city with a riverside promenade down to the exceptional Exhibition Centre, is undistinguished by any architecture of note on the waterfront.

However, having spoiled the previous administration's ambition to build a museum on the river to allow for the reconstruction of the State Library in whose building the museum had been established, Kennett did run an open competition for the museum building and this was won by DCM (2002). Their design allowed for the restoration in the round of the domed 1881 Exhibition Buildings – not to be confused with the Exhibition Centre – paving the way for World Heritage listing of this Brunelleschi-inspired design in 2004. DCM's design here is calmly set parallel to the rear of the 1881 buildings, and symmetrically organised around a central aviary and rain forest enclosure with a soaring shed roof. This is possibly the handsomest building in the city, certainly

Above: Melbourne Museum (2000). Having been heard, the gestures are muted and well attuned to the axiality of the adjacent World Heritage-listed Exhibition Building

Left and below: On the civic spine – Sensis HQ in the QV complex on Swanston Street (2005). In the strange new world of Asian urbanism, the architects had to design a building that began three storeys from the ground, with only its foyer at street level. DCM used their signature 'Yellow Peril' colour to indicate where their work began

Opposite left to right: Bill Corker, Barry Marshall, John Denton in the office they have shared for their entire career

the most generous in its public spaces, and a rare assertion of the importance of the communal in forging the city's culture. The offices of the museum are lined along the facade over the entrance, looking towards the old building, giving this fine open square a liveliness at most times of day.

While partners in DCM have been early advocates and implementers of the return to living in the heart of the city, occupying the loft building adjacent to the Adelphi Hotel and designing the Anna Schwarz Gallery on its ground floor, their peripheral works are continuing experiments that energise the practice. The Barry Marshall House (1992) inserts a courtyard into the dune-scape of the nearby Phillip Island and is a precursor to the winning design for Stonehenge, just as its interior is a clue to the ambitions of the rooms at the Adelphi Hotel. DCM's design for Sensis on the QV site, on the other hand,

seems to foreshadow the twisting rectangular form that is now emerging in a more refined form in the Emery House nearby. This is almost certainly a critique of the Sensis Building, which, sophisticated as it is in concept, leaves much to be desired in its constructed form.

1 Nigel Westbrook, 'Phantom Grids and Master Views: The Melbourne Domain – Emergence of an Urban Park', in Peter Brew (ed), Transition – Discourse on Architecture, No 47, RMIT (Melbourne), 1995, pp 6–19.
2 Rupert Sheldrake, 'The Rebirth of Nature', in Pavel Buchler and Nikos Papastergiadis (eds), Random Access 2: Ambient Fears, Rivers Oram (London), 1996, pp 100–21. For morphic resonance, see pp 114–20.

EDMOND AND CORRIGAN

In 1994 Edmond and Corrigan arrived on to the civic spine with RMIT's Building 8, a masterpiece of civic narrative expressionism, the prevailing avant-garde in Melbourne in the 1980s and 1990s. Thus they emerged early into the public realm of the city in the build up to the blooming of Melbourne as a design city in the 21st century. In 2004 they completed the Newman College Study Centre at Melbourne University, at the northern end of the spine, and a passagiata down the spine encounters their work on the School of Drama at the Victorian College of the Arts (2003) too.

The early 21st-century phenomenon that is Design City Melbourne commenced on the civic spine of the city with RMIT commissioning Edmond and Corrigan to design Building 8 (1990–4).[1] This was the first major commission by RMIT since the 1970s. The brief was to double the size of the institute's library and house the Faculty of Business. During construction, the functions were changed and two storeys were added to house Architecture and Design. This commission broke a 20-year relationship between the institution and a long-established architectural firm, and marked the introduction of a criterion-based selection procedure for architects that I had devised to ensure that RMIT appointed architects who had a demonstrated track record of ambition in design. It was also the beginning of the end of a tacit agreement among the city's elites that the commission for any building of importance had ipso facto to be awarded to

an architect from Sydney, Japan or the USA. It was the single most important act of curation in the encouragement of the local architectural culture 'since Robin Boyd'.[2] Importantly, I framed it as an act of curation, with the architects being advised that RMIT intended to establish a collection of fine buildings by all of the most ambitious architects in Melbourne.

Building 8 shocked the central city, bringing to it a colourful theatricality very different to the drab grey or beige conformity of most of what was being built. But it won local and national awards and, situated on top of Sydney architect John Andrews's sunken ziggurat, it declared war on Modernism. This war was waged most effectively in the internal planning, which was arranged as a series of urban villages on deep plan plates with a network of street-like corridors on each level. It was this relaxed approach to planning that enabled the building to survive the radical change of function imposed on it during construction. The library, constrained within minimal floor-to-ceiling heights, is peppered with small studiolo-like spaces that relate to the ancient traditions of scholarship. The main, two-tiered architecture lecture theatre has the intimacy of an anatomy theatre, and owes much to Alvar Aalto in its sinuous cross-section.

Peter Corrigan, informed by his extensive and now internationally acclaimed practice in stage set design, advised everyone that the novelty of Building 8

Above: Prahran Fire Station (1997). The architects' respect for the suburbs is evident in the incorporation into the fire station designs of amplified elements from suburban houses

Left: Newman College Study Centre (2004). The rehearsal room. Love of libraries and love of theatre ignite these spaces

Below: Ringwood Library (1994). The soaring profile towards the rear over the service lane between the library and the shopping centre

Opposite: Ringwood Library (1994). This night scene shows the building reflected on wet paving in the forecourt, emphasising the way in which it masks an entire regional shopping centre beyond

would soon wear off and that it would settle into the urban scene and become an unremarked part of the streetscape. It has, however, retained its ability to shock and delight visitors. Tom Nairn, the prominent Scottish globalisation theorist, describes his delight in the edifice when he first encountered it in the early 2000s, and how as he photographed it he was accosted by a passer-by who growled: 'We don't want any more of that here!' The commission was won on the basis of a series of buildings on the outer fringes of Melbourne's (then) 6,000 square kilometres of suburbs, now extending to 7,500 square kilometres! These buildings, many of them for the Catholic Church striving to minister to a spreading population, were photographed in a spectacularly new way by photographer John Gollings, then just establishing his reputation as an innovative documenter of buildings.

Edmond and Corrigan continue to work in the suburbs, the centrality of which to Australian culture they ardently affirm, with a series of fire stations, their design affectionately derived from suburban domestic architecture as part of a homage to the daily housekeeping roles of firemen, as in the Windsor Fire Station. The most recent in this genre has had to take into account the changes wrought by the Equal Opportunities Act, one of the pieces of legislation that serve to make inner-city Melbourne the most liberal part of Australia, which are now beginning to have effect and are seen in the appointment of many women to these stations. This frankly Postmodern approach continues to result in robust works of architecture that connect well to the everyday experience of the citizens of the city, even as they just as frequently appall some elites, notable among whom is the former State Premier Jeff Kennett. But these fire stations also belie the accusation that this approach leads inevitably to the inflated 'project home' syndrome, so called because this has become an easy way out for those building new institutions in the suburbs. Most significant among these cuckoo's egg projects is the Ringwood Library (1994) in which Corrigan's conflation of suburban form,

Above: Return to the (off) civic spine – School of Drama, VCA (2003). Sparkling alluringly at night, but stagey in the daylight, like a nightclub seen in sunlight

Opposite: Peter Corrigan in Phillip Hunter artist's studio in Brunswick

architetture povera detailing and Aaltoesque profiles result in a wonderfully generous interior space. Such a space is rarely seen in such institutions in the suburbs and has been fought for here to act as a counterweight to the vast regional shopping centre that appends from the rear of the library, a building that fronts on to a salvaged urban space behind the original strip shopping precinct of Ringwood.

When these projects are understood as a viewing of popular culture together with high international culture, the breathtaking ambition of the architectural project of this firm becomes evident. RMIT Building 8 is clad in the colours of local Australian Rules Football teams,[3] but it is also lined on some floors with tiles in the colours of Harvard University – a deliberate goad to the ambitions of those (as it was originally intended) within. Recently, as if to challenge his own predictions about the 'normalisation' effects on these expressions of civic narratives, Corrigan designed a theatre complex for the School of Drama (2003) at the Victorian College of the Arts (VCA) a block away from the civic spine and located in the city's Arts Precinct across the river from the central city. In many lights this looks like the inside of a nightclub in daylight, seedily tawdry; but in some lights and at night it simply sparkles with mischief! The interior is full of pranks with grids and meshes, using the cheapest of materials to create an interior of difference, a truly theatrical world.

The elision between high seriousness and irreverent fun is a heady and avowedly theatrical mix – think Shakespeare – and it certainly aims to appeal to what is called the 'popular imaginary' (though Corrigan would scoff at this term); yet there is a sombre substratum to the work, an 'Alas, poor Yorick,

I knew him' moment lies in wait at every corner. There is an element of folly in high seriousness, after all – we all die, no matter how immaculately our details are conceived. At his latest building, Newman College Study Centre (2004), his second to reach the civic spine,[4] Corrigan finds himself head to head with the Burley Griffins, giants from another age. In 1990 he might have gone 'head to head', but in 2005 he plays a subtler game and takes, as he would say of a player in his favourite game, Australian Rules Football, 'another option'. The building repeats in a different form many of the elements of the college; an upper-level ambulatory is strung around the outside, affording views to the playing fields beyond. But it is a deliberately dim resonance. In some lights it is hard to see that the building is there at all. In that term beloved of low-brow taste, it 'blends in'. Until you go inside. Here there uncoils one of the most delightful library spaces on earth, replete with Aaltoesque acoustic ceilings and tightly contained soaring space, designed for thinking. But even here the users are not left unchallenged. It is as if the Melnikov House in

Moscow – that extraordinary architect-designed and architect-owned survivor of purges and wars – has been threaded through the design. Against all odds the determined have found a way to keep architecture engaged right there in the flux of our politics, waging the battle between the liberals of the inner-city and the affluent conservatives of the new suburbs.

1 For an account of the new process see Leon van Schaik, 'Building 8: The Appointment Process', in Leon van Schaik (exec ed), Nigel Bertram (ed Vols 1 and 2), Winsome Callister (ed Vol 3), Building 8: Edmond and Corrigan at RMIT, Schwartz Transition (Melbourne), 1996, 92–6.

2 Norman Day, Age, 20 April 2005. http://theage.com.au/articles/2005/04/19/1113854190816.html

3 For an account of Peter Corrigan's connoisseurship of the game see: Leon van Schaik, 'Building 8: The Appointment Process', Vol 1, pp 92–6.

4 See Leon van Schaik, 'Newman College' [Edmond & Corrigan], Monument, No 64 (2004), pp 52–7.

PETER ELLIOTT

Peter Elliott received the Order of Australia for his work on housing in Melbourne in the 1980s, work that was perhaps Postmodern in inspiration. Certainly, it was completely at home in its surroundings, and it featured in the seminal article by Rory Spence on the architecture of Melbourne and Sydney published in the *Architectural Review* in 1986.[1] In this article Melbourne's urban culture was described as 'rebarbative', which looks as if it means 'sharp' – something which locals would have embraced – but which actually means repellent, unattractive or objectionable, which last description many might then have welcomed as a counter to Sydney's 'sensuality' or charm. The term that came so easily to this modishly dualist review simply does not apply to Peter Elliott.

When in an early career act of self-curation Peter Elliott, who studied architecture at Melbourne University, undertook the by-invitation postgraduate programme at RMIT[2] in the late 1980s he was working on alterations to the Carlton Baths (1989), a swimming pool complex in the inner suburb to the north of the central city. Here he shed any latent vestige of Postmodernism as a style, conducting a searching investigation into his role as an architect in the city. As Michael Sorkin, one of his panel of examiners, remarked of this work, what Peter discovered was a way of clarifying and amplifying the situations that he found in the sites and urban quarters in which he was working. This realisation prompted him to a consciously less rhetorical design approach, an

approach first in evidence on the civic spine of the city through a few delicate interventions in the more lumpen, Swanston Street-facing buildings of Melbourne University (MU). He added information offices shaded by widely overhanging canopies with an optimistic Modernist upwards slant, giving MU a street presence it had previously lacked (1994). He also designed the Warden's House at St Mary's College, a building that sits well with its many-styled neighbours, quietly asserting its own scale, a bridging between the domestic and the scholastic that is curiously disruptive of expectations of either. MU did not recognise the impact that this work was beginning to have, and turned its back on innovation for a few more years.

Peter Elliott was then commissioned to provide a development plan for the RMIT city campus, and so took on the job of opening up RMIT to the civic spine, creating progressively in a process not yet completed a series of highly acclaimed urban spaces between the tightly knit buildings of this campus. RMIT having adopted the City of Melbourne inner-city guidelines as the default position for works on the campus, Peter's design task was to create a series of spaces that were clearly of the city, but also distinctly of RMIT, providing external spatial connectivity between the growing collection of new buildings (most of them by his peers in the masters programme) and the existing ones. Sometimes bleak, as in the 1970s' polytechnic 'superblocks', these include some parts of the

Below and opposite: On the civic spine – RMIT Bowen Street Loggia (1998), a covered way linking Buildings 8 to 14. Using the yellow that in Melbourne is declarative of rebellion, the architect stitches together a series of fine spaces for the city's liveliest, most street-smart student body

Melbourne Gaol with fine bluestone buildings in a sub-Vanbrugh style, and a number of neo-Gothic, neo-classical as well as handsome streamlined buildings that call to mind early radios with their horizontal bands of window and engineering brick. Peter Elliott has devised several strategies for linking them: one is a covered walkway held up on enlarged yellow paper clips (rather like Claes Oldenberg's sculptures which take everyday objects and inflate them to an urban scale); another consists of a series of shade structures linking plinths designed for sitting, for the staging of small events or to accommodate temporary sculpture installations. Bowen Street, the central space of the campus, was reclaimed from car-parking and from the level changes introduced in John Andrews's design for the student union in the 1970s, and returned to a single planar surface, recognisably a street in origin. This space is transformed by students and staff on particular days of the year, and on open day in mid August it becomes a vital tent-city of booths promoting everything the university has to offer. Spaces between buildings have been cleared out and turned into beguiling courtyards and laneways. The transformation is so complete that it is almost impossible now to understand the imagination that was required to envisage these possibilities amid the former clutter of security fences, locked gates, temporary cabins for security staff, abandoned engineering plant and parked cars and motorbikes. Every one of these interventions takes what is there and gives it a new intentionality, enhancing its architectural lineage and building it into an assemblage that seems always to have been there.

Peter's other major contribution to the civic spine is the conversion of the old Melbourne Observatory (1999),[3] in the governmental Domain opposite the Melbourne Shrine, into a visitor centre and cafe. Here Peter used the lanterns of the new building to resonate with the odd collection of small observatory domes and sheds, creating a complex in which each part has been brought into play like assorted buckets in a sandpit. This is an enormously

popular venue for breakfast and lunch, and for Melbourne's famously Italian tradition in coffee drinking. In a review I wrote:

At the Observatory Gate to the Royal Botanic Gardens he has linked a scattering of small historic structures (restored by heritage architects Allom Lovell) with a new visitor centre, forecourt and paths to the gardens. This almost archaeological work reveals the original hill top site of Melbourne's Observatory from 1861 until 1944. Up the side of Birdwood Avenue, gravel paths and sweep out into a spacious court at the top of the hill. This is the brow that has always been the cusp between the Shrine of Remembrance and the Observatory site; now it is also a bridge to the flowing lawns of the Domain. In Elliott's strategy for the Observatory precinct, La Trobe's cottage was removed to a less congested site, revealing the remaining turrets, towers and roundels of the Astrograph house, the South Equatorial and Photo-heliograph houses, the Magnet house and the Italianate

Observatory. A serpentine seat wall weaves between these buildings and the Victorian Astronomer's residence, picking out the relationship between the collimating marker and the split observatory that lined up with it on Melbourne's longitude. As a powerfully local gesture, all of these elements and the tower of Government House are captured in a composition generated by the two lanterns of Elliott's new visitor centre. And as a persuasively theatrical performance, the facade of the centre and the syncopated paving of its forecourt turn the visitor around to walk down hill into the magic canopy of the western lawn and on into the picturesque treasure of the gardens.

In the regional city of Ballarat he devised the Robert Clark Horticultural Centre, a conservatory that takes a component of the domestic greenhouse and by folding the profile devises a structure that handsomely takes on the scale of a public facility.

Opposite: Robert Clark Horticultural Centre, Ballarat (1996). Here the architect began an experiment with folded-skin structures

Below: Peter Elliott in his inner city office

building, new and old. From the walkways linking the old and the new the fine detailing of both are close at hand. The archive has been cleared out to form two lecture theatres. The complex is a wonderful affirmation of Peter's enhancement and amplification strategy, a demonstration of how an architect with a strong sense of the need to curate the city can make a difference that both enhances the old and adds delight through the new. Again, in 1999, I wrote:

His work is not the rebellious: instead an almost curatorial intelligence is at work. Cleaning out cluttered sites, setting a visual and experiential hierarchy and orchestrating sequences, he is retelling Melbourne's story bit by bit: expanding the utility of the city and explaining its delights to a wide audience. Paradoxically, he is doing the local in a minimalist language that is internationally recognisable.

No wonder that Peter Elliott is one of the city's most widely liked and respected architects; someone who achieves all of this and is yet always felt to be approachable by colleagues, clients and the public at large.

Most recently his work on converting the former Public Records Office in Melbourne's legal precinct into a Law School for Victoria University (2004) epitomises what can be won from this sensitive pragmatism. The shallow 'U' plan of the neo-classical building was closed with a low single-storey fireproof archive block, on top of which Peter has concertinaed a double-storey library. The library itself is an elegant space on two levels linked by a staircase alongside a curtain wall that forms one side of a new quadrangle. A new lift shaft attached to one arm of the 'U' of the original building gives access to all of the levels in the

1 Rory Spence, 'Australia: Sydney/Melbourne', in *Architectural Review*, ed Peter Davey, Architectural Press, London, Vol CLXXVIII, No 1066 (Dec 1985), pp 23–94. Melbourne is introduced as 'Melbourne: City of the mind. The intellectual, rebarbative urban culture of...'
2 Peter Elliott, 'Forays in the Contemporary Institution: An Architecture of the Public Realm', in Leon van Schaik (ed), *Fin de Siècle and the Twenty-first Century: Architectures of Melbourne*, RMIT A+D (Melbourne), 1993, pp 41–64.
3 Leon van Schaik, 'Local Connections: Elliott's Garden entry and Yarra footbridge', *Architecture Australia* (May/June 1999), pp 84–9.

Opposite: On the civic spine – RMIT Building 9 Desk (1988). With this design, Garner Davis arrived on the civic spine. The desk signals much that they achieved in their design for the Civic Centre at Wagga Wagga

GARNER DAVIS

Jillian Garner and Lindsay Davis were among the first architects I ever commissioned at RMIT. In 1986, when I was appointed to RMIT Architecture, the department was located in Building 9 in an elegant conversion using corrugated-iron water tank sections to create internal elements complementing the parquet flooring and white plastered horizontal spandrels of a handsome engineering brick building from the 1950s. For this Ivan Rijavec had been the project architect, working for the long-time university architects, Bates Smart McCutchen (BSM), soon to celebrate their 140th birthday. Garner Davis were asked to insert into this a communications desk with a series of compartments that would help the different sections of the faculty achieve rapid paper communication. This was somewhat before the civic spine had become once again a reality, even though it was already surfacing in policy documents from the RMIT 1985 centenary conference. During the conference Winsome McCaughey, then Lord Mayor, had convened a committee to make recommendations for the institution's relations with the city; it lamented the huge BSM-designed grey 'polytechnic' blocks that lined the RMIT portion of Swanston Street with an almost impermeable grey block wall and called for RMIT to open itself to the city and to address once again the civic spine.

It was with reference to this document, and to the city's own subsequent determination to save

Swanston Street, that we were able to overturn RMIT procurement policy and initiate a renaissance in the local architecture culture. But it all began in Building 9 with the Garner Davis desk, followed by another desk, designed by Howard Raggatt and made by John Cherrey in August-September 1988 for the 'Collaborative Design – Working Together in Architecture' exhibition at the Meat Market Craft Centre in Melbourne. This desk, a quarter-full scale model of a house in Alphington, a suburb to the northeast of the city, became a *cause célèbre*, infuriating students of planning and social science who failed to understand the significance of its purchase as a symbol of the importance of material culture in a city. It clearly rankled for years, for when

the head of social science took over the office 10 years later, it was banished. This moment encapsulates the lack of understanding that permeates Australian planning culture, inhibiting innovation and clinging to past norms as if these were eternal truths, a culture that promotes mediocrity as democratic.

Be that as it may, Garner Davis completed a series of very elegant houses inspired by the optimistic Modernism of the 1960s, houses whose roofs open up to the light, whose sections are refined to feather edges, and where programme and construction are brought together in a sweet fitting that embraces the principle of parsimony. Their postgraduate research, credited to Garner[1] because

Below: Wagga Wagga Civic Centre, New South Wales (2000). The gallery is a double volume space, one floor below the Council's 'one-stop-shop'

Opposite: Wagga Wagga Civic Centre. The deck up the flight of stairs has become home to one of the best coffee shops in the city

circumstances in the shape of their winning entry for the Wagga Wagga Civic Centre overran Davis's completion, revealed how their reading of the wider context is reflected in their decisions about the design of the project itself.

It is strange to think of the Wagga Wagga Civic Centre as a postscript to a desk, but as a consequence of their approach the building sits in its civic terrain alongside an existing theatre, the original Town Hall, the 'shard' that is their exquisite design for the Art Glass Museum arranged around the lily-carpeted head of the lagoon about which the city arranges its core, all as if in an oversize living room. The way the building is screened behind perforated metal also renders its scale ambiguous – it could be a sideboard, but a coffee shop extends drawer-like from one end, a Lilliputian lush situation. This was a major under-taking for this young firm, and combined with the business of starting a family, Jillian and Lindsay dropped out of sight for a while, except on the weekend

breakfast circuit in St Kilda where they live and work. Many talk of how difficult it is to restart a practice after winning a large project, and Garner Davis have sometimes wondered how their lives might have developed if Lab Architecture, runners up in the Wagga Wagga competition, had won in New South Wales rather than in Melbourne. But they are back with a triumph of their quiet architectural intelligence with the Mornington Branch Library (2004), an hour's drive along the bay from St Kilda.[2] Here they originated the design with the same over-scale mapping process, refining this down until only those nuances that support the internal logic of the organisation are still in play. A horizontal slab of space is subtly articulated through the ceiling, perforated, incised and dropped in sections and beams to signal clusterings of different activity below. This disarmingly simple process reveals just how intensely thoughtful these architects are, as is the manner in which they have attached the library to existing and rather humble municipal offices, ennobling them rather than effacing them.

Top left and right: Surrey Hills House (1993), revealing Garner Davis's enduring interest in feathering junctions

Middle: Wagga Wagga National Art Glass Museum (2000). Harking back to the desk, the building is a thin, two-storey display cabinet

Below: Mornington Branch Library (2004). The kinship to Wagga Wagga Civic Centre is emphasised by this view, and there are hints of the stretched skin that haunts their work, be it furniture, interior space or architecture

Opposite: Jill Garnerand Lindsay Davis in the meeting room of their office in Barkly Street, St Kilda

It is worth noting that this work arises in a thin context: Australia does not spend on its cultural institutions in the way that has become common in the Northern Hemisphere. In a review I wrote:

Part of the intelligence I seek to define here lies in an understanding of the realities of policy/budget tension, an accepting of the constraints and a strategic focusing of design energy on ways of making a difference through architecture. This requires a certain detachment. Garner Davis did not have the luxury of being able to site the library; its location was decided in a pre-existing master plan, as was the situating of the municipal officers' car park in an under-croft. Yet the architects' conceptual skills, first revealed in public building at their municipal complex in Wagga Wagga, enabled them here too to create the breathing space necessary for the deployment of a series of strategies for accomplishing the client's brief.

The building won the regional 'My Favourite Place' award in the Year of the Built Environment competition, a contest determined by popular vote. Their work is not only immensely intelligent and subtle, with a lack of a hectoring urgency in its form, but it is a determined orchestration of space while the connection through views to the larger context appeals to a wide constituency who learn about its different layers through time. Their next appearance on the civic spine is overdue.

1 Jillian Garner, 'The enigmatic Qualities of the Map', in Leon van Schaik (ed), *Interstitial Modernism*, RMIT (Melbourne), 2000, pp 128–39.
2 Leon van Schaik, 'A Place for Intelligence, Mornington Library by Garner Davis', *Architectural Review Australia*, No 092 (2005), pp 122–7.

SEAN GODSELL

When, progressing along the civic spine, you reach the Arts Centre forecourt, it is time to meet architect Sean Godsell.[1] Not that you will find any of his work here, but it was here once, just as it has been in the garden of the Cooper Hewitt[2] in New York, but is no longer. These works that find their way into the hearts of cities are traces of the social agenda of modern architecture, almost old-fashioned in the clarity with which they ask of architecture what it has to offer the homeless and the dispossessed. For the period of a festival, a bus shelter designed to be friendly to those sleeping rough in the city stood in this forecourt on St Kilda Road. For a while, in the Treasury Gardens off Spring Street stood a bench, Park Benchhouse, designed to protect a sleeping person from attack, its creation prompted by accounts of someone who was stabbed in a park as they slept. And in front of the Cooper Hewitt in 2004 stood Future Shack, a shipping container fitted out to hold the basic 'Existenz-minimum' needs of a family, and with a roof that sheltered it from insolation as well as providing an under-cover deck. These ephemeral works may have passed on, but the critique of what is presented on the civic spine lingers. What is architecture if it connects only to the civic narrative of the fortunate? This anguished question leads back to Godsell's position as, aside from Tom Kovac in a totally different sphere the most internationally recognised Australian architect of his generation.

Godsell has won prize after prize for his houses, commencing with his own house in Kew,[3] completed while he was participating in the by-invitation masters at RMIT. This house, the Carter Tucker House at Breamlea and the Peninsula House[4] at Sorrento that followed it have been more widely documented internationally than any other work in the past decade. In these architectural enterprises Godsell has been partnered by photographer Earl Carter, who is so enamoured of the work that he and his partner commissioned the Carter Tucker House, set in the lee of a dune beyond Victoria's second city of Geelong. These are superb rationalist buildings that defy the slick glossiness of the Neo-Modern style that is the dominant vernacular in international architecture

today. The houses are not open to the public, but one of his finest buildings, the Science Block at Woodleigh School, Baxter[5] (an hour and a half's drive down the Mornington Peninsula) can be visited by appointment. Here you can also see the Art Centre which he designed as an extension to the original buildings by Darryl Jackson. The materiality of this building and of the Science Block comes as a surprise to some who have interpreted the photographs within the norms of the prevailing Neo-Modern internationalism. In an echo of Peter Corrigan's philosophy of realism, these buildings eschew any notion that an idea can be perfectly realised in material form. Rusting steel, weathering marine ply turning grey by degrees depending on the exposure to the direction of the prevailing rain, eroding gravel

Top left and right: Future Shack (2001) in the yard where it was constructed. It was later exhibited in situ outside Cooper Hewitt Museum, New York

Below left and right: Peninsula House (2002). Almost the inverse of the Carter Tucker House, this house for a film-maker descends away from the street into a series of intensely protected and private spaces and yet, paradoxically, it is a glass box protected from the heavens by laths

Above: Woodleigh School Science Block (2002). The building sits in a landscape modified by the architect, addressing it with what seems from a distance an almost Miesian determinism. Close up it is revealed as a warm and – in the Japanese sense of unwrought – raw construct, lyrical and engaging

pathways, corroding reinforcing mesh – all of these point to the mortality of the building, and to the regimes of conservation needed if we are to continue to inhabit this planet. Curiously, as Jonathan Hill, my guest on a recent visit observed, this very temporality reinforces in a Platonic sense our appreciation of the purity of the idea that is encased in this rough worldly fabric. This is precisely the opposite effect of what one experiences when encountering a Minimalist or Neo-Modern work, where every flaw in a surface detracts from the idea of the building, revealing indeed how shallow (and endlessly expensive) is the essentially pictorial 'money shot' concept of this image-based approach to design.

Godsell's buildings are not easy buildings. They demand our care and our intelligent interaction. The Carter Tucker House requires its inhabitants – if they do not simply succumb to its initial crate-like state – to read the weather and adjust the house all through the day. The house is thus a weather-machine, and it rewards its users by reconnecting them to the realities of confronting the weather, storms and still moments alike. While the Carter Tucker House rears up towards the street running back towards the dune, the Peninsula House runs away from a road behind the dune, presenting to the street as a carport. As it drops away to the north, lateral stairways on each flank provide a public and a private route through the house, and a skirt of screens lifts to open the northernmost double-volume space sideways to a sheltered barbecue area, frontally into the Ti Tree woods on the far side of which Godsell is designing a guest block. The house is a glass box inside a jarrah lath cage and the double-volume space is always in a sense in touch with the weather and the passage of the sun. Dug back from this is a den with a fireplace and thick bookshelves. Here Godsell provides solace from the exposure to the world of these 'machines that someone is living in', as his colleague Lindsay Holland quipped. A different redoubt is formed on the upper level, reached from below by the here hidden private stairway, where the bathroom gives on to a tightly contained courtyard from the tranquillity

of which the swirling winds can be observed. This is the ultimate luxury, as Stevie Smith[6] noted – having a direct understanding of the force of the wind, and yet being able (in her case) to observe it merely as the thrashing of the trees outside the bathroom window.

If you look again at the Science Block, riding its grassy wave (part of the design) it seems small, a contained graspable idea of a framed box, and then as you enter the cloister along its long sides, it pops into a larger scale. This is a building that needs to be operated, with a passive climate control system requiring seasonal adjustments to vents at ceiling height – open in summer except on days with a north wind, and closed in winter. This is an architecture that demands that we take responsibility for what each of us is doing to the planet, that we do not air-condition, that we work for our comfort. That we work too to understand the idea of the building which sits there poignantly behind the rough – the Japanese would say 'raw' – surface reality that presents itself to us. Often the pencil sketches of an architect will evoke in us a wonder at what our innate patterning capabilities can make in the world. But mostly that sketch soon disappears in a smoothing that results from passing instructions from designer to builder. Often the sketch then outlasts what has been built as the emotive conveyance of what was intended, and

sometimes, when it has disappeared in construction, a photographer can take us back to that moment.

The very raw, almost wounded materiality of Godsell's buildings, forces us to see the drawing in our mind's eye – this is a sublime achievement, and it is no accident that this spirituality leads the architect to contemplate, out of his own cash flow, what this architectural magic might do for those seemingly, but not necessarily, out of its reach. Fragments of this vision are visitable in the inner-city, the Craft Victoria Gallery at 31 Flinders Lane (2001), the Centre for Contemporary Photography in George Street in Fitzroy (2005), and the Urban History Centre in South Melbourne (2006).

1 Leon van Schaik, *Sean Godsell*, Electa (Milan), 2005.

2 The Smithsonian Institution's Cooper Hewitt Design Museum.

3 Sean Godsell, 'The Appropriateness of the Modern Australian Dwelling', in Leon van Schaik, *Interstitial Modernism*, RMIT (Melbourne), 2000 pp 140–53.

4 Doug Evans, 'Elemental Forces: Sean Godsell's Peninsula House', *Monument*, No 50 (Aug Sept 2002), pp 57–61.

5 Leon van Schaik, 'Molecular Matters: Sean Godsell's Woodleigh School Science Centre', *Architectural Review Australia*, No 83 (2002), pp 34–41.

6 Stevie Smith, *Novel on Yellow Paper*, Penguin (London), 1972, 1st edn, Jonathan Cape, 1936, pp 53–5: ' ... and so you come to the heavy door... and you go in and shut the door behind you, and bolt it, and inside there is a wide stone hall and lights hanging down perfectly steady...'

NONDA KATSALIDIS

Nonda Katsalidis is increasingly an enigma, at least in his curatorial impacts on the architectural culture of a city that his thinking has done so much to shape over the past 20 years. Always chary of the profession, on graduation he was possibly alienated from its quite evident Anglo-Saxon hypocrisy, which espoused the cause of small or commencing practices while simultaneously endorsing the activities of what amounted to cartels. These last controlled approved development processes to such a degree that Leonie Sandercock[1] characterised Melbourne as 'a city for sale' regardless of the architectural or heritage consequences. Katsalidis avoided traditional practice and worked as a contractor for some years after graduating from Melbourne University. While the city was laid waste in a process stemmed only by the arrival of Rob Adams as Director of Urban Design, and by RMIT's emergence as a patron of design, he built up a wide knowledge of the construction industry. Working initially within the emerging Greek community (Melbourne is the third largest Greek city in the world), he found a way of producing speculative office buildings of ambitious design without having to contend with conservative and closed city politics and, as it happens, along La Trobe Street, the long neglected northern edge of the city centre. On the strength of these the profession felt the need to reintegrate him into its ambit, and Dimity Reed, then president of the local chapter of the RAIA, persuaded him to host a series of discussion meetings with a

group of architects who became the first cohort to undertake postgraduate research at RMIT into the nature of their mastery.

Nonda surveyed all of his domestic and commercial projects and designed his own beach house at St Andrews on the wild coast of the Southern Ocean in the process, just as Sean Godsell would later design his own Kew House during his research. Here[2] he deliberated on his spatial and material preferences, and stored up a brace of new ambitions that found their expression in his pioneering St Leonard's Avenue apartments and Melbourne Terrace near the Victoria market in the centre city grid. These buildings, completed in a partnership with Karl Fender and at times Bob Nation, heralded a new standard of interior space, one that Fender and Nation had developed in their work in the cities of Hong Kong and Bangkok, where the Tiger Economies had produced a new entrepreneurial class in search of urban living in a style to which their experience of luxury hotels had accustomed them. These expansive and handsome interiors created a new market in the city, luckily foreshadowing the long period of prosperity that has prevailed since the mid 1990s. Designers and allied executives snapped up these early apartments. They were in such demand that at one point a new residential block on St Kilda Road sported a billboard announcing: 'Nonda Katsalidis-Style Apartments'.

Top: Melbourne Terrace (1994) near the Victoria market in the centre city grid brought a new standard to apartment living in the city

Bottom: The Eureka Tower (2005) transforms the city skyline and indicates the growing importance of the Southbank as a focus of the city

Opposite: The Potter Museum at Melbourne University (1998). A modernity that melts to accommodate an offshoot of Lygon Street's finest coffee shop, Brunettis

Above: Republic Tower (1999). There are shades of Rem Koolhaas's Delirious New York in the tower, with a 25 metre lap pool on the top floor and restaurants, bars and a public art space at street level and below

Opposite: Nanda Katsalidis in his apartment overlooking the Bay in Port Melbourne

The Tiger Economies faltered, and working in the late 1980s' downturn in Melbourne under the terms of Postcode 3000, a policy framework introduced by the city to enable the conversion of existing empty office blocks and infill residential apartments in areas previously zoned exclusively commercial, Nonda created a series of development packages that has rolled from one innovative building to the next. Republic Tower[3] followed Melbourne Terrace, located on the corner of Queen and La Trobe, the interiors introducing a loft-style spatiality removed from traditional signifiers of luxury and becoming ever more assured in this approach. This tower sports a 25-metre lap pool on the top floor, and curious bat-ear plan living areas glazed to a point on both sides, imposing a new twist on the 'tyranny of glass architecture' introduced by the Farnsworth House, but capturing the imagination of the market all up and down the east coast of Australia, if the numerous imitations are anything to go by. The base of the building is occupied by a restaurant, bar and cafe and, in a deliberate gesture to the high culture of the city, a double-storey convex/concave billboard arrangement that every season showcases public works by artists.

Thus Katsalidis has had a profound effect on the culture by working out how to create developments that are in the control of the architect, at least to some extent. Where the firm has worked under the control of other developers, as in the Docklands, the results have been far less remarkable. As we have already seen, Katsalidis arrived on the civic spine with the Potter Gallery at Melbourne University (1998),[4] for him a chance to show his peers that his head was not completely consumed with finance-design, a fate he feared, as he admitted in conversation at the time, would compromise his reputation as an architect. His next step, however, has been to design and assist the

Grollo family in the financial structuring of what was for a time the tallest residential building in the world, the 92-storey Eureka Tower (2005).

The alliance with Grollo brings together a number of vital strands in the emergence of Melbourne as a design city. The ambition of this tower is immense. For years the Rialto, a Grollo-initiated development, has been the tallest building in the city, its plan set on the diagonal and thus capturing the rising and setting sun and making it a regular winner in polls for the most popular building in the city. As we see elsewhere (see Simeoni, p274), the family has a proud involvement in innovative architecture, and this project marks the second generation's emergence on the city scene, a scene that is viewed from an unusual angle. The naming of these buildings is not trivial. The Republic Tower is seen as a way of displacing the still exclusionary Anglo ascendancy in finance, and Eureka refers to the 1854 rebellion of miners against the colonial state that demanded human rights that were not obtained for another generation. If Nonda is elusive today for other than personal reasons, then it is probably to shelter from the free-flowing comment about this tower while under construction. When it can be assessed in its finished state, opinions will change, as they already are among his peers, Godsell for one admitting to being awestruck by the sheer beauty of the tower and the golden head that sprays light above the city as the sun rises and sets. Certainly, its successful completion against determined opposition from the old establishment demonstrates once and for all the multicultural heritage of this now determinedly cosmopolitan city.

1 Leonie Sandercote, *Cities for Sale: Property, Politics and Urban Planning in Australia*, Melbourne University Press (Melbourne), 1975.

2 Nonda Katsalidis, 'Three Residential Projects', in Leon van Schaik (ed), *Fin de Siècle and the Twenty-first Century: Architectures of Melbourne*, RMIT A+D (Melbourne), 1993, pp 65–88.

3 Leon van Schaik, 'The high life', *World Architecture* (May 2000), No 86, pp 68–71.

4 Leon van Schaik, 'Street Credentials, Melbourne University's Potter Museum of Art', *Australian Architectural Review* (Sept/Oct 1998), pp 50–5.

5 Rem Koolhaas, *Delirious New York*, 010 Publishort (Rotterdam), 1994.

LYONS

Lyons arrive on the civic spine with the BHP Billiton HQ Building. Paradoxical, this arrival through a corporate HQ building, because their practice has developed through an innovative approach to architecture that has built them a loyal clientele on the periphery of the city, mainly in health and education.[1] The approach that has brought them this success is, however, certainly manifest in a purified, almost diagrammatic way in the HQ. Many of the principals in Lyons come from an architectural dynasty that has worked on projects for the wealthy end of town, but their interest in architecture and what it can give to a culture has far transcended the venal. In the 1980s they took a cool look at the environment governing commercial practice and decided that the room for autonomous architectural investigation had been shrunk down to a 100-millimetre zone around the facades of a building.[2] Rather than despairing at this state of affairs, they decided to push the zone for everything it could give, and discovered that treating both sides of the zone as facades opened up possibilities for their clients that had not been realised before.

Detaching the facade from the cores of buildings that are increasingly tightly determined by functional and financial constraints gave the architects the opportunity to create public spaces between the skin of the building and its interior at no extra cost. And dealing with the outside surface as a

system of signage independent from the building's functional requirements enabled them to signal the client's purposes to the citizens of the outer suburbs, where the elements of urbanity are thinly distributed.

At BHP Billiton, you get a concentrated glimpse of the approach. A simple slab block contains the office floor stack, a crystal glass face oriented away from the sun, while a concrete face confronts the north. The 28-storey stack is brought directly down to the pavement on Russell Street, but on Lonsdale Street the facade delaminates from the slab and becomes an apron at the scale of the three- to four-storey buildings of the Greek Precinct opposite. Out of this apron is carved the corporate foyer, one face of

which is lined with an aluminium relief generated in a manner researched for the external rendering of the urban surface of their designs for the city periphery. Also accommodated by the apron are access ways to the underground car park, shops facing the street in alignment with the city's active street-front policy, and a weather canopy over the pavement.

A fine precursor for this approach is Lyons's building at the St Albans campus of Victoria University of Technology (VUT) (2001) where a thoroughly undistinguished set of campus buildings was rescued by a multimedia facility designed to appeal to a funky youth demographic. Here foyers created by detaching the skin surround the core programme space, and the

Top left: On the civic spine – BHP Billiton HQ Building (2004). Lyons's surface architecture comes in to play in the city centre. The glass facade of the building is pulled out to form a series of atriums

Top right: St Albans campus of Victoria University (2001) interior. Here too the skin is used to develop extensive foyer spaces

Bottom: BHP Billiton HQ Building (2004). Looking back to Lonsdale Street the way in which the pulled out facade makes the atrium becomes clear

Opposite top: St Albans campus of Victoria University (2003) exterior. The skin, with an optical pattern suggesting depth, is manipulated to accomplish basic climate control

Opposite bottom: St Albans campus of Victoria University (2003). Lyons's surface architecture is in full play here, marking the ground and cloaking the media facility beyond

Below: Marine Environment Research Centre at Queenscliffe (2005). The
building is covered with a turf roof, designed to read as a simple lifting of
the earth. Passive climate control design makes for lofty interiors and the
soft tones of recyclable natural materials

exterior of the skin is covered with a computer-generated fractal pattern that repeats and furls in on itself in an endlessly provocative way. This sits on a base of granite boulders and faces an uncompromising plane of preserved native grassland.

A postscript is the Marine Environment Research Centre at Queenscliffe (2005).[3] Designed over a seven-year period, this building alongside Swan Bay, a World Heritage-listed shallows on the far edge of the 60-kilometre bay on which Melbourne is situated, uses its total external surface to deliver the client's programme needs – in this case a laboratory and marine discovery centre without air-conditioning. The roof is grassed over and the entryways are formed as if from the tarmac of the car park. The interiors are lofty and solid as befits the need for air volume and thermal mass, while the fittings (all sourced from sustainable producers) are playful and light. The building is a tribute to Lyons's contention that any programmatic requirement of a client can be met through the application of architectural intelligence.

Lyons should have emerged on Swanston Street much earlier, with their Swanston A'Beckett Street Sport Centre project for RMIT (1996). This wrapping of a tube with an inner and an outer facade around the Heritage-listed Oxford Hotel would have confirmed RMIT's leadership in the reawakening of patronage beyond any question. Unfortunately, the project went to tender at the precise moment that the local market overheated, and its moment passed.

Below: Carey Lyon, Corbert Lyon, Cameron Lyon, Neil Appleton and
Adrain Stannic in the meeting room at their office, in front of a painting
by Louise Forthun

Lyons's role in the curation of the QV site was considerable, as is indicated in the conclusion. This firm is closely involved in several of the curatorial systems that make Melbourne the design city that it is, not least in their self-curation.[4] As is indicated in the section on art, the firm collects the work of local artists. Members have been practitioner/academics, are still engaged in teaching and mentoring, and are committed to the struggle to make the institutions of the profession focus on the furthering of architectural culture.

1 Leon van Schaik, *Mastering Architecture: Becoming a Creative Innovator in Practice*, Wiley-Academy (Chichester), 2005, pp 152–6.

2 Carey Lyon, 'Towards a Brand New City', in Leon van Schaik (ed), *Transfiguring the Ordinary*, Printed Books (Melbourne), 1995.

3 'Queenscliff Centre: Lyon's Queenscliff Centre' reviewed by Leon van Schaik in *Architecture Australia*, ed Justine Clark Vol 94, No 1 (Jan/Feb 2005), pp 54–61.

4 Van Schaik, *Mastering Architecture*, pp 152–6.

Opposite: The Sphere House (2005). The house is literally carved out of a
copper-sheathed hemisphere

McBRIDE CHARLES RYAN

Debbie Ryan is an interior designer with an entrepreneurial flair. Her partner in work and life, Rob McBride, is one of the most original architectural thinkers in the city. Together they have found ways of realising their designs that are an inspired leveraging of situations. Where others find alibis for doing nothing, they open up new pathways for others to follow.

My strongest recollection of meeting Rob McBride was in 1987, when Susan Ryan, then a minister in the federal government, launched the first edition of *Transition* to be underwritten by Architecture at RMIT. For 25 years this journal of architectural discourse was the most important vehicle for capturing local knowledge in architecture. Bearing in mind Alvin Boyarsky's long search for such a vehicle at the AA, and seeking a way of achieving just that, I readily agreed to Peter Corrigan's suggestion that I take responsibility for funding the journal, while maintaining its integrity through an independent editorial board. From that date until the journal's demise over a dispute about selecting an editor, we funded the editor's position and underwrote the publishing costs. After the launch we retired to Kimchi in Little La Trobe Street, a short distance from RMIT and one of a series of cheap eating-places favoured by Peter Corrigan. Few visitors to the city in that decade escaped meeting him in this low dive or its Italian equivalent, La Cacciatore in the nearby inner suburb of Carlton. On this night, memorable for many

reasons, the minister and McBride began to sing Irish keening songs with an extraordinary harmonic edge. Soon after, I recruited him into the by-invitation postgraduate programme. His investigation into the nature of the mastery that he had established in practice and his speculations on his future practice in the light of what he had discovered were published in 1995.[1] While he referred to *Complexity and Contradiction*,[2] what shone through his investigation was a Melnikov-like interest in finding a large figure into which small projects could be nested.[3] In a series of small dwelling projects two figures are run alongside each other, giving very different impressions when viewed from the front or back. Then in the design of row houses in Port Melbourne

he found a way of creating a super order facade that united the houses in a contemporary version of the facades of Nash's terraces in Regents Park in London which unite numerous individual dwellings. The ambition is most tellingly indicated in a concept diagram for the design of a church hall renovation and house conversion in Hampton, a bayside suburb. The hall is shown being absorbed into a larger sphere. The sphere organises the extension and is expressed in the interiors. This super-figure approach has been the focus of the practice ever since. The Sphere House in Toorak is cut from a copper-sheathed sphere that appears two-thirds buried below the site, a solution that persuaded neighbours initially hostile to the development of the

Below and opposite: The Sphere House (2005). From some sides, as promised to the neighbours, it appears almost a simple mound in the landscape. Courtyards are cut in, while the interiors show no sign of being impaired by their confinement within the shell

site that there would be minimal intrusion on their views. The courtyards and interiors carved from the sphere are ingeniously designed, there being little sense to the observer of any constriction from the overarching geometry.

McBride and his partner Debbie Ryan arrive on the civic spine with an apartment building on the QV site, their most accessible project to date. Here the super-figure is in the plan rather than in the section. An eight-storey slab sits on the QV podium (designed by the QV coordinating architect, Hamish Lyon of BN Architects), gently cupping the lawns in front of the State Library that it overlooks. This form also projects over Little Lonsdale Street between the Library and QV. The interiors are planned on an ingenious pinwheel principle, with all of the services in the centre of each apartment, and access between rooms provided along the perimeter walls. The soft form of the project and its dark grey granite, light-absorbing skin, flushed with aubergine from the painted soffits of the balconies, play a dynamic role in the overall composition of the QV complex.

McBride Charles Ryan's most recently completed project is the Kent Court House, Toorak. Here, on a landlocked site in a cul de sac, the super-figure is the maximum developable envelope clad in dark grey and presenting as an opaque box. This form is undercut to create living spaces, while at the upper level a court is cut into the centre of the box to provide light and outdoor space to bedrooms. Here, as in the Sphere House, the architects have solved enormously difficult issues of overlook into neighbouring properties through the imposition of a super-figure, raised up as a dark, light-absorbing and therefore recessive monolith, while thus undercut every inch of the site becomes part of an inside/outside spatial couple that is both intimate and immense in its effects – a quality identified by Bachelard as one of those that most resonates with human senses of comfort.[4]

Soft spoken and retiring, Rob McBride's tenacious pursuit of a design principle that is quite distinct from that of his peers is supported by Debbie Ryan's entrepreneurial vision. In 'Melbourne Masters Architecture', the exhibition showcasing the work of 16

This page: Kent Court House (2005). The design starts from the top down, projecting upwards the developable envelope. For a site that is surrounded by other houses, and carving out living spaces within this envelope, it faces inward at the top, cutting up from the ground at street level and extending the floor surface to the site boundaries as decking. At night it presents a breathtaking confirmation of the efficacy of an approach to design that has been consciously developed since its early expression in the RMIT mastery programme in 1995

Opposite: Debbie Ryan and Rob McBride at Spoonful, where they often have breakfast with their young family

architects with whom I have worked over the past 20 years, their work seems at first to fit in with a position in the discourse somewhere between 'techne and poetics'. The super-figure mode that they use to such extraordinary effect is, however, not something they share with anyone else. In fact it is hard to think of anyone who is using this approach to reconcile the often deeply intractable spatial and planning constraints on inner urban and suburban design. We are more used to the approach when examining the rationalist, super-figure works of Aldo Rossi, who drew his inspiration from the way in which ancient Roman superstructures were recast over time, as at Arles, where the stadium became the armature for a ring of housing. In the way in which they organise their practice, they relate more clearly to an existing Melbourne tradition, following, like Nonda Katsalidis, in the footsteps of the 'Hollywood style' developer architects of the 1930s.[5] Their early ventures into multiple housing (Port Melbourne and Wynnstay Road in Prahran) have each been engineered around their own housing needs and those of friends. For them the

path to architectural innovation and quality in the design of apartments has been more readily achieved when the architect is part of the developer team, and the distinctive voice they have thus created has led to their participation in the design of their QV Apartments in the QV complex on the civic spine. What they have achieved sits now in the popular imaginary, and will haunt the future design moves of other architects.

1 Rob McBride, 'Form Rules', in Leon van Schaik (ed), *Transfiguring the Ordinary*, Printed Books (Melbourne), 1995. In the same volume, in which the pages are not numbered, are the 24-page catalogues of Bruns, Giannini, Lyon, McDougall and Murray.

2 Robert Venturi, *Complexity and Contradiction in Architecture*, MOMA (New York), 1968.

3 S Frederick–Starr, *Melnikov – Solo Architect in a Mass Society*, Princeton University Press (Princeton, NJ), 1981.

4 Gaston Bachelard, *Intimate Immensity in his The Poetics of Space*, Beacon Press (Boston), 1969, p 183.

5 Seamus O'Hanlon, *Together Apart: Boarding House, Hostel and Flat Life in Pre-war Melbourne*, Australian Scholarly Publishing (Melbourne), 2002.

MINIFIE NIXON

Immediately to the south of the Arts Centre on St Kilda Road, the extension of the civic spine of Swanston Street, is the Victorian College of the Arts (VCA), a unique institution in Melbourne, combining a secondary school and a tertiary institution devoted to excellence in art, drama, music, dance, film and television. We have already encountered the School of Drama, designed by Edmond and Corrigan. Adjacent to this is the site of ARM's home for the Melbourne Theatre Company. Back across Dodd Street and towards St Kilda Road lies the heart of the VCA, the student union and library, extended in a design by Minifie Nixon to include the Centre for Ideas. This was the VCA's first assay into becoming a patron of serious architecture, and it came about through the determination of Julie Irving, an artist on the VCA staff who took the unusual step of doing her masters in architecture at RMIT, where she observed the initiation of the criterion-based process for the selection of architects. In close consultation with RMIT she devised a commissioning process for the VCA with the support of Darryl Jackson, a prominent architect who was advisor to the VCA board. Minifie Nixon were shortlisted and then selected. It is possible that their coolly cerebral, new mathematics approach to the design appealed to the VCA theoreticians, where more expressive, less systemic approaches might have cloyed.

How did this young firm come to be in a position to produce its first building here on the civic spine of

the city? The partners had both graduated from RMIT, Fiona Nixon choosing to spend several years working in Singapore in the office of Kerry Hill, a West Australian who has established a practice that operates right across Southeast Asia and Oceania. Nixon, a rationalist at heart, soon mastered the logistical side of the practice, all the while identifying strongly with the cool aesthetic through which it reinvented the Asian resort as a vernacular Modernism. In this Hill combined the finest vernacular architectures of the region with his contemporary approach creating a subtle architecture that has become the byword for luxury there, replacing the rather more vulgar Bali Hai South Pacific kitsch that was current previously.

Paul Minifie, who had pioneered RMIT's emergence as innovators in computer-aided architecture as an undergraduate, culminating in a virtuoso proposal for the QV site, remained in Melbourne, completing a masters in urbanism[1] with Howard Raggatt, Carey Lyon and Ian McDougall in the programme organised by Shane Murray. He worked at ARM, inducting that firm into its highly sophisticated use of computing in design. When Nixon returned from Singapore they decide to go into partnership, intending to establish a practice operating across the entire region. Their work first surfaced on the international scene at the Archilab exhibition 'Futurehouse' in 2001,[2] to which they were introduced by Tom Kovac. Here they exhibited Orleans

Batwing, a mathematically derived complex surface, both structure and wall, which served as a support for apartments. The design for the Centre for Ideas is formed by locating a series of Voronoi cells (polygonal sections generated from cones, the sections' ridges defining the points at which the surface is closer to another cone) over oculi, located on the face of the building relative to internal needs, at which there are openings into the new spaces extended behind the new skin. This perforated stainless-steel skin may be cool in conception, but it captures the sky in reflection all day long, steely grey in some lights, ashen blue in others, and glowing gold in red sunsets.

In their trajectory the precursors were all charismatic proposals for unrealised projects, exhibited in Melbourne and Orleans. The postscript to the Centre for Ideas is the Australian Wildlife Centre at Healesville Sanctuary in the foothills of the Great Dividing Range, an hour and a half's drive to the east of the city. This is a hospital for wild animals, marking the return – as is also evident in the Cassandra Complex Platypusary – of Melbourne Zoo to the commissioning of innovative architects. The exterior of the Australian Wildlife Centre is composed of two different concrete blocks organised in a pattern generated in a cellular automata process. The innermost space is a Costa surface, a surface that is the smallest area it can be without intersecting itself, given its constraints. A helix or a parabaloid are such surfaces. This one serves as a contemporary form of the dome, lit by skylights, giving to visitors a sense of being outside while in fact inside, complementing the basic concept of the sanctuary – the appearance of observing animals in their natural habitat. Importantly, the central space is coloured gold to distance it from the pure white formal explorations of sculptors like Jean Arp and from the self-coloured fabric structures of lightweight structure designers.

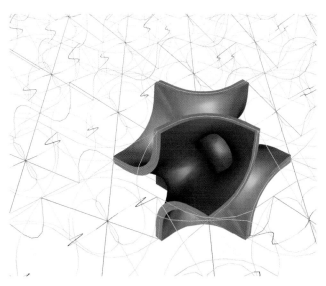

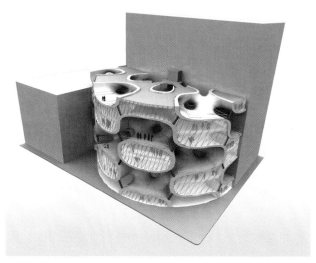

Top left, right and bottom: Orleans Batwing Archilab (2001). This project explores how a self-supporting folded surface can be utilised for housing

Opposite: Centre for Ideas, Victorian College of the Arts (VCA) (2004)

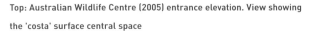

Top: Australian Wildlife Centre (2005) entrance elevation. View showing the 'costa' surface central space

Bottom left: Australian Wildlife Centre. The view to the apex of the dome is remarkably similar to the view to the lantern in the centre of Burley Griffin and Marian Mahoney's dome at Newman College

Bottom right: Australian Wildlife Centre. The paradoxical inside-outside space around the costa surface

Opposite: Fiona Nixon and Paul Minifie in their office on Swanston Street, not far from RMIT. Many lower rent spaces are available in this location, thanks to Melbourne City Council's policy of keeping this central part of the city grid zoned for lower-height developments. This protects the commercial role of this area and encourages residential and atelier usage

Both Minifie and Nixon are practitioner/ academics with a foothold in RMIT, where their contribution is currently vital to the maintenance of one of the three theoretical poles that define in that place the debate about the nature of architecture today. Minifie pursues rule-based explorations of programme and form, with one of his recent students, Roland Snooks, winning in 2005 a Fulbright Scholarship to study further at Colombia. In this he is engaged in a search for the contemporary discourse of architecture, looking for the forms now possible where predecessors Frei Otto developed tensile structures, Le Corbusier and Xenakis developed the Philips Pavilion, and their predecessor Leonidov used cooling tower forms. Nixon is documenting the emergence in Singapore for the first time since the 1970s of a vital architectural culture. The practice is energetically engaged in seeking opportunities to shape in a more idealist manner the development push in China, which all too frequently foregoes the intellectual pleasures of serious architecture in favour of Neo-Modernist slick or commercial Bangkok Baroque glitz. They are surrounded by brilliant disciples, all of whom

are looking for a way to break into practice that is not the easy lifestyle magazine route of the sumptuous surfaces of Neo-Modernism adopted as a way in by many of their less idealistic peers; uncharacteristically for the Melbourne of the 1980s and 1990s, but all too similarly to the decades preceding, depressingly conventional designers are prepared to ride on the coat-tails of an International Style that has generated none of its own cultural capital. The medium-term future of Melbourne as a design city depends on the success of this group.

1 Paul Minifie, Neil Appleton and Annie McIntyre, 'Picturesque: competing pictures', in Shane Murray and Leon van Schaik (eds), *38 South (II)*, RMIT (Melbourne), 2000, pp 68–70.
2 Minifie Nixon in M-A Brayer and B Simonot (eds), *Archilabs Futurehouse: Radical Experiments in Living Space*, Thames and Hudson (London), 2001.

PAUL MORGAN

It's hard to disentangle the physical from the intellectual in Paul Morgan's career. Paul Morgan dives. Accompanied by longtime friend, artist David Noonan, Morgan descends into the deep channel between Points Lonsdale and Nepean where the Port Phillip Bay meets Bass Strait. In a symbiosis that will be becoming familiar, Noonan captivated the architectural world in 1993 with an exhibition arranged by Paul and entitled 'Type 1:28' at RMIT Architecture showing 58 canvases based on models of Alvar Aalto. After a recent mishap Morgan rose too fast and ended up in the hyperbaric chamber at the Alfred Hospital, a futuristic trauma centre off St Kilda Road with its own helipad bridging Commercial Road and Fawkner Park, one of the grandest of the axial parks. This facility, packed with technically complex suites of equipment and resembling a large piece of industrial design, was devised on this difficult inner-city site by migrant architect Reg Rippon, schooled in the hard world of mining-facility design.[1] There are two aspects of this anecdote that seem to be telling about Morgan's design intelligence. The first is that where others retreat up into the hills around Melbourne or sit on dunes gazing into the wild waves of the Southern Ocean in order to create a contemplative distance between themselves and their lives in the city, he is part of a tiny minority who seek out that meditative energy by sinking below sea level and, as it were, looking up into city life from below. The second is that we can picture him within the hyperbaric chamber, his

life depending on a large technical apparatus, as if he is part of a new man/machine synthesis of the kind foreshadowed rather sensuously in the film *Barbarella*, or rather more bleakly in *Blade Runner*.

There is something of an engineering sensibility at play in his work, foreshadowed in his 'Arcadia at Speed' thesis on his postgraduate research at RMIT.[2] Here in a telling image he envisions the suburb as if generated through a cathode ray tube, sharing Lefebvre's concerns about the way in which technology inevitably changes our perception of the world.[3] This is combined with a preference for bounded forms – as evidenced in his early *Transition* 'Companion City' competition entry (1991), which looks as if he is

concerned that his buildings should work in outer space.[4] During a period in partnership with Michael McKenna,[5] Paul produced a series of works for RMIT and VUT, designing lecture theatres and computer studios that all share an aesthetic that seems to owe much to popular imaginings of a future in which we pass between from the environments of the surface of the earth, ocean deeps and outer space. Paul's design for the Spatial Information Architecture Laboratory Sound Studio at RMIT (2004) brings his work forcefully to the civic spine. His delight in resolving the complex requirements of the brief is more than evident: the laboratory nurtures a bathyscaph-like form with a variety of 'umbilical' chords attached to provide services, while the inside of the chamber meets the

Below: House at Cape Schank (2005). This too relates to the surface of the earth as if it is a space probe recently landed on a *terra incognita*

Opposite: The House at Cape Schank under construction

acoustic requirements with an energetic embrace of space ship aesthetics. This exposure and expression of the services of the new technologies form a consistent theme in his work, showing up in a number of his projects in a novel double helix system for bringing computing cables from ceiling to desktop.

Even when working in the domestic environment, as in a house outside Melbourne at Avenel, this architect seems to be suggesting that a spacecraft has landed, hovering above the ground somehow, has unfurled a pool deck, and is all set to leave when the time comes. The effect arises because of the bounded form, with the roof arcing back to make what looks like an almost ovoid form from above and curling down to meet the walls at the sides, while the underbelly of the house is visible from most viewpoints.

A house at Cape Schank for the architect and his sister may cause a change in Morgan's contemplative vantage point. Here a space mission

has been staged over time, with the first living pod arriving – or so one can imagine – as a closed timber-panelled box, that once landed has opened out to provide easy access to the hostile terrain. This second pod then arrives, more cellular in function, containing sleeping cabins and bathroom. This one is a modular metal-clad extrusion, and it may well have been let down from the mother ship in sections that are progressively bolted to the living pod via an air lock.

This aesthetic is more than philosophical in consequence, though it also certainly poses questions about the way in which we live in the surface environment of a planet that our acts of inhabiting are doing so much to endanger. These forms speak of autonomy, of waste-free fabrication from materials with calculated energy embeddedness in controlled conditions, of self-containment in their servicing on site. That they only partially realise this vision makes this a work in progress, but what an important work. Nor is the critic fanciful in suggesting the space

Opposite: On the civic spine – Spatial Information Architecture Laboratory
Sound Studio at RMIT (2004)

Below: Paul Morgan in his office in central Melbourne

metaphor. Artist friend David Noonan followed his work on Alvar Aalto with a series of video works set either in outer space or behind the windscreen of a moving car, a device that along with the television Lefebvre saw as creating a new and flattened perception of the world in us all.

Paul has played a role in many of the organs that have built the local culture to its present level of achievement. He edited *Transition*, the journal of architectural discourse, with Karen Burns in 1986 (Nos 18–19) and from 1992 to 1994 (Nos 39–43). He has undertaken postgraduate research with his peers, entered competitions, had his work exhibited in the first Beijing International Architecture Biennale (2004), and he continues to explore ideas generated in a network that crosses many disciplines.

1 Leon van Schaik, 'Stephenson and Turner: Alfred Hospital Road Trauma Centre', in Harriet Edquist (ed), *Transition: Discourse on Architecture*, RMIT (Melbourne), Nos 36/37, 1991, pp 71–80.

2 Paul Morgan, 'Arcadia at Speed' in Leon van Schaik and Paul Morgan (eds), *38 South*, RMIT (Melbourne), pp 53–8.

3 Henri Lefebvre, *The Production of Space*, Blackwell (Oxford and Cambridge, Mass), 1994.

4 Paul Morgan, 'Companion City: the Fluid City of Consumption', in Karen Burns and Harriet Edquist (eds), *Transition – Discourse on Architecture*, RMIT (Melbourne, 1991), No 34, pp 18–19.

5 Cath Rush, Michael Mckenna and Sue Wood, 'Between Surface and Re-emergence: Another Interpretation of the Blur', in Shane Murray and Leon van Schaik (eds), *38 South (III)*, RMIT (Melbourne), 2000, pp 46–7.

Opposite: EQ (2001). The interior is connected to the exterior with timber decking platforms. In most conditions inside and outside space is united

NMBW

The NMBW story touches on a remarkable number of the curatorial armatures that have made Melbourne the design city it is today.[1] The future partners met while studying architecture at Melbourne University (MU). Where, in the last year of Peter McIntyre's headship, they won the independence of subdivided studios where they each had a door key and access to a telephone. RMIT had abandoned studio teaching some years before, and its senior students made use of low rent office space in the inner city to set up quasi offices, in which they were joined by students from MU, forming alliances that have in many cases persisted as practices. A city that is intent on nurturing its own creative talents needs to be mindful of the importance of a supply of low-rent

accommodation. As Nikos Papastergiadis has pointed out, the disappearance of such space drives out newcomers, often literally to the periphery or to other cities.[2] Benign neglect, enforced in the city centre by height controls, has ensured that Melbourne has a complete range of rental accommodation – critical to any city nurturing a creative culture. As Melbourne's inner suburban factories relocate and their premises fall vacant, the city is benefiting from a migration of artists from Sydney, where space has simply become too expensive.

After graduating in 1991, NMBW curated an exhibition of Melbourne Architecture for the Weisenhof Seidlung, Stuttgart, an opportunity offered to them

because partner Andrew Wilson lived in Germany at the time. They moved into a room at Carlow House in Flinders Lane in 1995, a building full of studios, and now home to the publishing group Black Inc. They were all living in the city, and their first commission was for the Nudel Bar, a restaurant a few blocks away in Bourke Street.

One of the clients, Helen Saniga, was a sister of friends. During the day they worked in various practices. Nigel Bertram worked in Edmond and Corrigan's atelier and edited volumes 1 and 2 of the trilogy on Building 8,[3] then went to PLM, a large corporate firm; Lucinda McLean worked at Peter Elliott; and Marika Neustupny at Peter Maddison, out

of whose office, and with his encouragement, they ran the Nudel Bar job. This restaurant is located in a strip of restaurants that have been meeting places for architects for generations. In the 1950s and 1960s many practices also had their offices here, and the principals would meet each other in Florentino's Wine Bar, and their clients in the Bistro. Pellegrini's in the same block was the first Italian coffee bar in the city, opening in 1954, and it retains its original fittings to this day. The NMBW design for the Nudel Bar had a fresh crisp look to it to match its largely vegetarian cuisine, in a street in which mahogany panelling and Art-Deco interiors were aligned with more traditional European menus. It made clever use of its upstairs space, linking this freely to the

Below and opposite: Nudel Bar (1996). View from street and the interior

pavement tables outside. At the same time Andrew Wilson and Nigel Bertram undertook the Urban Architecture Laboratory programme of postgraduate research at RMIT.[4]

A desire to live, study and work in another country sent them away from the city on a parabola, all of them determined to return. In 1997 chance intervened for Marika Neustupny, who grew up speaking Japanese, when RMIT's Asssociate Professor Shane Murray invited Kazuyo Sejima to give a public lecture in Storey Hall, and he asked her to translate. This led to her going to study for three years at Tokyo Institute of Technology in an urban architecture programme under Yoshiharu Tsukamoto. Nigel Bertram went too, working for a Japanese design practice and returning in 2000 when Shane Murray offered him a job at RMIT in the Urban Architecture Laboratory. At the same time Lucinda McLean went to study at the Stadelschule under Enric Miralles, also returning in 2000. Independently each of them discovered the work of the Smithsons and became excited by its even rationality – as have others of their generation in Melbourne.

Their exodus was motivated partly by their determination not to be sucked into the polarised architectural situation prevailing in the city in the late 1990s, in which civic narrative expressionism and Modernism were locked into a stale, often aggressive, adversarial struggle. They were determined to find another way, not to owe allegiance to either of these camps. And to some extent their years away gave them a firmer hold on a different framework, partisan to neither. Like many of their generation around the world, they saw the way out through research, in their case starting with a wide survey of the terrain in which they are to work, establishing a position on the experience that their intervention is going to support, assembling a supporting palette of materials and bringing these together in a decidedly unemphatic way. They are determined that their designs should become platforms for spatial experience and not for demonstrations of skill in detailing. Their third-way approach has kept them on good terms with many practices that routinely pass work on to them (Kerstin Thompson, John Wardle, Peter Elliott and Carey Lyon all do so).

Below left and right: Somers House, Mornington Peninsula (2004). Views of the covered living deck adjacent to the new master bedroom, and of the connecting passage with a shadow cast by the water tank. This project uses the same approach to planning as for EQ

On their returns in 2000 and 2001, NMBW took its next step towards becoming a practice, with all three partners engaged in the practitioner/academic model through association with RMIT. By chance they acquired the same room in Carlow House which they had vacated three years earlier, and they are still based here. For Dur-é Dara, one of the owners of the Nudel Bar, they completed EQ, a restaurant in the Arts Centre on St Kilda Road. This they aligned with the major views across the river to the skyline of the Cathedral, sliding a platform into the opened up cylindrical form of the existing building and shifting it to the view. So persuasive is the relationship to the city view that most diners do not realise that there has been a shift at all.

Their next substantial completed project was an alteration and addition to a house and outbuildings on a small farm at Somers on the Mornington Peninsula an hour and a half's drive to the southeast, a project

that followed from an earlier commission for Lucinda's sister in the inner suburbs. The same deliberate architectural intelligence is at work here, orchestrating views, movements and levels. The existing project house is cleaned out to make it more what it might have been had its design been more considered when it was built. It could be seen to be descended, however dimly, from a Modern pavilion in which horizontality is emphasised. It is linked to two timber platforms that are arranged in an alignment to the site slightly different to that of the existing house, one encased in a deceptively simple corrugated-iron shed, the other surrounding a hot tub. The sides of the shed are largely open, and the flow of the landscape and the drift of the day can be observed from the shelter of this verandah throughway, while a new master bedroom and en-suite bathroom are located in the closed portion of the shed. Here, as in their other work, they avoid the ubiquitous plasterboard of Australian construction, preferring to use stained ply, butt-jointed with a 3 millimetre gap

Below: Marika, Nigel and Lucinda at the conference table in their studio
in Carlow House, Flinders Lane

and fixed with a flathead nail, providing a surface that is given a presence by the particular materiality of the ply and revealing the construction process to those who look hard enough.

Theirs is an architecture that aims for an evenness between its different aspects, such that the construction and the spatial experience are in balance, that the user feels that this is just a building, not something you have to notice, but one that really supports the best possible experience to be had in a place.

NMBW plan to sustain practice at this scale for a while, running about six small projects a year. They discuss all projects together at the outset, and then assign leadership and support for each, with rolling responsibilities across all jobs. Andrew Wilson, who moved back to Brisbane in 1999, continues a dialogue with NMBW through their Queensland Office and his teaching at Queensland University of

Technology (QUT). They feel supported in what they do by their involvement in the Half Time Club, a focus for the exchange of ideas among rising architects, especially since the two poles of discourse have been mediated by the introduction of a number of third ways in the making.

1 NMBW's work has been published: Alex Selenitsch, 'EQuilibrium', *Architectural Review Australia* (winter 2001), No 74, pp 66–71; NS Klickowski, *Restaurants*, Loft Publications (Barcelona), 2003, pp 72–80; Mauro Baracco and Louise Wright, 'Somers Shed, a rural shed by NMBW', *Architecture Australia*, (Jan/Feb 2004), pp 72-7.
2 Nikos Papastergiadis, *Spatial Aesthetics: Art, Place and the Everyday*, Rivers Oram/Pandora (London), 2005.
3 Leon van Schaik (exec ed), Nigel Bertram (ed Vols 1 and 2), Winsome Callister (ed Vol 3), *Building 8: Edmond and Corrigan at RMIT*, Schwartz Transition (Melbourne), 1996.
4 Nigel Bertram and Andrew Wilson, 'Re-appraising the Picturesque', in Shane Murray and Leon van Schaik (eds), *38 South (II)*, RMIT (Melbourne), 2000, pp 62–3.

ALLAN POWELL

Allan Powell arrives on the civic spine with RMIT Building 94 in 1996. This is the first manifestation of a new approach to architecture in Melbourne, one that puts the fostering of 'states of mind' in visitors at the forefront of the architectural endeavour. It is a way of working that complements the verbal intellectuality of expressionism and the search for techne, creating a third pole in the architectural culture of Melbourne; three poles are the prerequisite for a blooming of design in a city. Allan Powell emerges on to the architectural scene in Melbourne in the early 1980s because he appreciated before anyone else what the changes to the licensing laws in Victoria would entail for building. Prior to this, drinking was confined to the 'six o'clock swill', a very limited time period, and to a very constrained spatial circumstance – the inside of public houses with frosted windows. Melbourne was transformed as these laws were relaxed, in the mid 1980s, and restaurants were permitted for the first time to serve food and wine in full view of passers-by and on pavements. Powell was supported in his understanding of the implications of these changes by the experience of European cafe culture which his wife Gail, a graduate of the AA school of Architecture in London, brought to bear on this thinking. In early 1985 he designs the Metropole restaurant in Armadale, using off-the-peg components from a plaster shop – masks of Venus and other decorative motifs set against tiles in a grid. Later in 1985 he does Dechaineux, converting a fish and chip shop in an old

emporium and warehouse with cast iron columns down the centre and a saw-tooth roof above; the first warehouse-scale, fresh, fine-food restaurant in the city. So low was the budget that no equipment could be moved, so the cooking took place up front like a display, while waiters walked up and down to the scullery at back, giving the room an air of endless business. Tables were lined up like a barracks, counter to the prevailing informality; the lights were lined up too. This was the beginning of a social revolution in the city, breaking the moulds of convention in which different strata of people dined in different kinds of restaurants, attracting a new cross section of patrons and bringing new combinations of people together. In 1986 he designs Caffe Maximus in St Kilda with tall French windows opening the interior to the outside, a glistening, improbably solid edifice of black vitreous tiles. This restaurant took full advantage of the new regulations that allowed people drinking alcohol to be seen by passers-by outside. Before this, for the same restaurateur, in 1985 he designed the Latin in the city, featuring as a centerpiece a Futurist pink Bakelite-and-brass gondola that he had found in a shed behind the kitchen. It had been a leftist bohemian restaurant. Here Bryan Ferry first dined in Melbourne and leftwing parliamentarians met.

In 1987 Powell designs the more intimate Cafe Di Stasio in St Kilda, a restaurant a bit like a prop room that is also pavement cafe. Here the budget was

so low that when the flocked wallpaper was removed and revealed large stains on the underlying plaster, the residue of water damage reminiscent of Venice, it was continued as the theme. Allan delights in comments from well-travelled architects who, when taken there remark on nothing at all, but after an hour in the place observe: 'This has been designed!' Lastly there is Circa (1999) at the Prince of Wales in St Kilda, a dining room on the first floor of the Art-Deco hotel overlooking Fitzroy Street as it debouches towards the 60-kilometre diameter bay around which the city eases its way.[1]

There are those who dismiss this set of innovations, but they signify a rare social intelligence at work, seeing an opening and pushing it to its social limits. These were the first accessible restaurants to routinely and informally supply fine food and accoutrements such as linen table napkins, simple devices that set the stage for the diner's experience. And it is that sense of what it takes to create a lush situation that has propelled his work into other spheres in ways that often dismay architects raised on

Modernist shibboleths. It was in this unconventional frame of mind that Powell undertook his postgraduate research at RMIT,[2] seeking to uncover and proclaim this territory for architecture.

Much of this work is in villas like the 'precursor' Di Stasio House (1993)[3] and the 'postscript' Davies House (2003).[4] These houses are very unlike what the world has come to expect of the Australian house, coming from or creating a very different tradition to that of the lightweight pavilion in the bush. The Di Stasio House in the foothills of the Great Dividing Range, an hour-and-a-half by car from the city, seems to have been unearthed from the landscape by an archaeological dig. With the air of being an ancient ruin, partially restored and reoccupied, it bleakly rides a ridge above the vineyards of the estate. From its dumb and massy walls pierced with curtained slits a pavilion is extended to afford some sheltered overview of the panorama below and enfolds a sheltered courtyard with a shallow pond that catches light and aligns it with the horizon below. This creates a sense of embedded occupation that has not been asserted in

Opposite: Di Stasio House (1993) enfolds a sheltered courtyard with a shallow pond that catches the light

This page: Davies House (2003). Top left: A curtained pavilion between the north face of the house and the pool provides shade. Top right: Exterior from Hill Street, Toorak. Bottom right: Thick-walled corridors line the south face of the house. Bottom left: The reception rooms are linked enfilade along the north face of the house

Australia since the heyday of early settlement, when the squattocracy built Victorian piles to celebrate the wealth that came from the sheep's back. The Davies House does a similar thing in the inner suburbs of the city, inserting a blank-walled fortress, cranked like a cupped hand, on to a long sun-facing, south slope. Thick-walled corridors line the wall, while a series of rooms is linked enfilade along a glazed wall facing the sun, an arrangement mimicked above by the bedrooms. Cupped by this is a terrace that is defined by a swimming pool along its northern boundary, and on this terrace there is a gesture to the transient pleasures of the curtained pavilion, now merely a quotation from an increasingly distant past.

Allan's first work on the civic spine is Building 94, the School of Design (1996) on RMIT's City Campus, in which – as at MIT in Boston, whose mantle it aspires to assume in this city – almost all the buildings are numbered, not named. This is a building remarkable for its ease of use. The main accommodation is set back from the street to respect the scale of the neighbouring buildings, and the podium on the street frontage is slashed open with a slanting cut that prises into the facade a stairway rising to the first floor level. Here the landing stretches at right angles behind the first floor of the podium, itself resting on slanting black vitreous tiled columns, behind which a shop front stretches. Hidden from street views therefore is a main entrance to the library, and a further flight of stairs rising to the podium roof deck which functions as the outdoor area to a cafe that serves the building. Back at street level and on the other side of the stairway that itself marks the lobby entrance to the building at ground floor is a double-height gallery, glazed to the street, one of the most sought after venues for emerging artists in the city. The tower behind, heavily protected with horizontal Nile-green sun shields, incorporates a stack of studio spaces. Entering through the front doors you come to a wide foyer with a stairway that drops down to a set of three handsome raked floor lecture theatres. There are lifts, but in this building escape-stairs on one flank and at the rear are designed as wide and easy going stairways, with the fire doors held open on electronic locks. Movement is disarmingly simple, and people flow between levels with the greatest of ease. Corridors are

Opposite: The Tarra Warra Museum of Art (200X). Neolithic Modernism

Below: Allan Powell in his St Kilda office with some of his art glass

timber-composite-panel lined, the studios admit soft light. This is a building that users respect through enjoyment – very rare in institutional buildings – with a facade that is a spatial and occupiable landscape.

In Allan's case the building on the spine has a postscript that is more declarative about his architectural intentions than the fine Building 94 – the TarraWarra Museum of Art (2004) near Healesville.[5] Here in a retrospective vision one can see where all of the previous experiments are leading to: what Stefano Pujatti of Elastico has described as 'delicate brutalism'; and what visiting critic Prof Jonathan Hill has called a 'Neolithic Modernism', out of respect for the way that it speaks to our long-evolved and internalised sense of space. Through its strangely compelling assemblage of dumb Platonic solids, seemingly functionless tapered grey-blue columns fingering the usually bright blue sky, huge doors, long parallel vistas, some inside, some out, the museum effortlessly evokes a dreamy state of mind that almost all visitors succumb to with relief.

1 Leon van Schaik, 'Local Hero', review of Prince of Wales, St Kilda, Melbourne, *World Architecture*, No 81 (November, 1999), pp 92–3.

2 Allan Powell, 'Forgotten Zones: A Matiere for Architecture', in Leon van Schaik (ed), *Fin de Siècle and the Twenty-first Century: Architectures of Melbourne*, RMIT A+D (Melbourne), 1993, pp 89–111.

3 Di Stasio House; see Leon van Schaik, 'Magical Realism', *Monument*, Residential Special, 2003.

4 Of the Davies House I wrote in April 2004: *One does not experience space as it is photographed. We sit in a space aware of the spaces we have traversed to reach it, aware of what lies beyond. A windowless room on a beach is very different to the same room on the verge of a highway. That is why one so often finds people who live in grand houses are happily sitting in a pantry, a small space charged with the energy of the vast spaces around them. They would not be so comfortable if that were the only space to which they had access. These circumstances effect our 'states of mind' radically, as Allan Powell avers. Here is an architect who is so concerned with such states, so sure that they are what endures, that he rhetorically asserts that he does not know what a 'house' is today.* (see review 'Toorak House', *Architectural Review*, No 88, Residential, 2004, p 74)

5 Leon van Schaik, 'TarraWarra Museum of Art', in Maudie Palmer and Bryony Marks (eds), *Powell at TarraWarra*, TarraWarra Museum of Art (Melbourne), 2003, pp 20–34.

Opposite: Moor Street, Fitzroy (2000). This complex consists of the glazed skillion section to the left and the refurbished warehouse to the right. The night view shows how the new and old coexist

IVAN RIJAVEC

Ivan Rijavec sidled up to the civic spine of the city in 1997 with his Flinders Lane Apartment[1] in the heart of the art strip, four years after he completed a review of the nature of his architectural mastery, and speculated on its future directions.[2] This two-level apartment for an art lover encapsulates many of this architect's abiding concerns, focused on his research into how people perceive space. Many of his buildings are experiments into what we can be persuaded to believe about our situation through the minor and major manipulation of our peripheral vision. In this apartment a simple orthogonal box, lit by glazing at one end, is inflected by subtle canting and bowing of walls and ceiling until the scale of the box has become ambiguous. The effect is far from disturbing; it seems on the contrary to fix the occupant in a vessel afloat in a sea of spatial pleasures, playing on a thoroughly 20th-century sense of weightlessness.

This architectural engagement with contemporary fascinations in the popular culture has created some iconic inventions that could come to stand for the deeply internalised desires of late 20th-century culture, barely perceptible to us now. His Chen House (1997) is a show house in a number of senses. It displays the design connoisseurship of the owner in the street, and the architectural virtuosity of the stairwell through a picture window designed to allow views from the outside to the inside. Not to mention the dog and the car, which latter features in the interior

through a plate-glass wall, one of the first houses to include the car in the living room as a matter of course. In the reception area above, the kitchen floats on a plane of polished timber like a spacecraft soon to depart, the planar ceiling above dematerialised by deep incisions painted yellow and blue.

Rijavec has come close to realising a number of major projects in the inner-city of Melbourne and Singapore, but sadly – in spite of his successful advocacy for them in hostile planning milieux – these have not eventuated. However, what we are missing is clearly demonstrated in a project that has materialised: the Moor Street complex in the inner suburb of Fitzroy. The glazed section attaches to an existing building in a classical Australian skillion roof section punctured with two over-scale dormers. These are office/studios, and inside we are immediately aware that the spatial virtuosity of the architect has in no manner deserted him. The top-level mezzanine with the dormers is a particularly beguiling space, carved out of the section, while the pre-existing brick wall and its painted-on advertising legends are lovingly preserved in a deft curatorial move. In the existing building a laneway has been carved through to enable multistorey residential occupation, culminating in a three-level studio penthouse.[3] The lower two levels operate as interlinked sleeping and washing areas, the existing masonry walls plastered white while the new

Top left: On the periphery of the city – Chen House, Doncaster (1997). Situated in an area that attracts well-to-do migrants, this house exhibits Rijavec's formal play, building a setting for living and display

Bottom left: Chen House. The kitchen is composed of discrete boat-like objects adrift on the shiny plane of the floor

Top right: On the financial spine – Flinders Lane Apartment (1997). The space is inflected by subtle canting and bowing of walls and ceiling

Opposite top: Moor Street (2000). The behaviour-directing, Baroque effects of Rijavec's approach are confirmed in this rooftop room, with the view of the surrounding city horizon denied until you are seated

Opposite bottom: Moor Street. The interior of the new addition displays Rijavec's signature plasticity of form

Opposite: Chen House (1997). The amazing plasticity of the staircase draws attention away from the fact that the garage is separated from the reception rooms by a glass wall

Below: Ivan Rijavec in front of the preserved remains of an advertisement formerly on the outside of a warehouse in Fitzroy, an inner suburb of Melbourne

insertions, including full-height sliding doors to the upper sleeping area, are lined out in plywood, giving a warmth to an otherwise rather cold internal space. Above, the lounge, that also contains a kitchen dining counter along one windowsill, pops up through the exiting roofline and affords views back into the city and to the hills beyond. Here Rijavec's complete mastery of perceptual manipulation shows in the simplest of possible ways. The horizontal slot windows are at a level that cuts out the view if you are standing, and brings it into your cone of vision when you sit. The room is thus curiously activated, making cocktail parties intensely contained experiences, while more intimate seated affairs become contemplative exercises as the drama of the sliced view absorbs your attention.

It is little short of a tragedy that Rijavec's work is not accessible to more people through public buildings on the civic spine. What we are missing can be glimpsed at the Caulfield Town Hall (1990–1), where he designed an alteration and addition that twists up through a shifting ovoid form towards a lantern that joins old and new. The failure of the city to engage this talent properly is a curatorial lapse that is also an opportunity, indicating that here – as in a few other cases that we will note on our journey along the spines – enormous potential, as yet untapped in the current wave of innovative development, is in waiting.

1 Leon van Schaik, 'Elastic Collisions', *Architecture Australia*, Architecture Media Australia (Jan/Feb 1997), pp 30–5.
2 Ivan Rijavec, 'Working on the Perceptual Edge', in Leon van Schaik (ed), *Fin de Siècle and the Twenty-first Century: Architectures of Melbourne*, RMIT A+D (Melbourne), 1993, pp 173–90.
3 Leon van Schaik, 'The Hard Cell', *Vogue Living* (May/June 2004), pp 120–7.

Opposite: Skenes Creek House (1999). This section, high to the north to collect the winter sun, opening to the south to capture views of the sea, is a masterly distillation of the reconciliations needed to enjoy the continent's vast southern coastline

KERSTIN THOMPSON

Kerstin Thompson arrives on the civic spine at the QV site with a red building (2005) that sits between John Wardle's 40-storey residential slab and the 20-storey Lyons office slab. Laughingly, she describes how the problem of this sandwich of space was 'tossed' to her at the end of the design process for the other components. She immediately grasped that more than tidying up was needed. One wing of the red brick Queen Victoria Women's Hospital had been kept when the site was cleared, sitting rather forlorn between the DCM Sensis HQ and the BHP Billiton HQ facing Lonsdale Street, its rear face looking into the central square of the new development. It seemed like a leftover. She determined to anchor it back into the project by creating a companion building, similar in

scale and colouring. This strategy, welcomed by the client and the coordinating architect, has paid off handsomely. Seen from the corner of Lonsdale and Russell opposite the BHP Billiton HQ, the two red buildings reach out to each other and have become a consolidated part of the composition. Not that there is any mimicry involved here. Thompson's red building is only notionally a brick building, with a quite deliberate incorporation of pre-cast panels of embedded brickwork being used regardless of the line of laying, some horizontal, some vertical. Together with the matching red profiled steel, the structure has been arranged to create a general mass that deals with the sandwich of commercial space that spirals around the two levels engaged with the

walkways and inner square, and with a creche on the topmost floors. This is unalloyed inner-city realism, comfortably finding its own aesthetic from the procedures of solving its programmatic needs at the immediate and the urban scale.

Thompson's designs are anything but sentimental. A significant precursor for the QV work is the Merkel House in nearby Fitzroy, where she converted a warehouse into a residence by cutting a cylindrical opening into the centre of the building, making an urban court around which the public rooms of the house are arrayed, while the bedrooms look out of the back wall of the warehouse into a walled kitchen garden. Her Black Swan House at Lake Connewarre,

an hour-and-a-half to the southwest of the city, is another surprising result of following the logic where it goes without a prescribed sense of the outcome. Aside from its grounding in Thompson's abiding interest with the way in which the surface of this vast flat continent can be furrowed and twisted into the third dimension,[1] nothing prepares you for the long thin slice of space inside a black flange along a contour, one face opening towards the view, the other to the sheltered, sun-facing lee, a *parti* first established in her Skenes Creek House near Apollo Bay, three hours further southwest.

The most interesting postscripts are yet to come, with a series of new houses nearing completion and the work to be published. The battle for these

Top: On the Civic Spine – Thompson used the opportunity to give the remaining red brick fragment of the Queen Victoria hospital a context, creating the sense that it and the Red Building (2005) are the matrix in which the entire development sits

Top left and bottom: Merkel House (2002). Rooms are arrayed around the central living foyer. The courtyard has an uncompromisingly urban quality

Opposite: Skenes Creek House (1999). Here too the house defines an inland terrain sheltered from the prevailing cold-weather southwesterly winds

Opposite: Merkel House (2002). Thompson shows strategic daring, cutting a cylinder into an existing warehouse to create a home with a sense of inside and outside

Below: Kerstin Thompson's office is in the inner suburb of Fitzroy, Melbourne's first suburb. Fitzroy's mixed residential, commercial and factory space make it a prime location for loft accommodation. Thompson's home is in the same complex

houses has involved protracted consultation with local planners, who, it has to be said, are often not yet aware of the ways in which they can support the growth of the local culture, having been schooled in the main to fear innovation. Paradoxically, this mindset allows mediocre designs an easy passage, while serious design is usually contested. Thompson has become a fearless and effective advocate of serious design ambition in these circumstances and the resulting houses are a formidable accomplishment. They are for obvious reasons difficult to visit, though through publication they are certain to change our views about what is at stake in the design of villas. Most specifically, they will alter our perceptions of how houses should complement the landscape, a challenge that Thompson

set herself at Lake Connewarre working with landscape architect Fiona Harrison, an exploration she has deepened in her association with landscape architect Cath Stutterheim, with whom she submitted an entry for the National Arboretum competition. Her visitor centre, open to the public, is at Cranbourne Botanical Gardens – an outpost of the Gardens in the Domain an hour-and-a-half to the southeast of the city – and overlooking a design for an Australian garden by Perry Lethlean. Melbourne deserves more publicly accessible work by this architect.

Thompson is a strong advocate of third ways in the local discourse, having suffered from the adversarial bipartisanship of the past, and works effectively through the schools and in the profession in support of a wider view. She is also one of those who, having established their mastery in the city region and having launched into a series of innovations from that platform, have realised the need for an international network of peers with whom that innovation can be tested. It is no accident that she was the first Australian to be exhibited in the 'New Trends in Architecture Europe and Asia Pacific', a travelling biennale organised by Rei Art Forum (Tokyo), and that she used the opportunity of the RAIA Conference in 2005 to introduce her Australian peers to a new generation of architects from the same regions.

1 Kerstin Thompson, 'Interstitial Practices' in Leon van Schaik (ed), *Interstitial Modernism*, RMIT Press (Melbourne), 2000, pp 154–69.
2 Leon van Schiak, 'Box of Joys: Kerstin Thompson designs a Victorian beach retreat', *Architecture Australia* (Sept/Oct 1999), pp 44–9.

Opposite: '*It's a Boy*'. Hyperhouse (1992–8). In this project the focus is on the capacity of space to allow or encourage change and connection or networking by the home and its occupants to friends, family, work colleagues, news and entertainment along with the potential to make the outer skin of the building expressive. The skin filters out the unwelcome and celebrates the desired. Design team: Michael Trudgeon, Anthony Kitchener, David Poulton. Computer program implementation: Joseph Brabet. Visualisation: Glynis Teo

MICHAEL TRUDGEON

Industrial design is a conflicted territory in Australia. The economy bridges agriculture, resource extraction and the knowledge economy and rides on the momentum of a flywheel of services and construction in the main that serve the capital cities. While this is a house-owning democracy, there simply isn't much industry to design for. Innovative engineers such as Anthony Kitchener, who has constructed an international enterprise out of patented products that are prototyped in what was once a factory, work exclusively by licensing manufacture to overseas companies. Engineering talent is predominantly channelled into finding solutions for the mining industries. To observe at Nhulunby on the Gove Peninsula in the far north the kilometres-long belts delivering iron ore to crushing structures and on to trains and docks, or to join the locals at the hotel at Parachilna to watch a kilometre-long train wind past filled with ore, or to see the giant hole at Kalgoorlie is to witness the burgeoning industries of China and India in the raw. Architecture, even if only 3 to 8 per cent of housing is directly architect-designed, is driven by an unflagging demand for housing even with a slow population growth, as more and more Australians choose to live alone in larger homes.

Yet some architects are consumed by the ideals of industrial production of buildings – an illusive quest – but one that, as we have seen in Paul Morgan's work, nonetheless addresses important issues. Michael

Trudgeon is an architect who has never been satisfied to accept things as they are and fiddle around the margins. His preferred zone of operation is where a client finds that 'all else has failed'. When clients find that the conventional wisdoms of property managers, marketing executives and real estate agents have been shown up to be just that – projections of past solutions – they turn to Crowd, Trudgeon's design company, to re-frame the questions.

Crowd is, in a sense, a shell allowing collaborations and his collaborators include engineer Anthony Kitchener and architect David Poulton. Among their beguiling projects has been an autonomous kitchen that could be moved around a house at will.

Naturally, with this mindset, Michael is research driven. His initial postgraduate research involved a quest for the intelligent building through architecture as industrial design.[1] This work on distributed intelligence in the domestic environment led to extensive prototyping of a house that 'learned' from its inhabitants their preferred responses to climate and their communication needs, becoming evermore able to service these preferences. He is currently engaged in doctoral research concerned with the negotiating strategies necessary to take both designer and client into new conceptual spaces. We first encounter his work at ACMI, Federation Square, in a series of portable movie-viewing lounge capsules. The client had a major film archive that it wished to make available to

Below and opposite bottom: On the civic spine – Hyperlounge digital cinema capsules (2004), Australian Centre for the Moving Image (ACMI). The Hyperlounge capsule could be thought of as a mass-producible 'lounge room of the future'. A single capsule is shown with freestanding partition screen to help create a soft boundary between the screen lounges and the surrounding public space. These partitions also act as an interior street sign system, directing traffic around the spaces. Opposite is an installation view of capsules making up part of the larger Memory Grid programme at ACMI at Federation Square. Design team: Michael Trudgeon, David Poulton. Research engineering: Anthony Kitchener

Top right: Hoyts Cinema complex at Melbourne Central (2006). The designers say: 'Cinema is social, on a grand public scale. It's an event. Like the opera it can be as much about other people and other activities, a Passagiata that happens to converge at the theatre. The richness of the collective social experience is central. To address this we have pursued a new cinema typology; the Panavision Lounge, a double height space gives us a grand hospitality space that can be glimpsed from the entry. In fact it's still a cinema, with three of the original walls, original ceiling and all equipment including the sound system. Its just that its also a bar/cafe reception space and unique in Australia. Pendant lighting from the ceiling creates intimate spaces within this large void. Each time you come to this space it is different and that difference celebrates the cinematic seasonal shifts and calendar. This space is designed to extend the social possibilities of the traditional foyer.' Design team: Michael Trudgeon, David Poulton. Visualisation: Glynis Teo

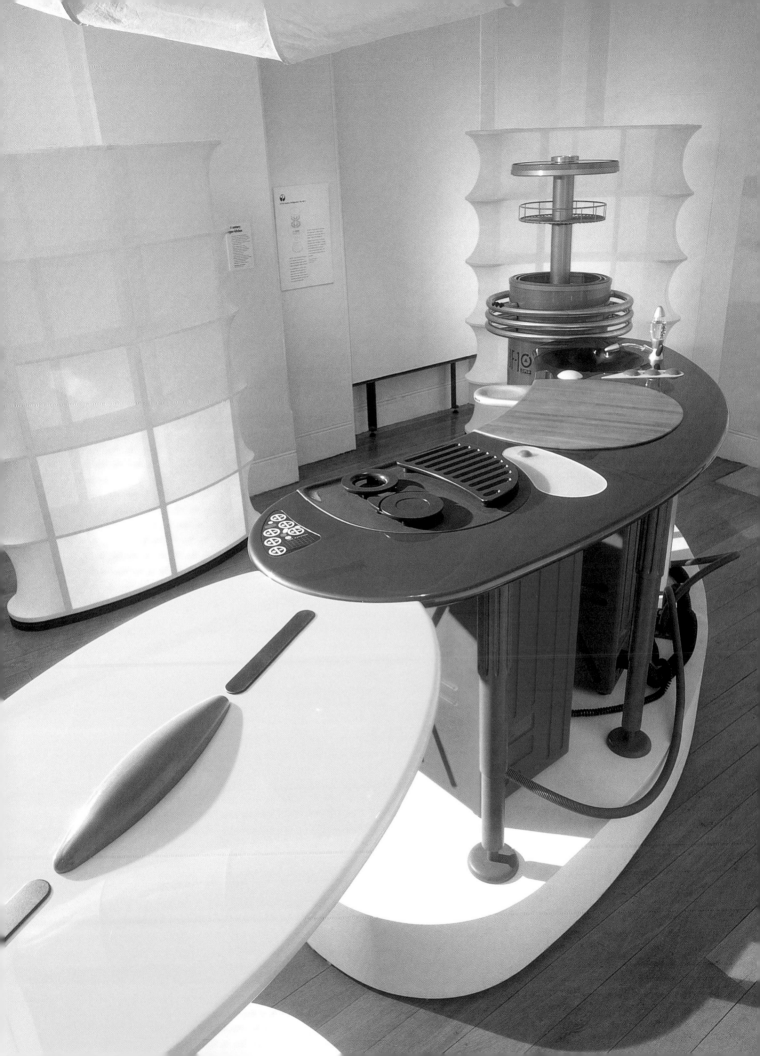

Opposite: Hyper Kitchen (1994). A central-island, wrap-around work surface with electromagnetic cooking tools and pivoted breakfast bar with horizontal rotary condiment pallet and contact-activated heating strips in the foreground. Flexible umbilical cables connect the Hyper Kitchen to electricity, fresh water and sewage services with a quick-fit Drybreak universal coupling (similar to those used for refuelling in Formula 1 motor racing). It does not require professional assistance for hook up. The coupling sockets for these services are mounted in the floor. Design team: Michael Trudgeon, David Poulton, Anthony Kitchener (Hyper Kitchen was developed for the exhibition 'The Domestic Revolution', curated by Michael Bogle at the Hyde Park Barracks, Sydney 1994)

Left: Michael Trudgeon in his office, running a class with Industrial Design students from RMIT

small groups of people to browse. These capsules are situated on the *piano nobile* of the institution that sits on a vast underground gallery as large as the biggest at the Bilbao Guggenheim that in an inexplicable collapse of architectural intelligence has been cut up into a maze of small black boxes, each containing rolling images. The capsules return to us the possibility of a contemplative experience of the archive, rather than repeating the strangely horse-and-carriage mentality of the underground gallery in which films seem to be curated as if they are pictures in a museum.

In his most recent work, Michael is rethinking the multiplex cinema complexes in the private sector. These environments, consisting of clusters of tiny screening theatres, enjoyed an initial success through enhancing options for cinemagoers, but the experience offered cannot compete with the new flat-screen, home-theatre technologies. What should the cinema companies do with their vast property portfolios in a post-bingo age? Crowd has come up with a series of proposals that produce interactive environments of a quality that cannot as yet be achieved at home.

Curiously, the wicker screens used in the ACMI capsules connect to ancient migrations across the Pacific as much as the desire to recast architecture as a matter of industrial componentry is future oriented. The screens mimic the ancient Polynesian maps of the Pacific Ocean, also wickerwork constructs, and for Michael signal ways of working in the unknown from which we can still learn as we 'walk the plank' from the ship of our current securities and leap into the sea of possibilities where new, if temporary, certainties are waiting to be discovered.

1 Michael Trudgeon, 'The Intelligent Building: Architecture as Industrial Design', in Leon van Schaik (ed), *Fin de Siècle and the Twenty-first Century: Architectures of Melbourne*, RMIT A+D (Melbourne), 1993, pp 217–31.

JOHN WARDLE

John Wardle arrives on the civic spine with his 44-storey slab of apartments (2005) on the QV site. A walk around this soon reveals many of the qualities that his work has developed through his long research into the nature of his mastery,[1] culminating in his virtuoso postgraduate research at RMIT in 2003. If you look closely at the ends of the slab, you will see that they bifurcate and feather out in much the same way as does his precursor two-storey Graphic Technologies Building (2000) on RMIT's Brunswick Campus. This process of extruding a section, twisting it to suit site, views and programme without ever turning a corner, creates powerful interior spaces. In his many houses, commencing with Balnarring (1997) where a raw external sheath covers a finely wrought internal box,

John Wardle has explored surface structures through joinery experiments, many of which have a paradoxical impact, seemingly revealing depth while often opening in ways that at first appear to defy logic.

Where the 44-storey slab reaches the ground on the corner of Little Lonsdale and Russell Streets, we see the first manifestation of this research in his large-scale work, though it is also currently emerging in his work for the University of South Australia in central Adelaide. The glazed corner volume seems to have been sliced off at an angle and the upper portion shifted slightly outwards before being re-soldered together. A little further around the corner into Russell Street a flanged incision has been made into the glass

facade at first-storey level. The inclined planes of this cut are solid, seemingly improbably so in relation to the glass above and below so that one is almost forced to read the incision as projecting out from the building face, rather than inwards.

Above this the car park to the apartments is masked by other joinery manipulations, grey spandrels crinkled back and forth in a reverse rhythm along Russell Street; warm, timber-colour laminations stacked in layers above one another down Little Lonsdale Street. Neither of these manoeuvres trumps the illusion of depth created at the two levels related to the street. John Wardle may refuse to turn a corner, but he knows how to mark one.

The architectonic play is mightily engaging, not least because at first it is difficult to grasp what is going on. It works because it slips in and out of focus as a form, like a puzzle, but also because it slips in and out of scale, sometimes seeming huge, sometimes a casket that could be cupped in the hands. Old-fashioned Modernists, who find Melbourne difficult to deal with anyway, would probably dismiss this joinery-research-related play as trivial formal manipulation. Nor is their dismissal without some justification, because there is a subset of work in the city, not far from the projects singled out here, that is simply mannerist and complicated without reason, and which they argue would have been considerably less offensive had the architects not been given

Left and bottom: Graphic Technologies Building on RMIT's Brunswick Campus (2001). Here Wardle experimented with feathering an extruded section. Extrusions 'cut to length' characterised the interior too

Above: QV Apartments (2005). Corner view of Russell and Little Lonsdale Streets showing an approach to the architecture that is like enlarged joinery or cabinet-making

Opposite top and middle: Balnarring (1997). An early experiment in extrusion ran a rough-hewn timber carcass over a wrought inner sleeve. The inner spaces are warm and smooth, and inventive joinery cabinets, revealing Wardle's intense preoccupation with making, flank the fireplace

Oppsite bottom: House for two artists (2005). Large-scale joinery persists in more recent work

licence to indulge by the acrobatics of their more accomplished peers. Certainly, that was the initial reaction of purists to Storey Hall, most of whom found to their disquiet that they were involuntarily disarmed when confronted with its interior reality, and the joyful logic at work. This I believe will be their reaction when they study Wardle's disarming architectural intelligence at QV.

Wardle is at work with the magical in architecture, schooled in this through his long apprenticeship in house design. His particular clientele has been built up through his ability to nest his formal inventions, from the scale of a cupboard through to the carcass of the entire building. He shares with his clients a love of the ingeniously crafted and well-made. It is no accident that he is a patron of automata-maker Steve Hope and ceramicist Simon Lloyd, that he uses wicker screens where others might use stainless steel. Or that he has supported neon artist Peter Kennedy with a major installation across the facade of his office in Russell Street, a contribution to the city that has nurtured him of richly figured light shining out on a chill winter evening, or a welcoming of the dusk in summer.

What we are witnessing in his institutional and residential buildings is the ability to scale-up into edifices and spaces that capture the imagination of city users by reconnecting us to that delight in the operable miniature that lies in our childhood fascination with toys that move. The method is not one that adds complexity and cost, but one that – as in the joinery – discovers how to make every surface serve many purposes and derives multiple logics from the conflicts of programme and regulation, resolving them through the abstraction of joinery. So while the works look

luxurious, this is because of the depth of consideration, not because of the use of costly materials or construction techniques. This is achieved through intense teamwork, with the office being organised around key enablers Amanda Ritson and Stefano Mee. Recently, a project manager complained that a junction system between concrete panels devised by the office was $100,000 more expensive than it needed to be. When a proper analysis was conducted with the architect, the client discovered that the extra expenditure on these junctions saved many more hundreds of thousands of dollars by obviating the need for a temporary scaffold during construction. Few if any details in a Wardle design do not embed a similar in-depth logic, making some of his institutional buildings among the most cost-effective in the city.

As in the design and making of automata, there is in Wardle's work an almost uncanny ability to concentrate many layers of functionality under the misleading guise of formal legerdemain, an ability that once understood engenders surprise and enduring delight.

1 John Wardle, 'Cut threads and frayed ends: the character of enclosure' in Leon van Schaik (ed), *The Practice of Practice – Research in the Medium of Design*, RMIT Press (Melbourne), 2003, pp 204–221.

Opposite: Gottlieb House (1998) reception area. Furniture designed by the architects assumes the scale of a miniature city in the large reception area, cunningly shrinking it down to domestic scale

WOOD MARSH

Wood Marsh's presence on the rhetorical spine of the city was secured with their design for the Australian Centre for Contemporary Art (ACCA) (1996–2002). This is situated in the triangular zone of the Arts Precinct that stretches from the Arts Centre on St Kilda Road to the Malthouse Theatre complex on Sturt Street, where the entrance to ACCA is also located. However, Roger Wood and Randal Marsh, the principals in this firm, are no strangers to the spine. Their sense of the importance of a curatorial context is unparalleled in its depth and duration. Their designs of furniture that might be buildings were shown in the NGV on St Kilda Road in 1986, before they had formally graduated from RMIT, and on a regular basis they have added impetus to their work by communicating their

intentions through the intensifying lens of exhibitions, at what is now the Anna Schwartz Gallery, at the Venice Biennale in 1991 where they designed RMIT's stand in the Arsenale, in the Seppelt Design Awards at MOCA in Sydney, in film at the first Rotterdam International Architecture Biennale and in many other venues. Even so their work too has developed in a dialogue between city and periphery.

Perhaps the most significant precursor to ACCA is the Gottlieb House in Caulfield. The street face of this large house gives little clue to what lies behind, but the simple concrete form with the projecting box is a radical restatement of the villa, the prevailing house-type in this suburb. Once through the entrance, where

the volume promised by the facade explodes into space, you encounter a reception area designed accommodate house parties of up to 200 people. The sequencing of the spatial experience – from fort-like exterior, to soaring verticality and then into floating horizontal depth, with an opening through a slate wall up some stairs to a kitchen and dining pavilion at the scale of the five person family – gives some indication of the ways in which they have dealt with the sequence of spaces in ACCA, their largest public building to date. Typically, the house is also a laboratory for a series of investigations into materiality, a materiality Randal Marsh described as akin to the vast flat-sided form that Frederico Fellini created for his film *And the Ship Sailed On*. This mute quality is what they seek,

precisely because it undermines our ready-to-hand, internalised sense of scale and confronts us with possibilities that switch on our architectural sensibility once again with the eidetic intensity that it had when we were children learning about our physical world.

To walk down Grant Street from St Kilda Road towards ACCA is to encounter just such a pleasurable dislocation and reawakening, at any time of day, but especially at dusk. The building is situated on a wide plane of granitic gravel subdivided with a pattern derived from Michelangelo's design for the Campidoglio on the Capitoline Hill in Rome. This combination makes the paradoxical proposition that

Opposite far left: Gottlieb House (1998) entrance. Designed to accommodate up to 400 people, the house has the air of a public building

Opposite right, top and bottom: On the civic spine – Australian Centre for Contemporary Arts (ACCA) (2002). The foyer becomes one of the city's most popular crush spaces during openings and has an unexpectedly large gallery space

Left: Barro House (2004). Here the monumental form masks a relatively modest house

Below: Shadowfax Winery, Werribbee (2000). Wood Marsh trialled the use of Corten rusting steel at this winery on the western fringe of the city

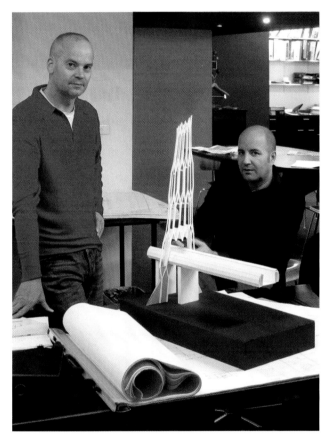

agent in the production and comparative evaluation of new art in the city. The interiors adapt so completely that the gallery does not seem to be the same place from one show to the next. On opening nights the foyer is a crush of people eager to see what has been brought to light from Melbourne and other cities.

Everything these architects do is notable. Their early work on nightclubs has a recent manifestation in the foyer for their Docklands Tower. An hour's drive from Melbourne, their Shadowfax Winery at the Werribee Park Hotel, a luxury hotel also designed by the architects, in one of the largest stately homes of the 19th-century squattocracy is another accessible work. Here you see the architects working on propositions similar to ACCA and the Gottlieb House, but in different scales.

It is however in a new house, the Barro House, that their continuing experimentation is most manifest. Here, once again, a dumb monolith faces the street. Enter, however, and space expands as in Dr Who's Tardis. And all within the compass of a standard residential block in an inner suburb. This contained spatial and material magic works on you just as ACCA displaces you, putting people in touch afresh with the wonder that architectural reality can provide, just as a great poem or passage of music affords us the mental space to contemplate the actuality of our experience, lifting us out of the humdrum of the normative awareness to which we slowly and inevitably succumb in our over-pressured lives.

ACCA is distinctive in its location in contemporary Australia, freed from the need to ape, through lawn and imported deciduous trees, the Europe from which the city has sprung, asserting the reality of our presence here on the most arid continent, asserting the support for the art of the moment rather than for collectable art, while at the same time aligning itself with a moment of high European design. ACCA, under the artistic directorship of Juliana Engberg, has continued to realise its goal of being a major curatorial

PASSEGGIATA DOWN THE FINANCIAL SPINE

Opposite: Newman House (2000), courtyard. Behind the facade Cassandra Fahey's skill with living spaces in tight places is evident

Previous spread: Fitzroy Warehouse (2003). This extraordinary interior (it won a national award) involved intensive research into materials and construction, pushing computer-controlled laser cutting skills to new heights in the city

Passeggiata Down the Financial Spine

CASSANDRA COMPLEX

Bursting on to the Melbourne scene and the world stage by silk-screening an image of Pamela Anderson's face on to the glazed facade of the Newman House (2000), designed and constructed for a local TV identity, the irrepressible Cassandra Fahey was catapulted on to the Collins Street commercial spine with a retail tenancy for Husk (2003), a direct challenge to the Minimalist orthodoxy of international retail. She then rocketed to national acclaim with the top award from the RAIA in 2004 for the interior of a warehouse space for Dr Michael Ben Mier in the inner suburb of Fitzroy (2003), one of the two main bohemian districts that bracket the central city. Currently her Platypusary for Zoos Victoria at the Healesville Sanctuary (2005), situated in the foothills of the Great Dividing Range

an hour-and-a-half to the east of the city, is changing the way in which zoos present themselves – transforming enclosures from a neutral backdrop to a joyful celebration.

Graduating first from what she laughingly refers to as 'inferior design' she graduated also from architecture. Her humour attacks head-on the prejudices of her more purely architectural colleagues, for she argues that much of her liberated approach to design stems from the open intellectual climate she encountered in Interior Design at RMIT. Fahey participated in the programme to which John Andrews, then teaching at the Architectural Association in London, was recruited to transform from a normative

skills-based degree into an idea-led degree. He is the founder of the worldwide conceptual design movement 'Bureau' that foreshadowed much of the new, research-led practice environment that is superseding the old professional norm. Andrews's intervention has been so successful that it has impacted on interior design education throughout the entire Australasian region. In this climate the ideal of idea-generated design was pursued without the constraints – mostly self-inflicted – that somewhat confine such explorations in an accredited programme.

Cassandra commenced her career under the mentorship of Tom Kovac, whose instinctive understanding that innovative work must be

conducted in an international context, even as it obtains all of its resonances from a deep rootedness in the resistances of local sites, clients and materials, has become second nature to her. She acquired a grant to travel the world interviewing every architect and designer that she admired for a video documentary. She returned to Melbourne with an international network and a canny understanding of the modes of behaviour that support a radical practice. This journalistic interlude brought her first clients and she seized the moment by designing a shrewdly solipsistic house for a celebrity, the Newman House, which became a *cause célèbre*, burnishing the reputation of her client and putting her firmly on the map as a designer to watch. It also brought her first

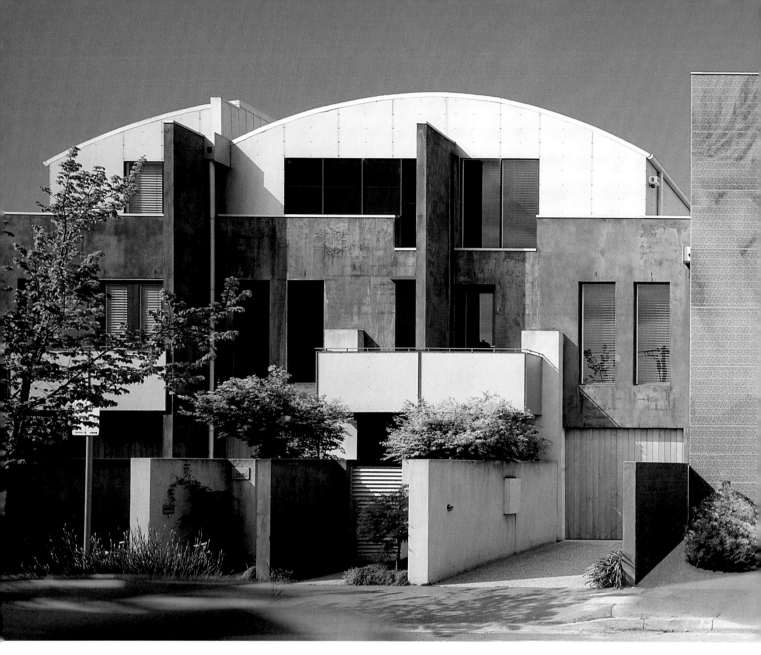

Above: Newman House (2000). The facade of this house, a portrait of Pamela Anderson, brought Cassandra Fahey into the public gaze

brush with the then legalities of planning and, like most of her peers, she has become adept at arguing the case for innovative design in the various legal forums that seek to control design in the city. As is so often the case, the idea of what she had done offended conservatives far more than the fact of what she had done – the house sits comfortably amid its Modernistic neighbours, a dreamy lyrical quality being the surprising outcome of greatly enlarging an image of the actress.

With Husk, Cassandra directly challenged the prevailing orthodoxies of retail design, inventing an interior that is in the tradition of the Aladdin's cave bequeathed to the city by the Burley Griffins, with an added touch of the casbah and a hall of mirrors, but doing this with a sure-footed sense of the rituals of shopping that makes this a very successful retail outlet in a rather drab part of Collins Street. Once past the displayed goods the browsing buyer is confronted with multiple but fractured images of themselves, which are as flattering and alluring as the images captured in tram windows on rainy nights or the reflections of people in the city's many bars. Beyond that again, purchase in mind, there is a cool softening of the space, a relaxing of the intensity forming a place for reflection that slows down impulse and reduces the propensity for buyer's remorse at a later stage. The psychological insight of the design arises from Cassandra's intense (and amused) self-awareness.

The Warehouse for Dr Michael Ben Mier is located in a district evacuated of industry by the shift to China of footwear, textiles and clothing manufacture. A handsome multistorey brick building housing what would be recognised as loft space from New York to East London, here Cassandra has articulated the space into zones of differing intensities for private and social use with a luscious red glass wall that bulges with all of the emphatic sensuality of Marilyn Monroe's lips and a series of white shards that have the luminosity of icebergs. The computing for the laser-cutting of the wall components alone involved collaborations with her most innovative peers.

The Platypusary at Healesville marks a return to active patronage of architecture by Zoos Victoria and sits adjacent to the World of the Platypus pavilion designed by Greg Burgess in the 1980s and close to the Australian Wildlife Centre by Minifie Nixon. Cassandra's design houses a breeding pair of platypuses, the outcome of years of research by naturalists. The tunnels and burrows of the wild are mimicked engagingly in plastic plumbing and cooler boxes. This apparatus, clearly labelled and colour-coded pink and blue, is housed within a double bubble of bronzed steel donated by Bluescope Steel. The frame is a set of laser-formed structural tubes, a scaffold for holding plates of steel laser-cut with a pattern derived from eucalyptus foliage, that grade from solid to mostly perforated, giving the effect of overhanging trees. A pond that emulates the natural habitat of the platypus in swiftly running streams is framed completely unsentimentally from a surface of matt and reflective marbles that partly absorb light and partly reflect it, giving an impression of

Top: On the financial spine – Husk (2004). Half a block up Collins Street from Swanston Street, Cassandra Fahey has created her own Aladdin's cave with this retail fit-out. At the culmination of your shopping you confront yourself in a hall of mirrors. Buyer's remorse seldom results

Middle and below: Platypusary at Healesville Sanctuary (2005). The enclosure consists of a double bubble of bronzed steel tubing and sheeting. The metal sheet is progressively more perforated to simulate a forest canopy

Opposite: Cassandra argues that her thinking is done in the country, and supplies pictures of herself beside a creek in the hills around Melbourne, completely hidden by free foliage. Here, however, she is seen in pop surroundings that are a setting for her more familiar her colleagues

the flickering of light in a deep forest gully. This is an extraordinary moment in the zoo's history. Here is a building that finally admits that we humans are not simply background to nature, but part of it, and that we had better embrace this and ensure that we become agents for change. And that doing so is fun and will make us happy.

Cassandra has named her practice the Cassandra Complex in acknowledgement of its deeply collaborative nature – all of these works involve her with innovative peers in many fields. It also nails her future intentions: her direction is increasingly in the area of sustainable development, and she has commenced design research into the sustainable suburb with a grant from government that will play out in collaboration with the Centre for Design at RMIT. She is conducting this research within the parameters of the by-invitation programme at RMIT which was designed to assist practitioners to reflect on the nature of the mastery they have achieved and to speculate on future practice based on these new insights. The work engages people with a surface immediacy but, as with the rainbow, the wonder grows with deeper investigation.[1] This is an architect who is an exemplar of Melbourne's design culture at its best – idea driven, intent on enjoyment and fun, idealistic and determined to make a difference and working to extract everything she can from the different curatorial processes at work.

1 Philip Fisher, *Wonder, the Rainbow and the Aesthetics of Rare Experiences*, Harvard University Press, (Cambridge, Mass.), 1998.

Opposite: On the financial spine – Watergate (2005), an apartment building that touches the Collins Street extension into Docklands. These twin towers sit on a podium overlooking the major open space in Docklands

ELENBERG FRASER

Collins Street, as we have seen, is the financial spine of the city. In Melbourne the shifting of the port activity down river to new container terminals opened up a debate about how to utilise or urbanise this flat apron of land between the originating grid of the city and the meeting of river and bay. The prevailing idea was to extend the grid of the city southwestwards over the rail yards to several waterside developments of the finger wharves of the old port. Thus, Collins Street that begins in the east with the gold-boom period Treasury, a virtuoso neo-Renaissance palazzo by the 19-year-old John James Clarke (1857),[1] sweeps down past various establishment clubs to meet Swanston Street at a junction where the Town Hall faces Art-Deco commercial buildings, divides the arcades of the retail strip and then climbs towards the neo-Gothic banking halls and stock exchange, plateaus out in the midst of insurance company headquarters and then slides down, losing prestige with every block, to the rail yards along Spencer Street. Or so it used to, for since 2004 Collins Street has swept on up over the rail yards by means of a bridge and on towards the water. As the new Nicholas Grimshaw-designed Southern Cross Station (2006) nears completion, this new Spencer Street junction is rapidly emerging as a crucial node on the financial spine, down which the National Australia Bank has moved to new premises on the water's edge. Facing the new station is Liberty Towers, an apartment building erected where only a visionary would dare to build.

That visionary was publisher Morry Schwartz, whose imprints, in a country whose media are neo-conservative in outlook, are the only local medium for a socially radical critique. In 1988 Schwartz was reading *Edge City*, as much because of his interest in its publishing success as for its thesis about city development in the 'Beltway' suburbs of cities. With RMIT's *38 South* investigation into the peripheral city, there was some mutual speculation about whether this phenomenon would eventuate in Melbourne. Schwartz was canny enough to understand that the only edge that was likely to be bridged in Melbourne was along Spencer Street, and that the junction with Collins Street was the best option. In 1998, having built up a business case, he participated in a design and development tender competition run by the Melbourne City Council (MCC) for a site looking over the rail yards.

With the young architecture practice Elenberg Fraser, he won this competition. Formed by Zahava Elenberg and Callum Fraser, two outstanding recent graduates from RMIT, the firm had a garden shed ('some shed!' as Churchill might have said) and a bayside house to its credit at the time Schwartz was awarded the project. The principals were well connected into the architectural production processes of the city and with the developers of the venture convinced of the efficacy of the design, financial backing was readily forthcoming and they were appointed. Completed in 2002, the building is a

homage to several of their heroes, Gio Ponti chief among them. Perhaps the most striking of the practice's innovations has been the collaboration with artist Stephen Bram in the design of a neon installation in the foyer.[2] Stephen Bram is an artist in the stable of the Anna Schwartz Gallery, whose pioneering director Anna Schwartz has worked tirelessly to incorporate art into buildings, notably into the Commonwealth Law Courts on the corner of William and La Trobe Streets. Meanwhile Zahava Elenberg established a company called Move-in supplying furnishings and fittings, and in 2003 was named the Telstra Australian Young Businesswoman of the Year.

In 2005 Elenberg Fraser completed Watergate, an apartment development down the Collins Street extension, appending to it at one end. A striking zigzagging balcony system takes this design well beyond the earlier screen experiments at Liberty Tower. The foyers also have taken the germ of the idea at Liberty Tower and grown it into something quite remarkable: walk-in art spaces in which every surface plays its part in creating an immersive art

environment, while the floor is strewn with toy-like furniture. The architects provided the framework of the spaces and a materials palette of black-lacquered surfaces and a choice of stainless steel or mirror panelling while the artists worked on large-scale models of the foyers. The ceiling in the central foyer is flat and reflective, transforming it into a mirrored box glazed on one side. In this space and informed by his understanding of how reverberative are the reflecting images it causes, Bram's neon installation is now refined and simplfied to create a web of light that dissolves the space into indeterminacy; the real of the virtual, if one can imagine such a thing. This from an artist who has built three-dimensional models of two-dimensional projections of three-dimensional objects! The ceiling in the outer foyers curve down two points. In the southern foyer, artist John Nixon has placed a glowing orange work on the wall, a virtual sunset glowering in the dark surfaces, infecting them even as far as the pure black mail room to one side, the faces of its letter box lit by hidden light. In the northern foyer, artist Kerrie Poliness has etched a series of globe-like projections into the glass of the mirrors along two parallel walls, and these repeat like floating planets into the distance on both sides, while the letter boxes occupy a position on the floor in a circle plan configuration that matches the globular forms. The foyers provide access to a common facility on Level 5, where access ways between the two slab-blocks bridge to a meeting room lounge and a gym facing on to a lawn and a pool. Here that early garden shed is in evidence, with a latticework of steel forming walls and shading pergola. This is one of the most compelling club spaces in the city, with closely contained views to the buildings beyond but with a horizontal planar containment that creates a Case Study house or Eichler Homes-like sense of the modern good life. It is

Top left: The southern foyer of the Watergate (2005) features artist John Nixon with his characteristic orange and black

Top right: The northern foyer features artist Kerrie Poliness with a series of map projection like constructions that loom into the virtual space, created by the lustre black of the walls and ceilings, setting up a drift of floating galaxies

Bottom: Watergate's meeting room/lounge/gym and changing rooms face on to a lawn and a pool with an almost Hollywood like insouciance. You expect David Hockney to be observing

Opposite: The central foyer of the Watergate features artist Stephen Bram's neon installation and mirrored surfaces that aid his spatial deconstruction project

as if you have walked into a David Hockney painting: *Beverly Hills Housewife* (1966) or *A Bigger Splash* (1967), so insistent is the frontality of relationship between the facade of the pavilion and the painterly surface of pool, lawn and their Pointillist borders.

With Watergate (so named because Morry Schwartz argued that no one in this generation would recall the infamous Nixon burglary), Collins Street, the street of rooms, halls and foyers, has gained a virtuoso set, so striking in its realisation that it recalls the accomplishment of the Treasury Building at the other end of the street. Coincidentally, these rooms echo across to Wood Marsh's Xanadu foyer on the wharf to the east of the Yarra River. Between, on the fringe of the Docklands Park, are situated two sculptures, a large rabbit by Emily Floyd and an over scale, mirror-clad *IOU* by Mikala Dwyer that reads UOI from the building for feng shui reasons. These derive from the

Docklands Development Authority's 'one per cent for art' policy, a curatorial regime that has also resulted in the Webb Bridge by DCM.

Having formed Zacamomo, a development company, with Morry Schwartz, Elenberg Fraser are now engaged in financing and designing their own projects, including restoring Normanby Chambers, a long unused Victorian legal chambers in Little Collins between Queen Street and William Street and a laneway newly restored by the MCC to the west. The ground floor is devoted to a cafe and a pub, and at the back, reached through the red front doors that are on axis with Bank Place, is Vieu de Monde, among Melbourne's hottest restaurants. The floor is made from timbers from the demolished Southern Stand at the Melbourne Cricket Ground, as are two servery tables which are constructed from the timbers branded with seat numbers. Here Elenberg Fraser join Melbourne's

Opposite: Huski (2005), a ski-lodge in Alpine Victoria, exterior. Here the architects are in control of the development, their formal virtuosity considerably more than skin deep

Below: Callum and Zahava in Vieu de Monde, Little Collins Street, central Melbourne

abiding interest in its own history and in finding ways of bringing its casualties into play in its internal spaces – just as ARM reconstructed the sculpture known as the Yellow Peril in the foyers of RMIT Storey Hall, bringing it back surreptitiously to Swanston Street.

Their Huski, a ski-lodge in Alpine Victoria, opened for the 2005 snow season. It is a building in the new apartment format that is becoming common in the snowfields and one that is the architects' most architectonically dynamic design to date, taking the plasticity that has been developing in the screen systems in their apartment blocks in the city and applying it to the floor plans here in the mountains a few hours' drive from the city.

Be that as it may, Elenberg Fraser have benefited from a benign intersection of several curatorial projects in their city; a longterm nurturing of

the avant-garde in art, the canny readings of the city by a publisher with a fringe political position and the opportunities opened up by the extension of the city into the unfamiliar and untrodden terrain of the Docklands. They also subscribe to the curatorial ambitions of their peers and mentors in being passionately concerned to be of the city and to celebrate and extend popular consciousness of its history.

1 Rohan Storey, *Walking Melbourne. The National Trust Guide to the Historic and Architectural Landmarks of Central Melbourne*, National Trust of Australia (Melbourne), 2004, p 81: 'considered Australia's finest 19th century building...'
2 Leon van Schaik, 'Light', *AD*, Vol 74, No1 (Jan/Feb 2004), pp 126–7.
3 Kevin Alter, 'Modern Life', in Kevin Alter (ed), *The Good Building*, Center for American Architecture and Design (University of Texas at Austin), 2003, pp 81–8.

ROBERT SIMEONI

'Perhaps after all a parabola is the quickest way there.'
Andrei Vosnesensky, 'Parabolic Ballad'[1]

Although Robert Simeoni has a toe-hold on the spines of the city through a fit-out of an advertising agency in Bourke Street, he comes thundering into public consciousness through his work on Woolamai House on Phillip Island on the southern edge of Western Port Bay, Melbourne's second bay. Here he has restored an early homestead as a guesthouse and designed a companion piece that has become the new main house. The project came to him through his addition to the client's home in a northern suburb of Melbourne (2002/3). Here in Thornbury he inserted a pavilion between existing wings, one designed by Kevin Borland

and clearly an influence on early Norman Day house designs with their flat-plane, mortar-board type roofed pavilions, the other by Greg Burgess. Inserting a work between one by an architect who was among the few innovators of the 1970s after Robin Boyd died in 1966, and one by an architect who has been firmly in the public arena since he designed Bambruk Visitor Centre for the Aboriginal community at Gariwerd (see Greg Burgess, p 146) was a formidable challenge. Simeoni brought it off with a surprisingly insouciant move, using interlocking screens in two curved arms and floating a concrete slab behind these in a 'look, Ma, no hands' manner not seen since Boyd. The result has the disarming quality of intimate immensity,[2] and sits well with the work of Simeoni's predecessors. So successful was the

approach that Simeoni has replicated it at a larger scale and to good effect in his Preston multi-function room adjacent to a church in neighbouring suburb.

The pavilion is a place for sitting and relaxing and the client was so enamoured with it that the architect was asked to work on Woolamai House, which had been in their ownership for sometime and was to become a more visited place, now that the client was retiring. The architect set to work on the restoration of the Heritage-listed homestead and began discussions with the client on the new main house. One might have expected that the client, who is of North Italian extraction, would have envisaged a companion house in a Neo-Palladian style, but true to

his earlier patronage of innovative architects, he immediately warmed to an uncompromisingly contemporary design which Robert Simeoni presented. This drew on what the client already regarded as a successful *parti* in the small extension in Northcote. The client's business is concrete and construction and in his Woolamai design, Simeoni argued for an elegant post-tensioned concrete roof terrace rather than a flat roof. Here, the uncompromisingly new works supremely well with the restored house: from outside and inside the new showcases the old just as effectively as it frames the views of the ocean. According to John Gollings, who has seen many such new builds, the junctions between the fittings and the finishes in the bathroom and the kitchen are unusually finely resolved.

Left: Preston Holy Name multifunction room (2004) adjacent to a church in a neighbouring suburb

Below: Thornbury pavilion for Grollo (2002/3) showing Kevin Borland's extension to the left and Greg Burgess's extension to the right of the new Robert Simeoni pavilion

Opposite page clockwise from top: Woolamai House (2004). The elegant trace of the roof handrail is inscribed against the horizon; offsetting the formality of the concrete structure, the railings spring from the ground in a daring, continuing cursive line, while netting provides safety; the soft and the hard, an irresistible combination of curtains, breeze and fine concrete

This page: Woolamai House (2004). Freed from the constraints of the suburban grid, Robert Simeoni finds other sources of restraint. Just as at Como where Robert Simeoni's mentor Guiseppe Terragni created a modern form out of the surrounding neo-classical urban fabric, here the forms of the old house's verandah are ennobled into the new idiom. The soft and the hard, an irresistible combination of curtains, breeze and fine concrete

Below: Robert Simeoni in the front room of his office, standing in front of a door inspired by Terragni's Casa Del Fascio in Como. The office is a former shop in the inner suburb of Carlton, the old Italian district which is still dominated by Italian restaurants and coffee bars

A breezy theatricality is in evidence that may have been learned from Allan Powell. The new pavilion has the delicacy of its Thornbury predecessor, even though it is so much larger. The nautical cast of the stairs to the roof and the roof terrace avoids the mannerism usually attendant on yachting-inspired detailing.

Robert Simeoni graduated from Melbourne University and in 1991 undertook an 18-month course of study at the University Institute of Architecture in Venice under his North Italian compatriots Tafuri[3] and Rossi, whose work had fascinated him while he was a student. A workshop with Massimo Cacciari was particularly rewarding for him. In the mid 1990s he shared a studio with Kim Halik, one time editor of *Transition*, an architect whose breadth of interests and meticulous memory for detail have influenced numerous of his peers at different times (see NMBW, p218). Simeoni then worked for Allan Powell, whose architecture he continues to admire and advocate to his peers in the Half Time Club, a discussion club for emerging architects. He set up his own office in Elgin Street, Carlton, adjacent to the heart of the original Italian quarter of the city, and has constructed inside the Victorian double-storey terrace house that is his office a facsimile of the metal frame doors in Giuseppe Terragni's Casa Del Fascio in Como. This is a practitioner whose deliberate connoisseurship in architecture and whose careful curation of his intellectual milieu are now very much in evidence. Simeoni has created an impressive plateau of mastery and has been invited to consider the nature of the innovation that may flow from it in the context of the RMIT programme. The work encourages confidence that further surprising but sure-footed concepts will follow.

1 'Parabolic Ballad', tr WH Auden in *Antiworlds, the poetry of Andrei Vosnesensky*, tr WH Auden et al, Basic Books (New York), 1966. Sleeve notes to a record of the same name, same year, CBS MONO 70026: 'Parabolic Ballad is a declaration of the poet's belief that art and poetry must revolt against established traditions and seek renewal on a "parabolic trajectory".'
2 Gaston Bachelard, *The Poetics of Space*, Beacon Press (Boston), 1996.
3 BL Lapenta and M Tafuri, *Architecture and Utopia: Design and Capitalist Development*, MIT Press (Cambridge, Mass), 1979.

Emerging Asian Urbanism

In the QV complex in Melbourne the various strands of curatorial endeavour that are threaded through the city's history come together: infrastructure, patronage, skewing the canon and reflective practice. The QV site is a city block bounded on one side by Swanston Street, on another by the lateral Lonsdale Street and on a third by the parallel Russell Street. On the fourth side it is divided from the State Library by the secondary lateral, Little Lonsdale Street. Together these two sites form a square divided by Little Lonsdale Street. Formerly fully occupied by the Queen Victoria Hospital, the site was cleared except for a pavilion of the original red brick building centred on Lonsdale Street, now a Women's Centre, facing the Greek quarter of the Central Activity District (CAD).

The development's unusual character is deeply dependent on a determined curation of its infrastructural form. From the outset the City Architect Rob Adams made it clear that no development would be countenanced that did not meet both the principles thrown up by his painstaking work on reawakening political awareness of the infrastructural gifts from the visionaries of the past, and his grasp of the fundamentals underlying the regeneration of the Central Activity District. The latter meant getting people to live in the city centre, ensuring that no development kills off a street by facing it with a blank wall and that subdivisions behind street frontages are small enough to facilitate multiple usage, restricting the passage of traffic down major through fares, keeping and extending the lanes and arcades as a secondary pedestrian and activity system, widening footpaths and encouraging underground parking at the edges of the retail centred on lateral Bourke Street.

These conditions seemed to confound the developers who first attempted to exploit the site, and eventually the City Council bought the land and sold it on to another developer with an outline development plan. This plan, developed as a design by NH Architects, coordinates many functions and the work of several designers. The ground plane of the site falls a full two storeys across its diagonal from the Little Lonsdale/Russell Street corner to the Lonsdale Street/Swanston Street corner. Broadly speaking a multitiered 'H' of laneways is laced across the site from Russell Street to Swanston Street, with the base of the 'H' branching out to the site corners at Swanston Street. This system affords at grade access to the complex on three different levels. From the highest stem of the 'H' on Russell Street pedestrians ramp up slightly on to a mezzanine that overlooks a central square – a broadened cross bar of the 'H' that is focused on the rear of the remaining pavilion of the hospital. This upper level links into a white goods and furniture retail floor that occupies the full Swanston Street frontage. A laneway lower down Russell Street ramps up slightly to give access to the central square. Both stem and branch of the laneway from the corner of Swanston and Little Lonsdale lead to the central square, while the stem and branch from Swanston Street and Lonsdale Street lead to a large food-court below the square. The square is also linked by stair and escalator to Little Lonsdale at midpoint of the site, and a ramp along the lower side of the remaining hospital pavilion gives access to the food-court and to the square. From the food-court escalators lead down to two regional-scale super-markets and to the car park, which can accommodate 2,000 vehicles. What is laborious to describe is disarmingly simple to use.

The laneways are lined with small retail outlets, largely local fashion labels on the Swanston Street edge, office supplies on the Russell Street edge. Coffee shops and restaurants surround the square. The Lonsdale Street frontage between the Women's Centre and Russell Street is occupied by the BHP Billiton HQ building (Lyons 2004), its large corporate foyer separated from the Women's Centre by access to car parking and from the complex by a blank wall to the Russell Street laneway – one collapse in the permeability principle of the development wrought by fears created by 9/11. The Russell Street/Lonsdale Street corner faces the Greek Centre, emblazoned with slogans demanding the return of the Elgin Marbles to the Acropolis. Here, one storey above the foyer and in full view through the innovative glazing, the architects have located a gym, tribute to new corporate cultures and to Hellenism, perhaps.

On the other side of the Women's Centre, stretching from Lonsdale Street to the square, a pale translucent box floats skewered on slanting yellow columns. This is the foyer to an elegant glazed box that floats above the white goods and furniture floor two storeys above, occupying two-thirds of the Swanston Street frontage. This is another headquarters building, designed by DCM (2004) and

Above: Seen from Little La Trobe Street, McBride Charles Ryan's apartment building (2004) rides over the commercial base of the complex, deflecting away from the State Library Forecourt

occupied by a local telecom company. The remaining third of the Swanston Street frontage is taken up by a 12-storey apartment building designed by McBride Charles Ryan (2004). This curves softly in plan in response to the open courtyard in front of the State Library, and extends halfway up Little Lonsdale. The remaining frontage to the secondary lateral is fronted by a 40-storey apartment slab block designed by John

Wardle (2005). The remaining land parcel, between the apartment slab block and the BHP Billiton HQ is occupied by a multipurpose structure designed by Kerstin Thompson. This houses a creche on its upper level, some above-ground car parking, retail facing Russell Street and the laneways, and a brewery restaurant facing the square. Thompson has designed this building to be an echo of the redbrick Women's Centre pavilion, concerned to validate its presence in the complex by linking to it through the redness and brick panelling of her design.

The design of each component by different architects was a condition for the development, the City determined not to control the design quality – something Rob Adams believed beyond its powers – but to ensure a diversity that would reflect the heterogeneity of the surrounding streets. NH Architects proposed a shortlist of architects to Daniel Grollo, the developer (scion of a family originating in the Veneto that has constructed most major projects in the city and has a history of working with innovative architects). He added other names to the list, the architects were interviewed, and many of those appointed, had been graduates of the by-invitation, reflective practice programme at RMIT. Thus it was that the patronage exercise led to the first major

projects on the civic spine by Lyons, Kerstin Thompson, John Wardle and Rob McBride. The effects of these new presences on the spine are yet to be understood.

The poetic lyricism of the McBride Charles Ryan block, shaped in plan like an aubergine – grey granite, with the frames to the openings and deeply cut balconies coloured aubergine and with innovative, pinwheel planning of the apartments – brings something utterly new into play in the core discourse. Cutting, incising and rolling procedures have informed McBride Charles Ryan's work in the periphery for years, as in the remarkable XYZ house in which they 'were encouraged by the heretical act of

letting Matta-Clark loose on Grounds' Academy of Science', the latter being a copper-domed structure in Canberra.[1] The tough-mindedness of Kerstin Thompson's insertion is startling from many vantage points, but without a shred of imitative sentimentality it accomplishes its urban goal of linking to the Women's Centre and making it seem an integral part of the conception. Lyons demonstrate their decade-long romance with the skin of buildings, finding in that outer 100 millimetres a key to a design autonomy that has won for their clients (thus far on the city edge) double the facade – one facing out, one facing in. Here the clear crystal glazing of the 20-storey office block is swept masterfully down and forward like a billowing skirt that amazingly mediates to the

scale of the Greek Quarter. The Wardle building is a demonstration of his extrusion principle of design – up-ended, with fragments of extrusion peeling away as the building rises into the sky.

This complex demonstrates how the current generation is developing the canon in a local context, but it also introduces, to the surprise of many, a new urban form into Australia – one long sought after by Modernist urbanists, but that outside Hong Kong seemed to have failed. In this complex, the 'congestion' model of urbanism is accomplished with all the benefits of proximity between work, retail, leisure and living, and few of the disadvantages – because it is not as dangerously pressured by people as are some parts of Hong Kong.[2] Here, in a carefully considered process that has been amplified by serendipitous coincidence between differing layers of curatorial intent, Melbourne has achieved a piece of the New Asian Urbanism that so confounds Western critics.

While the adjacent redesign of Melbourne Central by ARM shares many of the infrastructural principles, especially those to do with active frontages, laneways and connectivity, it is a configuration of offices and retail in the core retail precinct of the city. The developer client here too – Lendlease – has acted with enlightened self-interest in appointing ARM to rethink the super block. The results are remarkable and the conversion of poor Kurakawa (the original architects) into good ARM is a wonder to behold. But QV combines in addition on its site all of the components of a vision of the CAD that up until this time has been spread across the city grid, lot by lot.

This is already having an effect on adjacent development processes, and the large CUB site, (formerly owned by RMIT, which is building a Design Research Hub designed by Sean Godsell on the Swanton Street–Victoria Street corner), and parenthesising the civic spine by facing the Shrine across the city at the point where Swanston Street bends to the north, is to be developed in a similar way by Grocon, but this time using a short-listed competition process. This will bring even more of Melbourne's architects into play on the civic spine, and opens up the periphery to the experiments of another generation of architects. If, that is, they are not – as seems currently to be the case – entirely wrapped up in a stylistic fascination with Neo-Modern forms, bereft of a local argument.

Is this extraordinary flowering on the civic spine, current and near future, the beginning of another generation of innovation, such that the city will continue to startle and surprise the design world? Or is it the apogee of what has already been laid down? I now, hope for the former. But unless the city is prepared to continue investing in what we have learned about curatorial processes at all levels, Melbourne's time as a design city will fade from the international consciousness. Design cities that do not take hold of these processes have to take breath between generations of innovation.

1 Anthony Parker, 'XYZ: McBride Charles Ryan Architects', *Architectural Review Australia*, No 092 (2005), pp 114–21.

2 Justyna Karakiwiecz, 'The Dimensions of Urban Density', unpublished PhD, RMIT, 2001.

Conclusion

I began this journey into the notion that Melbourne is a design city by wondering out loud about the appearance of such a city, and remarking on just how hidden are the architectural and interior wonders of Melbourne. So much so that when I was introduced to a leading local philanthropic couple with the indication that I was writing a book about new Melbourne architecture, they reacted with undisguised surprise. Really? Is there anything to write about?

Towards the end of the process of putting this book together I met Dr Gerard Vaughan, the director of the city's highest profile visual arts body, the National Gallery of Victoria (NGV) – a name that bespeaks the federalist ambitions of those who founded the institution in a country that still consists of city states. I wanted to talk about the possibility of an exhibition on the basic theme of the book: the way in which the 'civic spine' of Melbourne registers designs of the architects who work in this city in the popular imagination. We were meeting in his office, a double-volume corner room in the triangular building that was once the studio of the master of the painting school attached to the gallery. The Arts Centre in which we were consists of a series of buildings based on Platonic solids: cubes, cylinders, a triangle – and (in the original design) a cone. The NGV has recently been completely refurbished by Mario Bellini, and the director now presides over two enormously charged works of architecture: the Ian Potter Centre at Federation Square by Lab Architecture, and this internationally rewrought interior to the Grounds Romberg and Boyd gallery. What, Dr Vaughan wondered – almost as if he intuited my initial doubt – could be done to lift the complex further into international recognition? Replacing the somewhat unimpressive spire that had replaced the cone at a late stage in construction in the 1960s with an iconic element designed by Gehry? Concerned that a true design city should boast an icon that emerged from its own culture – and we agreed that the Eiffel Tower did precisely this for Paris, and Dr Vaughan reminded me that there was in the early 1890s a fully developed plan to build a full scale version of that in Melbourne – I asked why we did not support a plan to build the original copper-sheathed cone. This would do more than anything to lift the Arts Complex back into focus on the civic spine. And Dr Vaughan responded with an amazing story of how, as a school child, he and his classmates had collected copper pennies, aiming along with all the other school children in the state to make a 10-mile long line of copper coins, the amount it had been calculated would be needed to sheath the cone. What, he asked, had become of these coins? As he spoke it seemed to me that the first impression of mine, 20 years ago, that the heart had been taken out of the city when the copper cone was replaced with the lattice spire, was more than a question of form, it was indeed a question of following through on the ambitions of this community to be something other than an importer of design. Now that this site is surrounded by towering skyscrapers, wouldn't that softly verdigris cone rising from a series of arcs, shimmer that ambition on down to future generations, a visible symbol of the way in which Melbourne still, despite the mediocrity of so much construction, constructs its own culture, a culture of space and form that is of great interest to anyone who loves cities and their specificities?

Photo Credits

The author and the publisher gratefully acknowledge the following for permission to reproduce material in the book. While every effort has been made to contact copyright holders for their permission to reprint material in this book the publishers would be grateful to hear from any copyright holder who is not acknowledged here and will undertake to rectify any errors or omissions in future editions

Key: t=top, b=below, c= centre, l=left, r=right

Cover and all images except those listed below: © John Gollings (JG) p2-3 © Trevor Mein - Meinphoto; p9 (t) © Justin Pumfrey/Getty Images, p9 (b), p11 © Walter Bibikow/Getty Images, p16 © Hamish Blair/Getty Images; p35 Earl Carter; p36 (b) Kerstin Thompson (KTA); p56 © Trevor Mein - Meinphoto; p70 (tr) John Cherry; p71 (tr), p75 (t), p76 (tr & bl), p77 (tl & tr) © Leon van Schaik (LvS) with JG; p81 (cl) Elise Fraser; p85 Grant Hancock; p87 © LvS with JG; p89 John Betts; p90 Paul Knight; p92 John Brash; p96 Earl Carter; p103 Paul Knight; p108 (t) © LvS with JG, (c) © Jan van Schaik, (b) © Trevor Mein - Meinphoto; p113 Sue Anne Ware; p115 Ranulph Glanville; p117 (bl) Lena Lim, (br) © LvS with JG; p118 Victoria Lynn; p121-126 © Jan van Schaik; p130 © LvS with JG; p133 Baracco Wright; p134 (t) Harrison and Crist, (c) Peter Bennetts, (b) Paul Sampas; p135 Aaron Tester; p136-137 Tom Kovac; p153-154 Norman Day; p157 Norman Day; p169 © LvS with JG; p167 © Jan van Schaik; p175 Jonathan Podborsek; p177 Tim Griffths; p178, 180 (c) Patrick Bingham Hall; p179 Jeremy Simons; p180 (tl & tr) © Trevor Mein - Meinphoto; p180 (b) Derek Swallwell; p181 © LvS with JG; p35, 183, 185 Sean Godsell Architects - Hayley Franklin; p186 Earl Carter; p187 © LvS with JG; p199 Clare Connan - Lyons Architects; p209 Minifie Nixon; p210 Peter Bennetts; p211 © Jan van Schaik; p213-214 Paul Morgan; p215-216 Andrius Lipsys; p217 © Jan van Schaik; p219 Peter Bennetts; p220-221 Ian Davidson; p222 NMBW; p223 © LvS with JG; p239 (tr) Jeremy Addison (KTA); (tl & b) Patrick Bingham Hall; p240 Patrick Binham Hall; p241 © Jan van Schaik; p243 Glynis Teo; p244 Peter Clarke; p245 (t) Glynis Teo (b) Peter Clarke; p246 Dominic Lowe; p247 © Jan van Schaik; p251 (b) John Wardle Architects; p252 © Trevor Mein - Meinphoto; p253, 259 © Jan van Schaik; p272 Peter Bennetts; p276 (t) Simeoni; p279 © Jan van Schaik; p282-283 Jeremy Addison (KTA).